PENGUIN
COMPASS

THE SPIRITUAL ACTIVIST

Claudia Horwitz is the founder of stone circles, an organization
that helps individuals and organizations integrate spiritual and
reflective practice into the work of social justice. Claudia conducts
workshops, retreats, and training throughout the United States and
overseas. She has spent more than fifteen years developing youth
leadership, supporting struggles for economic justice, and
strengthening nonprofit organizations. A Kripalu yoga teacher,
Claudia lives in Durham, North Carolina.

The Spiritual Activist

Practices to Transform Your Life, Your Work, and Your World

Claudia Horwitz

Penguin Compass

PENGUIN COMPASS

Published by the Penguin Group

Penguin Putnam Inc., 375 Hudson Street,
New York, New York 10014, U.S.A.

Penguin Books Ltd, 80 Strand,
London WC2R 0RL, England

Penguin Books Australia Ltd, 250 Camberwell Road, Camberwell,
Victoria 3124, Australia

Penguin Books Canada Ltd, 10 Alcorn Avenue,
Toronto, Ontario, Canada M4V 3B2

Penguin Books India (P) Ltd, 11 Community Centre, Panchsheel Park,
New Delhi - 110 017, India

Penguin Books (N.Z.) Ltd, Cnr Rosedale and Airborne Roads, Albany,
Auckland, New Zealand

Penguin Books (South Africa) (Pty) Ltd, 24 Sturdee Avenue,
Rosebank, Johannesburg 2196, South Africa

Penguin Books Ltd, Registered Offices:
Harmondsworth, Middlesex, England

First published in Penguin Compass 2002

1   3   5   7   9   10   8   6   4   2

Portions of this work appeared in different form in the author's
A Stone Throw, published by Stone Circles.

ISBN 0 14 21.9606 1
CIP data available

Printed in the United States of America
Set in Stone Serif
Designed by Claudia Fulshaw Design
Illustrations by Andrew Boardman

For Fifer and Frances

table of contents . . . .

acknowledgments

Expressions of gratitude to those who have helped make a book – and a journey:

My brother, Stuart, for living and breathing these words from start to finish, and willing the text into being when I no longer could. My parents, Margot and Ellis; my sister-in-law, Bonnie; my niece, Fifer; and my Uncle Manny have loved me well and often. And to the ancestors who have passed, your presence is still very much with us.

Martha Abbott, Melanie Armstrong, Ann Ehringhaus, David Sawyer, and Nateshvar Ken Scott for opening the doors to the sacred a little wider.

Annice, Arrington, Billie, Brian, Cara, Charles, Daughtry, Ed, Ellen, Emilee, Kelly, Maura, Jason, John, Julia, Scott, Thérèse, and Tony for deep companionship on the journey.

Shawn Bohen, Mirabai Bush, Ed Cohen, Katherine Fulton, George Lakey, Wayne Meisel, Greg Ricks, Ralph Smith, and Marian Urquilla for setting the bar high.

Mitch Snyder, Lisa Sullivan, and Ingrid Washinawatok for bringing so much radical life into too few years.

Jane von Mehren and Sarah Manges, my editors at Penguin, for being true and compassionate allies – to myself, to the reader, to the work.

Amy Rennert, agent extraordinaire, for all the tenacity and faith necessary to turn the dream of publishing into a reality.

Claudia Fulshaw and Andrew Boardman for deft, exquisite work in the book's design and illustrations, respectively.

Miriam Biber and Tamara Ambar for support and valuable research assistance.

Blessing Way, Echoing Green, North Carolina Public Allies, Z. Smith Reynolds Foundation, Rockefeller Foundation, Triangle Community Foundation, and the hundreds of individuals for supporting the work that inspired this book.

All those who lent their stories, for your beautiful and powerful lives.

All who attended circles, trainings, and workshops over the years for your wisdom and your patience.

introduction

I didn't set out to write a book. I wanted to write a training manual, a guide for what I thought would be a small group of people who shared my passion for the integration of spirituality and activism. As I began to write, the project grew. When I disseminated the early fruits of my labor, the audience grew as well. And then I saw that this connection between inner journeys and outer commitments was actually quite relevant to many people.

The intention of this book is to share a perspective on an ancient belief, a simple idea that creates a more challenging reality for each of us in the short run and a healthier overall existence for all of us in the long run. The idea is that as we develop spiritual and reflective practices within the context of our personal lives and the pursuit of social change, we create a more solid and secure foundation for a new world. We build lives with greater expressions of love, more authentic relationships, and a deeper articulation of truth. We become less afraid of fear and less afraid of life.

When we turn inward, we find stillness and chaos resting together. We find craving and contraction and the seeds of liberation from both. We can ignore what we find or we can embrace it – all of it. When we turn outward, we see levels of suffering that mirror and exceed our own. We know this world is not what it could or should be for far too many beings, human and non-human alike. It takes courage to face the world with compassionate attention, to be candid about the injustices we understand, and to probe those we do not. We try, stumble, and try again. Consciousness is a daily walk.

And it is not a choice any longer.

We need a national culture of reflection that bends toward justice. We must develop the capacity and infrastructure for deliberate, ongoing, profound reflection, so that we might bring balance to the *other* forms of national culture we seem to be infinitely more comfortable with, the cultures of reaction, of military response, of traditional religion, of avoidance.

Reflection and spiritual practice will help ensure that our actions as human beings yield benefits to a sphere far beyond the horizon we can easily see.

When my scholarly uncle read an earlier version of this book, he congratulated me on my "how-to book." At first I shuddered. With my love of ideas, the written word and the interplay of theory, had I really written an instruction manual? Yes, perhaps I had. And then I realized that spiritual activists are always interested in the questions that begin with "how." We hunger for practicalities. We see how desperately we all need to know *how*: how to find that refuge where we can nurture our core, how to deepen the union we feel with others, and how to embrace life beyond our immediate experience.

The path may not be easy, but it is not rocket science either. (In college I had a friend who majored in astrophysics; the only one in our graduating class. This is not that.) Living a life where values manifest in daily actions – actions that promote the basic health and welfare of all we can possibly imagine – is within reach for each of us. It is not something that will rest only in the hands of a few master teachers, enlightened beings, or revered clergy. It is our birthright, and our responsibility. Spiritual activists move more freely between the inner quest for peace and the outer quest for justice, and we feel some comfort knowing it is a permeable membrane that joins our struggles, our commitments, and our transformations.

We are all seekers. In the midst of an ever-complex, ever-quickening universe, we crave the pause in which we remember what matters most. In the face of suffering, we desire new and better ways to respond. This book is inspired by these convictions. Welcome.

Claudia Horwitz
Durham, North Carolina
April, 2002

The Spiritual Activist

Part One

Refuge
Turning Inward, Finding Strength

Going out in the world every day takes energy, focus, and commitment. Individuals search for wholeness, and search for it everywhere. We want permission to be quiet for a while, each day, in a world that prizes activity. We want to rest and reconnect with what makes us brave. We want to stay present to our deepest truth.

So, what keeps us from this wholeness? Pain in all of its manifestations: anger, fear, insecurity, anxiety, and deep sadness. The first noble truth of Buddhism tells us that life is suffering. That's not all it is, but it is that. We get sick. We develop fears and we cling to them. We are angry. We get anxious. We experience incredible loss, and with this loss comes sadness, sometimes so great that we think it will break us. Stressful things happen and we must choose how to respond. We have been hurt by other people who were hurt themselves. And inevitably, we lose what we love.

How do we acknowledge and respond to this suffering? How do we embrace and transform it? Animals threatened with extinction and in need of protection often find themselves in a refuge, a place of safety and nourishment. To lead a sane and beautiful life, we need a space of quiet and deep rest where we can turn inward and find strength. In this place, we find compassion, tranquility, love, strength, and a sense of ease. The seed of our renewal lies in our ability to develop practices of mindfulness, a language of spirit and a reconnection with the body. If we don't find refuge within ourselves, we will always be asking others to be what they are not meant to be.

Through ongoing, deliberate experiences with our inner life, we cultivate stillness, open our hearts, nurture our personal expressions of faith, and deepen our capacity just to *be*. Rather than an escape, refuge is a return to the real. Turning inward allows us to develop our power from within, the power that makes real change possible.

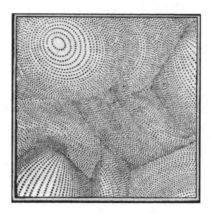

practice

Sustained exertion is not something which women and men
of the world naturally love or desire, yet it is the last refuge of all.
~ *Dogen-Zenji, quoted in* The Three Pillars of Zen *by Philip Kapleau*

Spiritual practice, by uprooting our personal mythologies of isolation, uncovers the radiant,
joyful heart within each of us and manifests this radiance to the world.
We find, beneath the wounding concepts of separation, a connection both to ourselves
and to all beings. We find a source of great happiness that is beyond concepts
and beyond convention. Freeing ourselves from the illusion of separation allows us to
live in a natural freedom rather than be driven by preconceptions about
our own boundaries and limitations.
~ *Sharon Salzberg,* Loving-Kindness: The Revolutionary Art of Happiness

The man or woman truly on the path [to inner peace]
seeks every moment as the one in which to activate life's highest blessing.
~ *Paul Fleischman,* Cultivating Inner Peace

what is practice? . . . .

A spiritual or reflective practice has three characteristics:
1. It connects us to the presence of the sacred or that which has great meaning in our lives.
2. It is something we do regularly (ideally on a daily basis) and without interruption.
3. It grounds us in the present moment, bringing us into awareness of what is happening right now.

A practice is simply a habit that gives us energy and reminds us of what matters most. Every moment in our lives is a chance to be present and to open our hearts. How do we take advantage of this? How do we live each moment to the fullest? One way is by taking concentrated time each day to notice the peaks and the valleys with a tender awareness and without added drama. We can acknowledge suffering in our lives – doubt, fear, anger, sadness, or anxiety – without having to identify with them completely. This detachment can help us transform the energy of pain into strength. And it provides us with a wellspring of clarity when a difficulty or crisis arises.

There is so much competition for our attention. The television blares, a child tugs at our leg, colleagues make their demands known. There will always be plenty of reasons for our attention to be elsewhere. We spend so much of our mental energy evaluating or rehearsing. We're sure our happiness lies in a memory of the past or what is just around the corner, but contentment lies in our ability to appreciate whatever truth is unfolding in the present. Spiritual practice brings us into the fullness of the here and now. It is a reprieve from the mind's fascination with rehashing the events of the past or preparing for the future. It is a relief to be where life does not need any alteration.

Having a practice helps us pay concentrated attention to the inner voice – a presence that has the power to continually reinform the activities of our daily life. So while spiritual practice can seem like a selfish activity, in fact it helps to dissolve our preoccupation with self. Through practice we cultivate a sense of peace and compassion that pervades the rest of our relationships and activities.

turning point . . . .

It was the summer I turned twenty-seven when I first learned what a spiritual practice was and began meditating. I had gotten myself into a work commitment that I didn't believe in, and probably wasn't qualified for, and the results felt disastrous. Shaken by what I could only see as failure, I realized that I had no idea which values were driving my decisions or how I could find courage when the going got tough. What is my anchor in the world? I wondered.

I made a pilgrimage to see two friends on their farm in Kentucky, and I described my dilemma. I was honest about the degree of pain this incident had caused me and the deeper insecurities that had been sparked in the process. I was at loose ends. My friends looked at me and very matter-of-factly told me that I needed a spiritual practice. "But, I have a therapist," I responded. They patiently explained that wasn't what they were talking about. I'd never heard this term "spiritual practice" before. I wanted a definition. Instead, they presented me with three possible routes out of my despair: read, meditate, or pray. (Now I know there are infinitely more types of practice, but this limited range of options was quite useful at the time.) I was already reading more than enough for graduate school, and prayer seemed loaded with the current ambiguity of my relationship to Judaism, my root tradition. I chose meditation. They shared some of the basics with me and I began to explore this seemingly bizarre concept of just sitting with my breath.

Back home later that summer, I set up a corner of my room with two plants, a photograph of the New Mexico mountains, stones, and a clay pot that had been given to me. And I began to practice. Every morning, I sat. Sometimes it was only five minutes, sometimes ten or fifteen. Regardless, within just a few days strange things began to happen. Every night I would get home and think, "Today was a pretty good day." I didn't overreact so much. I was nicer to people. I accomplished most of what I hoped to accomplish for the day. Within days, meditation was bringing me a sense of calm detachment that I'd never experienced before. I worried less about what other people thought and what I was missing in the world. My highs and lows weren't as gut-wrenching.

In the decade since, my practice has had its ups and downs. Some days I can't sit for ten minutes without looking at my watch. Some days I can sit for half an hour without flinching. Some days I skip it altogether and then pay the price later. When I neglect my practice, I simply feel off. The day begins to unravel and it's often too difficult for me to piece it back together again. I'm not as focused or patient, with myself or with others. Little things cause a lot of frustration. I'm less hopeful, more easily overwhelmed and distracted. I talk more, but the words seem to mean less. It is almost as if my ego expands into the space that usually fills up with the presence of spirit. I've come to realize that it's really not about being good or bad at meditation; it's just about doing it. When I meditate, my life feels more authentic and less of a struggle.

Over time, this morning meditation has become an act of remembering who I am and who God is in my life. I have realized that I need a period of solitude in the morning, anywhere from one to three hours, to function as a

spiritual quick hits

These simple actions can bring you to a different place, shift your energy, or give you a new perspective:

- Memorize a poem or prayer that you like and share it with one or many.

- Take one day to help people you know. Work at their organizations or at their homes. You might concentrate some energy on new/young parents with small children who need relief.

- Spend a whole day in silence.

- Spend a full day with children. Let them plan part of it and then take time to do what you loved most as a kid or feel like you didn't get to do often enough.

- Attend someone else's house of worship.

- Lie on the floor and spend thirty minutes listening to your favorite music in the dark.

- Go to a museum and spend at least fifteen minutes with one painting that moves you or that you don't understand.

- Get on your knees and ask for forgiveness.

(continued on next page)

sane and loving human being in the world the rest of the day. So I start my days with a quiet that lets me sink below the surface of my daily routine and my mind's chatter. I begin with yoga because I find it hard to concentrate unless I've awakened my body first. Then, I sit with the breath. After that I find I have emptied out some – there is a slight releasing of anxiety, memory, or negativity. So, that seems like the right time to set the tone for my day with a reading from a work of spiritual philosophy, poetry, or sacred text. Finally, I usually need to write, even if it's just a page in my notebook. This helps me codify what I'm wrestling with, declare my intentions, record the specifics I want to remember, and explore experiences that have been particularly impactful.

Of course, it doesn't always work out this way. There are mornings when I am lucky if I find fifteen minutes to stretch a little and meditate. Because I travel a lot, I am constantly finding creative ways to maintain my practice on the road. The bigger challenge has been to refrain from judging myself when I don't do what I "should" be doing. I've learned that a little is better than none. When my practice is strong, I am more aware of the energy that pervades every living being and more awed by the interaction between these living beings. When I take time to honor myself and my relationship to this life force I notice the extraordinary in the ordinary and beautiful things that happen in my life. I ask more questions and I tend to do only one thing at a time. My relationship with myself and with others deepens. I am more likely to embrace change and even to surrender control. I find I have more energy. I am more joyful. My practice is the foundation. Sometimes it is shaky and sometimes it is strong, but it is always there.

☉ questions for reflection . . . .

What are your associations with habit? Routine? Discipline?

Do you do anything on a regular basis that connects you to the sacred or to your sense of spirit?

How do these current activities enhance your life? What impact do they have?

If you do have some kind of practice, is it very different from the spiritual or faith activities you were brought up with?

What types of spiritual or faith-based activities or practices are you curious about?

℮ developing a spiritual practice........

As one matures in spiritual life, one becomes more comfortable with paradox, more appreciative of life's ambiguities, its many levels and inherent conflicts. One develops a sense of life's irony, metaphor, and humor and a capacity to embrace the whole, with its beauty and outrageousness, in the graciousness of the heart.

~ *Jack Kornfield*, A Path with Heart

Imagine carving out twenty minutes every day to renew your relationship to spirit. Is there something you already do sporadically or occasionally that could become a more regular practice? Use the grid below to notice what you already do that you might consider spiritual. This can be anything from a walk in the woods to reading sacred text in the morning to writing in your journal to attending your house of worship to meditation. It might be a work-related activity: a short, daily check-in with a coworker, an action that signals the beginning of your workday, or a regular cleanup of common workspace. Be as specific as you can. You may not remember everything right away, so fill the grid out over the course of a couple of days. Don't worry how many boxes are left blank.

	Alone	With others	At work
Daily			
Weekly			
Monthly			
Yearly			

Once you feel the grid is complete, reflect on what information it is giving you:

Which boxes are full? Which are empty? What does this reflect?

spiritual quick hits (continued)

- Write a letter to an ancestor.

- Meditate on a photo of yourself at a younger age.

- Spend a day answering every question you are asked with, "I don't know."

- Look everyone you meet squarely in the eyes for an entire day.

- Copy something in a foreign language without worrying what it means.

- Take a breath and hold it.

- Take off your watch and cover your clocks.

- Go to the library and wander around. Go to the children's section and check out three books for yourself.

Do you nurture your spiritual life mostly alone, mostly with others, or both?

How often do you do each activity or practice?

Do these activities cost money?

How convenient are most of these activities? Do any require a trip away from home?

Here are some possible practices. Note your reactions to them:

reading	art	keeping a Sabbath
meditation	music	silence
prayer	dance	planting/gardening
yoga	exercise	sports
writing	fasting	studying sacred texts
walking	t'ai chi	pilgrimage
cooking	crafts	service work/volunteering

Now revisit the same grid, only this time with the intention of writing down anything you might want to explore. Brainstorm. Write down everything that comes to mind as a possibility – whatever interests you. Maybe there was one thing you remember doing two years ago or something you heard about from a friend or something you read about that sounded interesting. Don't worry about how remote or unlikely it might seem – write it down.

	Alone	With others	At work
Daily			
Weekly			
Monthly			
Yearly			

Reflect on the questions below. Again, these questions do not have to be answered in one day; consider your responses over the course of a week or two. Different times and different moods will yield new reactions and ideas.

What do you want more of in your life? What do you want to know more about?

What activities or practices help you in difficult times?

What is the best time for you to incorporate a practice?

What is/are the best place(s)?

What do you need to make this happen? What might stand in your way?

Which relationships encourage you to be your best self? Which are holding you back?

What course or class might you be interest in taking?

The primary criteria for a practice is that it be something you can do every day with some degree of commitment and authenticity. This doesn't mean you should expect to love your practice every day. On the contrary, there will always be days where it is the last thing you want to do. This is resistance to be noticed and lovingly overcome. Jack Kornfield, author and co-founder of the Insight Meditation Society, talks about the need to "take the one seat," because it is through repeated commitment that true understanding and maturity are possible. To keep changing our practice will not benefit us in the long run.

℮ which path is the right one?

When we find a practice or a path that is right for us, we usually know it immediately. Here are three questions to ask yourself:

1. Does this practice fill you with awe?
2. Can you surrender to the practice?
3. Does the practice have heart?

If the practice fills you with awe, at least most of the time, it will likely be something that can sustain and delight you, even when it is challenging. We are too much in need of awe not to find it in our spiritual life. Though it can certainly be joyous, practice is not meant

emptying out to fill up again

There is a Zen story of a professor who goes to see a monk. The monk welcomes him, and the professor explains that he has come seeking wisdom from the monk. With that, the professor begins to talk endlessly about his knowledge and what he has done in the world. Finally, the monk asks the professor if he would like some tea. The professor nods yes, continuing to speak about his accomplishments.

The monk sets a cup in front of the professor and begins to pour. He continues pouring the tea until the cup is overflowing, and the tea is spilling all over the floor. The astonished professor jumps up.

"What are you doing?" he asks. "This cup," the monk replies, "is very much like your mind. It doesn't have room for anything else because it is already full."

to be easy. If we're prepared to be humbled by a path we have chosen, we may find it easier to maintain some discipline without judging ourselves for our shortcomings in it. Rather than worrying about how good we are at something, when we surrender to our practice, it leads the way. And if it has heart, it likely will have staying power.

℮ teachers and allies

Teachers and allies are quite useful along the spiritual path. In beginning or deepening a spiritual journey, consider who in your life can support you. The process will have its highs and lows. You may feel as though there is never enough time or the right time. It may feel strange at times, and it's easy to lose sight of why you are doing this practice at all. A teacher, ally, or partner can help you navigate all of this and stay committed when you may be ready to give up.

In the West, many of us struggle with the concept of a guru. This Sanskrit word is actually a combination of *gu*, darkness, and *ru*, removal. So it means "one who removes darkness," and this is what great teachers do. They reflect back to us our best selves, the spark of divinity within. They are people who have done, and continue to do, the kind of work it takes to clear as much of the ego as possible. The individual becomes a clear vessel and this is what enables them to be present and loving without a lot of projections, reactions, advice, or judgment. Not an embodiment of perfection, they are constant reminders of the best people we can be. There is an old saying, "When the student is ready, the teacher will appear." Your teacher might be someone you have known for a long time. He or she might come in the form of a friend or clergyperson. She or he may be someone who shares a significant lesson or resource with you, who teaches you a specific practice, or whose life experience is so resonant that you learn from sharing your journeys. Most of us will have more than one teacher in our lifetime.

Do you have any kind of spiritual support system now?

If yes, is it adequate? How might you shift or strengthen it? If not, how could you develop one?

Is there someone in particular with whom you can imagine sharing parts of your journey?

Can you choose a friend to exchange letters or E-mails with as you grow in these ways?

Have you met any spiritual mentors, allies, or teachers with whom you might establish regular contact?

✏ write it down: keeping track

As you begin developing a spiritual practice, consider keeping track of what you're doing and the effect it is having in a journal or notebook. You can use it to record experiences and your reactions to them. Writing about them will only increase your understanding of what is happening and the changes taking place internally. You will probably become aware of new information about yourself and the world around you, and more conscious of certain emotions that are surfacing. Add images that convey meaning. Write down prayers, meditations, and other exercises that have been useful to you. And, make a note of resources you hear about: books, articles, workshops, teachers, and groups.

℗ making time

Inevitably, when you start thinking about developing a spiritual practice, barriers will surface. The most common revolve around time, and our perception of how little of it we have. It's easy to take a look at our full lives and wonder how we'll find the space for practice when we're faced with the demands of a busy life at home, work, or both. I have heard that the Dalai Lama manages to do his spiritual practice six hours each day, even though he is pretty busy being the spiritual leader of Tibet and running an exiled Buddhist community in Dharamsala, India. I try to remember this when I am tempted to whine about time.

Over the course of a week, keep track of all the ways you spend your time. From the time you wake up in the morning until you go to bed, write down each activity that you spend time on and how long you do it. At the end, add up the hours spent on each activity. Make some choices from this. Do you consistently work late? Do you make four trips to the grocery store each week when two would suffice? Are there habits or hobbies that don't feed you that you might be willing to give up? Do you spend a lot of time on the phone with friends you see regularly? Ask a friend to help you think through possibilities and brainstorm options for revising your daily routine. Spiritual practice can thrive on twenty to thirty minutes each day.

labyrinth (continued)

thousands of people in this country have now walked the labyrinth, and many are creating their own out of elements as diverse as paper, canvass, stone, and grass.

Contact: Veriditas: Grace Cathedral Labyrinth Project, 1100 California Street, San Francisco California, 94108. (415) 749-6356. E-mail: veriditas@gracecathedral.org www.gracecathedral.org

℮ retreats

Retreats can be an effective way to deepen a new practice or rejuvenate one that is waning. Don't be fooled by the word "retreat." You are not escaping anything. A retreat can and should be a period of rest and renewal, but it can also be quite challenging. The best way to work up to a longer period of time away is by starting with shorter ones. A day spent in a quiet location with no distractions may inspire you to plan a whole weekend away or sign up for a workshop in something that interests you. That, in turn, may lead you to begin planning an even longer visit. Many retreat centers offer long-term options (ten days to three months and even longer) and some include a work component that can significantly reduce the cost. A list of retreat centers appears in the Appendix.

the right time

Julia Scatliff O'Grady, a time coach, helps people shape their days through a unique look at our relationship with time:

The biggest myth – it's legend now – is that there is a right time for an action to take place. Another myth is that you can manipulate time: save it, make it, smush it. Time is beyond our ability to save. Time is just a way we have found to interact with the sun and the moon and now we don' t even use the sun or moon anymore.

You will know how much time you have for a new endeavor by how you typically spend your time now. Often, when you launch a new practice, a new year's resolution, or anything big you're so incredibly ambitious that you implode by day three. Seeing how you spend your time now is, to me, the best indicator of how your practice will become a part of your life. If you know that you are a night person and you decide that you're going to get up every morning at 6:30 to meditate, that's a recipe for disaster, because when have you ever gotten up at 6:30? Maybe your practice needs to be at 11:30 at night.

It's hard to see your natural patterns and to follow those rather than what your head is telling you to do. The power of the body clock is so much more powerful than the mind. If I was trying to build in twenty to thirty minutes a day for practice, and I had never done anything in a daily way, I'd have to find ways to trick myself. I'd find someone to call me every day to make sure I was doing it. Or I'd do practice every other day at first. I'd have to have a hunger to begin. It wouldn't be because I felt I should. I'd have to have the hunger to bring a practice into my life.

The first stage of doing a time inventory for your life is so key. Just about everyone has some way she or he can look at the past six months. This is a good stretch because you can see seasons change and patterns build on themselves. Then, look at your energy levels, when they're low, when they're high. If you're trying to do something like start a practice and your best time is ten A.M. to twelve P.M. but you're at work, can you come into work early so you have that time from ten A.M. to twelve P.M. to do your practice, instead of trying to do it at seven A.M. when you might be better off doing your work?

What kind of community can you build around yourself to honor your hopes? If you figure out that your best time to build a practice is from eight to nine at night, tell people. Maybe a friend calls you at 8:15 and you pick up the phone and they ask, "Why aren't you doing your practice?" It's really hard to do a new thing alone, unless you're incredibly self-disciplined, and most of us are not. Your first response might not work and that's often when people stop and say they don't have time. There's some diligence required and some compassion. You may not know right now but if you sit in a chair every day, you will figure it out. The whole thing about 99.9 percent of life is showing up is really true.

– From a conversation with the author.

resources for practice

Arrien, Angeles. *The Four-Fold Way: Walking the Paths of the Warrior, Teacher, Healer and Visionary*. San Francisco: HarperCollins, 1993. A look at each of these four archetypes, their principles, and tools for cultivating them. www.angelesarrien.com

Bass, Dorothy C., ed. *Practicing Our Faith*. San Francisco: Jossey-Bass, 1997. A resource for Christians looking to deepen their faith. This book touches on economics, hospitality, the body, Sabbath, community, healing, and song. www.josseybass.com/catalog/isbn/0-7879-3883-1/

Bell, Richard H. *Sensing the Spirit: Spirituality and the Christian Life*. Philadelphia: Westminster Press, 1984. How we forget, and can remember, God.

Brussat, Frederic A. "27 ways to live a spiritual life every day." *Utne Reader,* (July/August, 1994, 91–95). Quotations that provide examples of concrete, day-to-day spirituality on topics such as "Washing your hands," "Doing chores," "Sharing gossip," and "Throwing out the garbage." www.spiritualrx.com

Chittister, Joan, OSB. *Wisdom Distilled from the Daily*. San Francisco: Harper & Row, 1990. Written by the former prioress of the Benedictine Sisters of Erie, Penn. This book looks at the Rule of St. Benedict as a foundation for listening, prayer, community, monasticism, work, leisure, and obedience. www.peacecouncil.org/chittist.html; www.erie.net/~erie-osb

de Mello, Anthony. *Wellsprings: A Book of Spiritual Exercises*. New York: Image Books, 1986. Beautiful meditative passages from a Christian perspective that blend Eastern and Western teachings.

Fields, Rick, with Peggy Taylor, Rex Weyler, and Rick Ingrasci. *Chop Wood, Carry Water: A Guide to Finding Spiritual Fulfillment in Daily Life*. Los Angeles: Tarcher/Putnam, 1984. A guide for using daily activities as a way to live and apply spiritual insights. Includes chapters on relationships, sex, family, work, money, play, body, and social action.

Fleischman, Paul R. *Cultivating Inner Peace*. New York: Tarcher/Putnam, 1997. Eight principles for making peace a way of life. Also includes stories of individuals who inspire the path.

Gatlin, June Juliet. *Spirit Speaks to Sisters*. Chicago: Noble Press, 1996. Written for Black women, "to inspire, praise, enlighten, elevate, and liberate." Minister, activist, singer, and writer, Gatlin's voice calls readers to spiritual fitness and a more intimate relationship with God.

Harvey, Andrew. *The Direct Path: Creating a Journey to the Divine Using the World's Mystical Traditions*. New York: Broadway Books, 2000. Eighteen powerful practices that grow out of Harvey's extensive study of the world's mystical traditions.

Kaufer, Nelly, and Carol Osmer-Newhouse. *A Woman's Guide to Spiritual Renewal*. San Francisco: HarperCollins, 1994. A step-by-step workbook for women seeking to renew their spiritual selves. Written in two parts, "Healing your Spiritual Alienation" and "Seeking Spiritual Connection." Includes chapters on nature, beauty, creativity, rituals, intuition, and relationships.

Kornfield, Jack. *A Path with Heart: The Perils and Promises of Spiritual Life*. New York: Bantam Books, 1993. Clear, compassionate, and authentic guide based on Buddhist teachings. Filled with specific practices. www.fourgates.com/kornfield.asp; www.spiritrock.org/html/KornfieldSched.htm

Lerner, Michael. *Jewish Renewal: A Path to Healing and Transformation*. New York: Grosset/Putnam, 1994. Lerner sheds modern light on Jewish texts, God, prayer, and the practice of the faith. www.tikkun.org

Nouwen, Henri J. M. *Reaching Out: The Three Movements of the Spiritual Life*. New York: Image Books/Doubleday, 1975. Catholic priest and theologian's moving account of the movement from loneliness to solitude, the movement from hostility to hospitality, and the movement from illusion to prayer.

Petsonk, Judy. *Taking Judaism Personally: Creating a Meaningful Spiritual Life*. New York: Free Press, 1991. The author weaves her own story with those of colleagues, friends, and mentors.

Richardson, Peter Tufts. *Four Spiritualities: Expressions of Self, Expressions of Spirit*. Palo Alto, Calif.: Davies-Black, 1996. A psychology of four spiritual paths corresponding to Jungian dimensions of personality: Journey of Unity, Journey of Devotion, Journey of Works, and Journey of Harmony. Each includes underlying tenets, practices, mentors, and texts to read.

Underhill, Evelyn. *Concerning the Inner Life*. London: Methuen & Company, 1926. An exploration of how we can strengthen our inner resources, Underhill's essays were initially delivered to clergy in the 1920s.

Vanzant, Iyanla. *One Day My Soul Just Opened Up*. New York: Fireside, 1998. Inspirational readings and exercises for forty days and forty nights. www.innervisionsworldwide.com/

committing to the path . . . .

David Sawyer

An educator, consultant, and executive coach, David Sawyer has spent three decades inviting people to explore the connections among leadership, service, and spirituality. He spent ten years at Berea College developing student servant-leaders. Sawyer led the team that designed the New Generation Training Program at Youth Service America and the national training for Summer of Service, the pilot for President Clinton's AmeriCorps program. Now he advises leaders in business and social change programs around the country. David is a native Kentuckian and lives in Portland, Oregon with his partner, Tierra.

My spiritual life now revolves around a formal practice, under vow to a spiritual teacher, but it hasn't always been so. At age thirteen, I became disillusioned with Christianity, and full of adolescent frustration, renounced it bitterly. As a junior in college, after a truly dark year, I encountered Eastern religion and philosophy, and discovered that the spiritual process did not have to be about "believing in God." It could be understood as a journey towards God. This idea was very liberating to me. One spring day, I had what I guess could be called an enlightenment experience. For three days my depression disappeared, and I experienced real clarity and happiness. I will never forget the horror – sitting in an economics class – when that state of grace vanished. Shook me utterly. Trying to recapture that gracefulness got me seriously involved in the spiritual path. I thought it might take a couple of years! Thirty years later it can still be a tremendous struggle.

I took vows in the Tibetan tradition in the mid-eighties, and had the sense that vows built a kind of spiritual container. Lessons didn't leak out so quickly, and the water level began to rise. My ultimate teacher though, turned out to be Western born Avatar Adi Da, also known as the Ruchira Buddha. His autobiography blew me away in 1973, but the demands of his community were way more than I was prepared for. In 1995 the chance to see Adi Da for the first time presented itself. On Easter day of 1996, he and I had our first personal exchange. It was quite intimate; we kissed. I was able to speak words of love and respect in his ear, and he responded very tenderly. It was a special moment in my life.

> I think of inner work as anything that helps us to navigate our issues and learn to shine.

After that I took an eternal vow – a scary thought, and a very real commitment. As for formal practice, I continued to meditate and pray every morning, but a subtle link had been established. I had the feeling that my own efforts were being met halfway. I could actually feel a new energy, a brightness, and I knew that I had encountered a remarkable teacher. These days practice is less a private struggle to get somewhere than it is about turning to a tacit spiritual presence. Of course I must do that turning, which given my talent for resistance, can be very difficult. Adi Da once humorously called me "spiritually challenged!"

In the West we have a basic distrust of spiritual teachers, which given the shocking lack of integrity so many have displayed, is entirely understandable. My feeling is that a relationship with a true teacher – in any tradition – quickens our journey and helps us to finally experience new states of being. This sort of bond is sometimes called the "guru yoga" in the East, but there are examples in our Western world too. Having said that, I don't believe that you must have a spiritual teacher to do a great deal of real inner work. Nor do I believe that you must meditate formally. I think of inner work as anything that helps us to navigate our issues and learn to shine: real therapy, strong friendships, long walks, great books, daily prayer, uplifting music. When asked to advise others, I usually recommend that they just choose something simple and start doing it every day. For years I used to collect my thoughts staring out the window with a cup of coffee or glass of wine, which was very centering. Doing something briefly every day – in a manner that you find congenial – gets your feet moving along the path without a lot of resistance. After that, things tend to evolve organically, as they should, and you discover new ways to strengthen your spirit as the journey progresses. For some that may involve a living teacher, as it has for me.

One day at Berea College I found an old Christian text that talked about our inner and outer journeys – another very liberating idea for me. I was worried that serious spiritual practice would weaken my work in the world, the outer dimension, but the opposite has been true. I have more clarity and listen much more deeply. My bullshit detectors are keener, but greater compassion has also awakened. I focus increasingly on the essential rather than the ephemeral. Kindness and directness have learned to coexist. Thankfully, people seem to be receptive. My experience has been that spiritual work has cleared away a lot of inner garbage and helped me to be more rather than less effective in the world.

The integration of our inner and outer journeys is terribly important. And can be terribly difficult. The ancient Greeks thought of these two journeys as circles overlapping side by side, and had a word for their almond-shaped intersection – the *majorca* – which symbolized the sweet spot where our inner and outer journeys are connected. This is where our deepest values and gifts find expression in our work, and where the work we do stimulates and enlivens our inward strivings. Buddhists refer to this conjunction as "right livelihood," and hold that our work needs to not only make a contribution to the world, but also to our own spiritual development – a sacred thing, and a rare one.

Some outer environments can be tough for spiritual practice. Recently I spent two years working with BP in Alaska, helping them strengthen and soften their organizational culture. I had a ton of stuff to work through, given my old feelings about the oil industry and about multinational corporations generally. I used to feel that entering that building every morning was like entering a lead vault – a no-practice zone. My learning curve was nearly vertical, and I came close to bailing out after six months. Now I count it as one of the richest periods of my life, full of inner and outer lessons, and full of strong, surprising friendships.

Dag Hammarskjöld, the secretary general of the United Nations during the dark years of the Cold War, said, "In our era, the road to holiness must pass through the world of action." That pretty much sums up my sense of who I am and what I must be. I've always been very much a person of the world, and I keep believing that it's possible to live an American contemplative life – a life that is intensely involved in the reshaping of the world but also profoundly committed to realization. This is my challenge and my commitment.

David can be reached at davidsawyer@att.net

real world practice . . . .

Julie Iny

Julie Iny is the Advocacy Director at Kids First, a youth organizing and advocacy organization in Oakland, California. She worked at the National Community Building Network for four years as the Outreach Coordinator. Julie is also the co-founder of A Jewish Voice for Peace, a grassroots organization in the San Francisco Bay Area promoting coexistence and a just peace for the Israeli and Palestinian peoples.

I grew up Jewish and started going to synagogue when I was young. My brother and I joined a Jewish socialist youth group when I was about eight years old. It was an amazing part of my development as an activist. At the age of nine I was asked about my values; we got to grapple with what we thought about the world. The youth group was avowedly secular so I accepted this as the way I was. We did cultural celebrations, looked at Jewish history, and celebrated Shabbat in our own way. I ultimately decided to quit synagogue, because what we were doing didn't compare to my youth group. I had a strong political and cultural identity and found myself alienated from established Jewish institutions, believing that I was not like other Jews. I think a lot of Jews go through this.

> For me, part of spiritual practice is about recovering a fuller expression of myself and healing whatever limits my ability to express myself in a full, vibrant, powerful way.

There's something about this secular identity that was a barrier to me connecting or exploring organized religious practice. I went to college in Berkeley and I noticed that I liked singing prayers with a group of people. The communal experience of chanting was moving. I never pursued it in a regular way but the singing did help to open me up more. There is a division in the Jewish community between those who are religious and those who aren't. Many of those who aren't are close-minded in terms of trying to see value in people's spiritual practice.

A turning point for me was my relationship with a man who organized his life around his spirituality. He had a very rich spiritual journey himself. From his culturally Christian, non-religious African American family background he delved into Pentecostalism, Orthodox Judaism, and Zen Buddhism before putting down deeper roots in Tibetan Buddhism. He pushed me to look at my practice and it coincided with my own questions about growth, especially healing from anti-Semitism. As a child I had decided that anger wasn't healthy so I completely shut down that emotion. For me, part of spiritual practice is about recovering a full expression of myself and healing whatever limits my ability to express myself in a vibrant and powerful way. It was clear to me from talking to my partner that he had done a lot of that work. I saw it in the quality of attention and thought he brought to our relationship. It was about mutual growth and support, seeing people for who they really *are* versus who you *want* them to be. Being with him opened me up to looking at spiritual practice and meditation as a potential tool. One of my realizations came during this time. He had always worked less than full time so he could devote time to his spiritual development and I always filled my life up back to back; I didn't spend a lot of quiet time by myself. There was something appealing about slowing down and creating that time for some kind of practice. Because he'd done so much spiritual work and had a disciplined practice, he showed me there were a range of tools out there that would support me.

I had a period of time where I wasn't taking care of myself and finally felt the effects. I hit burnout and defined a personal goal of having balance and taking care of myself mentally, physically, spiritually, and emotionally. Then, I received a letter from Vallecitos[1] saying I'd been nominated for a fellowship. It was all the things I had asked for. Going there gave me a week to put into practice various tools for taking care of myself in fundamental ways. It was my first opportunity to try meditation daily.

My goal is to have a daily practice but I don't have one yet. It's a process; it isn't something that comes easily. Looking at people who do have the practice, I see the value, and it helps me to be patient. It's important that I remain tender with myself, and part of that is recognizing that I've made progress in terms of getting to a place where I'm open to a spiritual practice. I've done some exploration, and that has value. I struggle around making time and not overworking myself. I've been making progress, not making plans for every minute of my life. I'm still exploring what practice will speak to me and be meaningful. The intention is the doorjamb – it holds the door open a little bit. I see that the world of self-growth isn't a linear progression; you will move back at times, but as long as you focus on moving forward, you keep growing. And that's my hope for the work I'm doing.

> If we want to sustain this work, we need to be taking care of ourselves and creating spaces where we can take care of each other.

It's clear to me that part of working with young people is creating a community where people can bring their full selves, support each other, and affirm each other. It's about building relationships where people can be real. When I make an effort in that area it feels like part of my spiritual practice.

What drives me to do more spiritual practice and more reflection is the desire to have my actions consistent with how I want the world to be. I haven't always treated people in the way I want to. I want to create organizations where the values we put out there are consistent with the values we have within. Audre Lorde said, "You cannot dismantle the master's house with the master's tools." I want to hold that in my mind. A lot of organizations articulate the external vision without thinking about how they operate internally. It makes them more vulnerable to practices or attitudes that negatively affect the mission and health of the organization. You have ageism or racism and it might not be challenged because there isn't a space for people to look at what they're creating.

---

[1] a retreat center in New Mexico that is specifically for social change activists

If we want to sustain this work, we need to be taking care of ourselves and creating spaces where we can take care of each other. There can be an emphasis on economic and social justice but if we don't focus on human transformation, it doesn't bring us the quality of life that I would like us to have.

life as practice . . . .

Darryl Lester

Darryl Lester has worked in adult and youth development since 1990 with organizations like North Carolina Public Allies, the Counseling Center at Shaw University, African-American Student Affairs at North Carolina State University, and the 4–H Youth Development School-age Care Project. He is also a trustee for the Warner Foundation. Most recently, he served as the Program Officer at the Triangle Community Foundation and now consults on issues of community problem-solving and ethnic and race relations. He lives in Raleigh, North Carolina with his wife, Dionne, and their daughter, Danielle.

I grew up in a small town in South Carolina, somewhat rural, in a large family. Going to church was a tradition. The church was the center, and you went out of habit. You got involved, went to Bible school in the summer, participated in the choir, you were an usher; it became a ritual. I came from a family whose values came out of that foundation of the church.

As I've grown older, I've widened my lens on southern religion and I see it as more of a spiritual path. I still go to church, but now it's more about principles and values and things that need to happen outside of that building. And I realize that as I grow, I can connect

> The more I walk this path, the more humble I want to become.

with other folks whose foundation may not be the same as mine. I'm trying to keep the peace in my own life, and my faith allows me to keep that peace, but it also helps me make sense of some of the things going on in the world and of how folks can get peace in their own lives. And it doesn't always mean, "Come into this building."

I'm a part of this church, and it's a small southern church, but when I hear some of the Church folks make comments, it almost makes me not want to be a part of it. But I realize everywhere I go it is like this. So I get what I need from there, and I back away from what I don't need. When we did the Annual Black Church Week of Prayer for the Healing of AIDS, there were comments made around the table that showed people's ignorance and I had to educate people without backing them into a corner. I wanted to snap their heads off, but I couldn't; I had to educate them, so that next year they'll be in a different place. There's this unconditional love.

Integral to my practice is a time of prayer and acknowledgment that there is this force. You can't see it, but you do know it has some control over things that are happening. I think through prayer you're able to communicate with that force. There are also guiding principles that go along with that. Being humble is one for me – the more I walk this path, the more humble I want to become. Another is the value of being genuine. You don't say one thing and do another. You try to be consistent in how you live your life. It's not a rigid walk; I'm always trying to connect with people where they are. Even though you might be on a different side of the coin, you can still have some appreciation for where they stand.

> It's not a rigid walk; I'm always trying to connect with people where they are.

I try to connect with people that help me reinforce those same things. I love basketball. In the mornings for the last year and a half, fifteen guys have met to play, and we start off with some quiet time. Some guys bring a prayer or something inspirational. Then we play ball, and we play hard, intense. But guys aren't arguing with each other, aren't cursing. We don't get slowed up by arguing about a call or something like that. We all play hard, but it's about guys trying to get their bodies in shape, because part of their spiritual walk is trying to take care of themselves. Now we're looking at how this same group of individuals can come together and address what is happening in our community.

And I fast often. As you're able to clear your system, it puts you more in alignment with that spiritual force. Now I try to do it anytime before I do something in public. I'm really asking for the supreme being to clear my mind. It's not about folks looking at me, but about trying to get them to hear what I'm saying, what has meaning for me.

In the work environment, folks try to separate out their faith if they have one. Folks that are at peace with themselves, you can tell by how they operate at work. If we've got a deadline to meet, I don't have to snap at you. My faith is going to determine how I'm going to treat people at work.

I pick and choose my battles. I can't afford to spend energy dealing with trivial stuff at work; when I leave work I'm trying to deal with other stuff. Being a person of color, when I walk out of work I'm going to encounter different things than my coworkers will. History has shown that my chances of sometimes being taken the wrong way are increased. I've been in the grocery store, and I can watch folks' demeanor with their pocket books. I try to laugh it off, but it's still frustrating. When you don't have faith and you encounter that kind of tension on your life, you don't always know where to go with it. My faith has given me a high threshold; my faith gives me peace.

practice.

mindfulness

Mindfulness is loving all the details of our lives,
and awareness is the natural thing that happens:
life begins to open up, and you realize that you're always standing
at the center of the world.

~ Pema Chödrön, Awakening Loving Kindness

Let us be silent that we may hear the whispers of the Gods.

~ Ralph Waldo Emerson

It is a central stillness of spirit that is so vital that it can tame the wildness
out of almost any tempest, however raging it may be.

~ Howard Thurman, Meditations of the Heart

what is mindfulness? . . . .

Mindfulness is balanced awareness in every moment, a kind of loving attention that is detached but present. We might choose to practice mindfulness
during certain periods, through a practice like meditation, and then we are
more likely to be mindful the rest of the day. We can walk or drive or work or
play with a greater sense of attention. Cooking, eating, and cleaning can
become acts of mindfulness. Each interaction becomes an opportunity to
practice mindfulness in our speech, our actions, and the way we listen to other
people; in each instance meditation can help us make the choice to be present.
Staying present, we can listen more closely and without needing to respond as
quickly. As we become more aware of our actions and our interactions, we also
begin to notice and be mindful of our emotions – anger joy, frustration, fear,
excitement, despair – without becoming attached to them.

     Mindfulness nurtures our ability to ask, sometimes almost subcon-
sciously, What is my truth? What is my response to this situation? What else
do I need to know? What is the best course of action? Do I have the energy to
do it? Who else can help? The more mindful we are, the more we can respond
in a way that is truthful and wise. There seems to be a greater and greater sense
of urgency in the world. We don't always feel as if we have time to think
things through before making a decision. Mindfulness increases our ability to
think clearly about our work and ourselves. We get a chance to be aware of
what is going on, our breath, our sitting, a mantra, a candle in front of us—
whatever we choose to focus on. And all we have to do is be aware. These
things ask no response from us. What a switch from daily life, when we are
constantly asked to respond. Pick up the phone when it rings, and you have to
say something. Someone presents us with a problem, and we automatically
begin to solve it. A crisis hits at work or at home and we have been conditioned to come up with something, and fast. It is easy to overlook vital
information and the range of potential responses. What if we created another
option for ourselves, not to react but to be in full, present, and loving awareness? And what if, in that space of being, we left lots of time for the voice of
our true wisdom to emerge?

turning point . . . .

In 1994, I made what would be the first of many visits to the Kripalu Center
for Yoga and Health in western Massachusetts. It was my first introduction to
both yoga and something called Danskinetics – a combination of dance, yoga,
group interaction, and an aerobic workout. My first Danskinetics class was
taught by Ken Scott, who also goes by his Sanskrit name, Nateshvar. For an
hour and a half he led us through a series of powerful dance movements and

into free-form dance, with an energy and excitement that I had never seen before or since. Through it all he radiated a sense of goodness and joy.

And he did not say a word.

Later that afternoon I noticed another guest approach him in the hallway. He smiled at her, listened, smiled again, touched his finger to his lips, shook his head, smiled a third time, and moved on. I watched in wonder. I found the woman at dinner that evening and told her I couldn't help being intrigued by their exchange. She laughed and informed me that Nateshvar was on a silent retreat. He was only engaging in nonverbal communication, which allowed him to continue teaching Danskinetics, yoga, and other movement classes.

This silent retreat was to last for one year.

Through this encounter, I became fascinated with the power of silence and its effect on the mind. I used to think I had to talk all the time. This was an unconscious response to the fear that I'd be perceived as boring, unintelligent, or clueless. If you send a very loud parade down the street, maybe no one will notice the street itself or the house where you live. I began to realize that many of the most intriguing and intelligent people I knew did not seem to feel this similar compulsion. I started to think about what my talking attempted to hide but often exposed: nervousness, angst, ignorance, arrogance. I wondered how I might rely less on verbal communication. And I started to incorporate intentional silence into my daily life, eliminating conversations for at least an hour after waking up and an hour before going to bed.

In early 1998, I returned to Kripalu for a month for a work-study program and spent five of those days in silence. In this mindful quiet, I marveled as idealized images of myself melted away, and I became more content with reality. I made decisions with greater intentionality and I was less likely to jump to conclusions or make assumptions. Other people's faults and bad habits barely even registered. I was exempt from mindless chatter and small talk, engaging less with people and more with myself and my spirit. I was amazed at how easy it was to go about my day without words: doing yoga, working in the kitchen, brushing my teeth, eating, wiping tables in the dining hall, walking in the Berkshires, dancing. And my silence made more space for other people as well. I paid greater and greater attention as friends shared parts of their own story that had been previously unheard. The internal storms that raged were ones that had been brewing beneath the surface for some time, waiting for the signal that hurricane season had begun. Somehow the mindfulness triggered the tempest but instead of being afraid or wanting to escape, I was grateful. The pain that rose up was almost welcome. Somehow I knew it carried with it the seeds of rebirth.

My last day in silence was a difficult one, culminating in a particularly challenging afternoon yoga session. My friend Jay came up and motioned to ask if I wanted to take a walk. I was grateful for the invitation. I had already begun to think of Jay as a refuge and without quite knowing how, I knew our time together would offer some healing. That winter in the Berkshires the snow fell every second or third day, so I pulled on my boots, sweaters, scarf, hat, and gloves. I almost felt I was burying myself beneath all those layers. More familiar with the various trails around Kripalu, Jay led the way. We walked side by side, content to be in each other's presence without needing to play charades or point things out along the way. I was grateful for a traveling companion, someone who, as writer Rainer Maria Rilke says, will "border and protect each other's solitude." About twenty minutes later we reached our destination – Monk's Pond – a place Jay had promised to show me the week before. I hadn't anticipated the beauty of this small pond, iced over, covered in white, surrounded by more of the same, as snow-laced trees and bushes. Even the late afternoon sky chimed in with milky gray. We walked out to the end of the short dock that jutted into the pond and Jay looked at me for the first time, as if to present the treasure. I smiled in grateful response. The wonderland instilled a renewed sense of peace. I became mindful of my senses, tasting snow, hearing the ice drip off the trees, watching the many shades that white can be. We took time to explore the outskirts of the pond on our own, and I knew this afternoon would stay with me for a long time.

Monk's Pond would not have been striking if we'd chatted the whole way there and back. If Jay had felt the need to tell me a story about *his* first trip to the pond. If I'd asked where we were going when we set off on our walk. If I hadn't been focused on l istening to the pond, instead of talking my way around it. The experience gave me a glimpse at how quiet enriches both activity and rest, and how it opens us to the power of waiting in presence.

 questions for reflection . . . .

Our soul makes constant noise, but it has a silent place we never hear.
When the silence of God enters us, pierces our soul and joins its
silent secret place, then God is our treasure and our heart.
And space opens before us like a fruit that breaks in two.
Then we see the universe from a point beyond space.

~ *Simone Weil,* Random Thoughts on the Love of God; *translated by Robert Bly*

Do you notice yourself becoming distracted or trying to do too many things at one time?

How do you refocus your attention?

Can you imagine your mind less full of distractions, allowing you to go through your day more mindful of each experience?

What kinds of silence are present in your life? How are they different?

When are you most comfortable with it? Uncomfortable?

@ silence: an invitation to mindfulness

In the presence of silence, the conditioned self rattles and scratches.
It begins to crumble like old leaves or worn rock. If we have courage,
we take silence as medicine to cure us from our social ills,
the suffering of self-centered alienation. In silence, sacred silence,
we stand naked like trees in winter, all our secrets visible under our skin.
And like winter's tree, we appear dead but are yet alive.

~ Joan Halifax, The Fruitful Darkness

Silence is an opening that encourages mindfulness. It is the voice of intuition and of soul, of depthful reality. This is the voice that we search for when we have to make difficult decisions, prepare for a life-changing event, or deal with great pain. It is also the voice that keeps alive the memory of great struggle and tremendous joy. Once we get past the possible discomfort, silence can enhance the communication and relationship we have with friends and loved ones. Silence quiets our nerves and the endless chatter in our minds, brings us to greater states of rest, and provides space to regain perspective. Carving out a place for silence is an act of paying more attention to one's self, to other people, and to the world. It is an act of resistance to abstain from unimportant conversation and thoughtless communication.

We live in an age of sound. At work, telephones ring, machines hum, people talk, faxes fax. We come home, and we turn on our radios, televisions, CD players, and VCRs. We can barely imagine our life without this wall of noise, this flow of information, but we also need the silent spaces between sound to transform so much information into wisdom. How much information do you deal with every day? Think of the written information: faxes, E-mails, regular

the sounds of nature

In May 1998 a local paper reported the somewhat startling appearance of six species of cicadas in the Raleigh-Durham area. After living underground for thirteen years, feeding off tree roots, the cicadas had crawled out of the ground. They were ready to attract a mate, lay eggs, and pass on to their next life in bug heaven.

I heard the cicadas that weekend and at first thought they were locusts. Their noise was full of celebration, the sounds of gratitude for their liberation. The article, however, reported, "People have mistaken it [the buzz] for airplanes flying overhead, construction equipment, even burglar alarms. The sound is so loud, so annoying, and so puzzling that they're calling 911, wanting to know what's going on."

We no longer recognize the sounds of nature.

Buddhism, enlightenment, and the four noble truths

Meditation comes from the Eastern tradition of Buddhism. Buddha is the Sanskrit word for "awakened one." The story of the Buddha begins in 560 B.C.E., when a young man named Siddhartha was born a prince in northern India. His father the king hid all unpleasantness from him. It wasn't until Siddhartha got outside the palace walls at age twenty-nine that he caught a glimpse of suffering: sickness, aging, and death.

This experience transformed him forever and sent him on a pilgrimage. For years he wandered throughout India, studying Hindu teachings, fasting, and practicing yogic exercises, all in search of a solution to the suffering he had witnessed. Eventually he abandoned religious teachings but continued to meditate. He sat and struggled until finally one day he experienced what Buddhists now call enlightenment: a feeling of complete oneness, no separation. Soon afterward he began to teach his message of hope, that there is a way beyond suffering.

(continued on next page)

mail. Then there's verbal communication – conversations, phone calls, meetings. We often arrive at a new place full of thoughts or emotions from the last place – the traffic jam, an interaction with family or friends, a frustrating or stimulating phone call. The question becomes, How does information become wisdom? How do we find time to process and reflect on all that we are taking in? The more we attempt to do more than one thing at one time, the more relevant this question becomes.

⊚ silence in your daily life

Noise, it seems to me, is one obvious manifestation of the clutter, confusions, and overstimulation of modern life that interferes with spirituality.

~ Elizabeth Warren Forsythe

How might you incorporate silence into your day? Could you be silent before nine A.M. or after eight P.M.? This is harder if you have children, but some of the sanest parents I know make a habit of finding quiet time for themselves at one end of the day or the other. Other people stop at their house of worship in the mornings or afternoons to sit quietly in the sanctuary. The experience of being in a church, synagogue, mosque, or temple is different when you are the only one.

There are also many ways to integrate some quiet time into your workday. It takes creativity and commitment, and a willingness to resist the urge to fill up every moment. Whether you work in or out of the home, beginning or ending your workday with even two minutes of silence can make a big difference. This time can help you set an intention for the day, reflect on your primary accomplishments and highlights, or just breathe. If your life requires that you spend time in transit – in a car, truck, subway, bus, or on foot – consider how you use this time. Are you scrambling to make phone calls, catching up on your reading, eating your lunch? Could you imagine dropping these additional activities just for one day?

Maybe you could spend one whole day in silence. Pick a non-workday, if possible. Inform your family or living companion(s) of your intention ahead of time, even ask them to join you. Try not to stay at home all day, even if it's a weekend. Enjoy opportunities to interact with others nonverbally. At Kripalu, they have nametags inscribed with the words, "In Loving Silence." You can try that, or carry around a card that explains briefly what you are doing. In his article for *The New York Times Magazine* entitled "Silent Sundays," author James Otis explains that over the past three years of staying silent every Sunday, he has carried around printed cards that read "I don't speak on Sundays." These are given to anyone with whom he must interact. You may very well open the door for someone else to discover the power of silence. The more humor and openheartedness you bring to the experience, the less uncomfortable you'll feel with other people's reactions. Your commitment will inspire and intrigue some, even while it is confusing and strange to them.

Let the silence be all-encompassing: no radio, television, or CD player. Throughout the day, jot down your thoughts, reactions, the difficulties and joys, the reactions you receive from others. Or, just move through the day without stopping to process it. Let your thoughts and feelings come to the surface and then sink down into the depths of your being. Later you can reflect on what was important about the experience. Silence is a great opportunity to become what you know.

℮ silence and the senses

I once found myself in the Snake River Wilderness Area of northern New Mexico with a group of people. As someone who grew up in a green suburb, and now lives in a city full of amazing trees, the desert of the Southwest is a place of mystery to me. I marvel at the hues, the vegetation, the vastness. It catapults me to another part of myself, not familiar at all, but welcome all the same. So it was with this visit to Snake River. I felt the blessing of being so far from home, literally and figuratively. As we got closer to the edge of the canyon above the river, I started to hear the faint sounds of rushing water. Everyone was talking, excited by our journey and being together, and it was hard for me to take in the incredible beauty that surrounded us. I wanted everyone to just be quiet. I confided this to one friend who encouraged me to ask the group for what I wanted. I didn't know everyone all that well, so I took a few deep breaths and finally spoke up, asking the group if we could be silent for a few moments together. People looked a little surprised but everyone quieted down. As we stood in silence, the sound of the water filled my ears, the colors became more vivid, and I could feel the wind howling at my skin. Others seemed to appreciate this slight pause in the chatter.

Try this in a backyard, a park, or in a place of natural beauty. Sit in silence for ten minutes. Use this time for prayer, meditation, or thought, but don't read or write. At the end of ten minutes, begin to

His message is conveyed through the Four Noble Truths:

1. *Dukkha,* or suffering, is a necessary condition of life.

2. The cause of suffering is *tanha,* or the desire for private fulfillment. We must accept this suffering and take full responsibility for it if we are to find a way out of it.

3. Everyone is capable of relieving suffering by overcoming this desire.

4. Suffering can be relieved through the Noble Eightfold Path: right knowledge, right understanding, right speech, right behavior, right livelihood, right effort, right mindfulness, and right concentration.

With all I have thought and read about silence, I have found nothing more beautiful than the words of writer Pico Iyer in his essay for *Time* magazine, "The Eloquent Sounds of Silence"

We have to earn silence, then, to work for it; to make it not an absence but a presence; not emptiness but repletion. Silence is something more than just a pause; it is that enchanted place where space is cleared and time is stayed and the horizon itself expands. In silence, we often say we can hear ourselves think; but what is truer to say is that in silence we can hear ourselves not think, and so sink below our selves into a place far deeper than mere thought allows. In silence, we might better say, we can hear someone else think.

Silence, then, could be said to be the ultimate province of trust: it is the place where we trust ourselves to be alone; where we trust others to understand the things we do not say; where we trust a high harmony to assert itself. . . . In love, we are speechless; in awe, we say, words fail us.

(*Time*, 25 January 1993)

explore your senses. Take three slow steps in any direction and stop. Check in:

What do you see?

What do you hear?

What do you feel?

What do you smell?

What do you touch?

silent retreats

A silent retreat of even two or three days can be a time of integration, elimination, and stillness. You might seek out a local retreat center, monastery, or convent, many of which have space for guests for a low fee or donation. Many meditation centers sponsor workshops in silence, with a nightly talk by one of the meditation teachers. These places are more common than you might expect. Bring a journal and maybe one inspirational book, but take care not to overload yourself. Don't rush to fill up your days. Watch how your body slows down, how your eating habits change, and what shifts in your experience through your senses. A short list of retreat centers is provided in the Appendix.

meditation: mindful being

The spirituality of it [meditation] ambushed me.
Unwittingly, I was engaging in a practice that has been at the heart
of religious mysticism for millenniums. To separate 20 minutes from the day
with silence and intention is to worship, whether you call it that or not.
To be awakened to the miracle of existence – to experience Being not only
in roses and sunsets but right now, as something not out there but in here –
this is the road less traveled, the path of the pilgrim, the quest.

~ Marty Kaplan, "Ambushed by Spirituality," Time

Meditation is a form of silent concentration – being mindful of one thing and observing it with intentness. The clearing of the mind. It can be practiced either in the context of a religious tradition or completely independent of one. There may be no greater need for us than to learn to be still. Through meditation, we can detach ourselves from hoped-for results and whatever is consuming us in the moment. Meditation allows us to relax our grip on life, our need to make everything work out, our desire to stay completely in control. The trick is not to avoid the bad days, the frustrations, the stress, the pain. Rather we can watch it, as one might watch the weather, knowing it's bound to shift.

There are as many definitions as there are practitioners, but the basis of many forms of meditation is the breath. Our breath is a mirror of our emotional landscape, the one thing we always have with us. If we're nervous or scared, the breath reflects this. If we slow our breath down, the body automatically begins to feel a sense of calm. With each breath in, if we are conscious of it, we are breathing in energy. With each breath out, we breathe out something we no longer need. All organisms breathe; it is one of the few things that all of nature has in common. The *Oxford English Dictionary* defines spirit as "the animating or vital principle in man and animals; that which gives life to the physical organism, in contrast to its purely material elements, the breath of life."[1] To focus on this miracle is to pay close attention to the most important physiological and psychological process we have as human beings. We breathe, and with awareness of breath, we begin to clear our minds. The endless stream of words and images begins to slow down.

℮ basic meditation

The practice of meditation can reduce tension and promote relaxation, improve concentration and self-discipline, give a sense of improved well-being, increase energy, aid the development of the psyche, enhance spiritual growth, lower high blood pressure, decrease the frequency and severity of tension-related diseases, aid the body in its recovery from physical fatigue, promote serenity, and improve your ability to listen.

·· *Jessica Macbeth,* Moon Over Water

We might think of meditation as solely an Eastern practice, but in fact many of the world's religious traditions embrace meditative silence. Clergy and lay people alike have found innovative ways to deepen religious prayers and rituals by incorporating periods of meditation. There are now numerous books and retreats focusing on Jewish and Christian meditation; some are listed in "resources for mindfulness" at the end of this chapter. Each book, teacher, and religious tradition offers different ways to meditate. Experiment until you find something that works for you. Here is one way to get started.

1. Before beginning a period of meditation, it helps a lot to stretch or do some yoga to get energy flowing through your body. If you have an alarm that is not

too loud, set it for the desired length of the meditation period. That way you can meditate without having to worry about how long it has been or how much time you have left.

2. Find a comfortable, quiet spot. Sit in the same place every day. Over time, it will become a quietly enchanting corner in your house, apartment, or room. Your body temperature will drop as you sit, so dress for warmth. Sit either in a straight-backed chair or on the floor, cross-legged. If you sit in a chair and your feet don't reach the ground, find a box or pillow to rest your feet on. If you choose the floor, put a cushion under your buttocks so your knees rest on the floor. Your back should be as straight as possible. You want a posture that will allow the maximum energy to flow through you. At some point, you may want to explore sitting on a prayer bench or Zafu cushion, used in Zen meditation.

3. Rest your hands either in your lap or on your thighs in a position that is both comfortable and intentional. See how long you can make your spine and your torso. You may want to begin with a short ritual – lighting a candle, saying a short invocation, or reading an inspirational prayer or poem to yourself.

4. Close your eyes or bring them to a soft gaze, looking down and about six inches in front of you. In many forms of meditation the eyes are usually left open. The belief is that if you practice mindfulness in meditation with the eyes open, it will be easier to maintain that mindfulness during the rest of the day, when your eyes are open. In the beginning, closing your eyes may help eliminate distractions.

5. Begin to notice your breath. Let it deepen and lengthen as your body starts to relax. Get settled in your body, your breath, and the space around you. You don't have to do anything deliberate to the breath, just watch it. Feel the rise and fall of your belly and your rib cage. Notice where the breath flows in the body and where it feels tight.

6. Bring a more concentrated awareness to the breath by counting to ten breaths. On the in breath, silently count "one" in your head; on the out breath, listen to the sound of the exhale. On the next in breath, count "two," and so on. If you lose count (which you surely will – our minds need practice to stay focused), just start over over again with "one." When you do get to ten, start over. Try consciously to notice your breath as it moves up and down through your body. Continue this for a period of five minutes at first;

gradually you can lengthen this period. A variation is to pick one word like "peace" or "love" to say to yourself on the in breath.

7. End your meditation as consciously as you began it. If your eyes were closed, open them slowly. Give yourself a couple of minutes just to rest in the quiet of the moment. The moments following meditation can be some of the most blissful. You may want to end with a closing ritual or prayer. Take time to stretch out your legs, back, and shoulders after you've finished sitting. Stand up slowly and take your time transitioning to the next part of your day.

Try this practice early in the morning and/or in the evening. Five to ten minutes twice a day can make a revolutionary difference; eventually you can work your way up to fifteen to twenty minutes or more.

℗ meditation as metaphor

Breathing is the fundamental link between all things in nature.
It is our conscious relationship to life. Breathing connects our awareness
to every movement, every thought, every emotion we have.
How we breathe is how we live.
And the way we breathe can allow us to recover our wholeness,
our balance of body and mind.

~ Bija Bennett, Breathing into Life

It's hard to engage fully with the world when the mind is frantic. We're distracted, we drift, we're somewhere else, and suddenly we've missed the confession, the information, the question, the assistance we needed. Some days you will feel many of the benefits meditation has to offer; other days you may not feel any. Recognize that you will have a range of experiences with meditation just as you would with any other spiritual practices. All of these experiences are part of the practice. It may be helpful to realize that the challenges that arise during meditation are metaphors for what we face in the rest of our lives.

DISTRACTION. If there's one thing you can count on during meditation, it's distraction. Our minds are not used to the kind of quiet meditation can sometimes bring, and initially we do not know exactly how to handle it. You start to sink deeply into a breath, and a few items for your grocery list float through your head. Or you remember something you wished you'd said in an earlier conversation. Or an idea for a new project appears. Suddenly you are not meditating; you are thinking. What do you do? First of all, relax. Try not to get discouraged; this happens to everyone. Meditation is deceptively simple, but there is nothing easy about it. And then just notice what is happening. Buddhist nun and teacher Pema Chödrön suggests that you say to yourself, "Oh, I'm thinking. Oh, I have an itch on my left foot," then refocus your attention on your breath. Let the distraction lead you back to the breath. And then observe how you begin to deal differently with distractions in the rest of your day.

JUDGMENT. Being disciplined about meditation is one thing. Being hard on yourself is quite another. Be kind to yourself, especially in the beginning, and don't worry if you think you're not meditating well, not doing it often enough, or not doing it for long enough. It may take a while before you are actually able to concentrate on your breath for more than a couple of seconds. This is proof enough of how cluttered and busy our minds are and how we can benefit from time set aside simply for concentrated awareness. Even when we're struggling with the practice, we can still reap the benefits. And, as we grow in compassion for ourselves, we become more compassionate with those around us.

DISCOMFORT. Westerners usually have a harder time letting their bodies adjust to sitting meditation. It is a good idea to relax your body before meditating. Some light stretching or yoga can be enormously helpful. (See the "Healing" chapter for more information.) Trust your body – any kind of gentle movement that helps relax your back, shoulders, legs, and arms will allow you to sit for a longer period of time, with less fidgeting. You can also guide yourself through a full body relaxation meditation described below.

FATIGUE. Falling asleep during meditation is perfectly normal, especially at first. It may be a sign that your body needs a kind of relaxation even deeper than meditation. You may not be getting enough sleep, or your mind may be resisting this level of concentration. You may want to change your position or alter the time of day in which you're meditating. Many of us don't always see fatigue for what it truly is – a sign that we need more rest. If you find yourself continually nodding off during meditation, you might consider getting more hours of sleep or finding space for a short nap in the middle of the day. (Extreme fatigue can also be a sign of depression or illness; consult a health practitioner if additional rest does not seem to help.)

℮ walking meditation

Walking meditation is a chance to pay attention both to your breath and to your footsteps. The basic instruction is to be aware of every step you take. Be mindful as you pick your foot up, as it hangs briefly in the air, as your body shifts its weight, as that foot comes down and the other one comes up. Zen master and peace activist Thich Nhat Hanh has a beautiful saying: With the lifting of the left foot, breathe one full breath and say to yourself, "I have arrived." With the lifting of the right foot, breathe on full breath and say, "I am home." Your hands can be clasped in front of you at waist height, or hanging loosely by your sides.

You might be amazed at how slowly you can walk. You can do this anywhere. Beautiful, scenic locations offer wonderful opportunities for walking meditation. It's also interesting to try this on the streets of a big city. Small spaces like your living room are great and even better for concentration, because you may not be easily distracted. It's nice to stop periodically and just breathe. Thich Nhat Hanh's *A Guide to Walking Meditation* (Nyack, N.Y.: Fellowship Publications, 1985) is a good resource for guidance.

℗ full-body meditation for relaxation

Lie down on a comfortable floor or sit comfortably (but straight) in a chair. If you lie down, put a pillow under your knees. Make sure you're dressed warmly enough. What follows is a "script" for full-body relaxation. You can:

1. Read it over a few times to get the general flow, memorize a few key phrases, and then repeat it to yourself. Keep this next to you and refer to it periodically. You may find this less relaxing the first few times you do it, but you'll find in time that you've committed much of it to memory and no longer need the script.
2. Record it on a tape player and play it back.
3. Pair up with a friend and lead each other through it.

NOTE: Each time you see ". . ." pause for one full breath. The main thing here is to take it very slow, but not so slow that you fall asleep in the middle of the meditation.

Begin by settling into the space underneath you . . . feel your body sink into the floor or the chair . . . feel it getting heavier . . . let your body relax . . . loosen any clothing that may feel tight . . . readjust your body if you need to to feel more comfortable . . . turn your attention to your breath . . . just watch your breath . . . notice it getting deeper . . . focus your attention only on the breath . . . as you breathe, become aware that each breath in is a chance to breathe healing energy from the ground below you . . . each breath out is a chance to rid the body of tension . . . use whatever distractions may arise as reminders to return to your breath . . . this is time just for your body and your mind to relax . . .

Now bring your awareness to your feet . . . they carry you around every day . . . let them relax . . . breathe into your feet, noticing any points of tension or stress . . . just let your feet relax . . . clench the muscles in your feet and toes for a moment . . . feel the relaxation deepen as you release . . . let your feet and your ankles sink into the floor beneath you . . . now move your awareness to your calves and your knees . . . notice any tightness or tension here . . . tighten these muscles and let them relax . . . keep breathing deeply as you begin to focus on your thighs, your pelvis, your buttocks . . . tense up the muscles in your thighs and your pelvis . . . then enjoy the release as you let this part of your body relax . . . continue to breathe deeply and evenly . . . notice the calm in your lower body . . .

Next, begin breathing into your back . . . you may notice many different points of tension in your upper and lower back . . . this is a common place to hold stress . . . tense up the muscles of your back and let them go into a state of calm relaxation . . . breathe into your back and breathe out, letting yourself sink deeper into the ground or the chair . . . bring your awareness next to your chest and your stomach . . . tighten the muscles in this area and then let them relax . . . notice your breath as it moves through you . . . the chest and stomach moving in and out in an easy rhythm . . . let this part of your body relax . . .

Imagine drawing a breath in through your fingers and letting it drift slowly up your arms . . . let your fingers and hands, elbows and arms relax . . . tighten the muscles in your arms and let them relax . . . bring the breath and your awareness to your shoulders and your neck . . . notice how you feel . . . notice if there is any stress or aching in this part of your body . . . you may want to let your neck roll slowly from side to side, being careful not to strain any muscles . . . breathe slowly into this part of your upper body . . . let the gentle breath bring healing to your shoulders and your neck . . . let them release . . . let every breath out carry tension away with the body . . .

With the breath, begin to notice your head and your face, your mouth, nose, eyes . . . become aware of any tension . . . let the breath flow through your face and let it relax . . . give your face and head permission to just let go and release . . . drop your jaw . . . let your eyelids droop . . . notice your face and head getting heavier as they become more relaxed . . .

Breathe relaxation into your whole body . . . let the breath wash up and down like a gentle wave . . . let it flow over every muscle, every bone, every cell . . . with your breath, notice how relaxed your body has become . . . know this is a state you can always return to . . . that is the breath, your breath, which brought you here . . . your body and mind and soul are relaxed . . . this relaxation will stay with you . . .

Slowly, return your awareness to the floor beneath you and the room around you . . . leave your eyes closed . . . when you're ready, begin to wiggle your fingers and your toes . . . stay focused on your breath . . . slowly roll over to one side . . . very slowly, when you're ready, sit up . . . notice how different your body feels . . . when you are ready, open your eyes . . . move very slowly as you stretch your legs and arms . . .

You can also find recorded guided meditations to listen to, or books with meditations that can be recorded and played back. Many use imagery as a way into relaxation. There are plenty of great tapes around, and many public libraries have them.

resources for mindfulness . . . .

Adair, Margo. *Working Inside Out: Tools for Change*. Oakland, Calif.: Wingbow Press, 1984. Full of guided meditations to use with groups engaged in social and political action. Focuses on energy, planning, healing, relationships, and visioning. www.toolsforchange.org

Bennett, Bija. *Breathing into Life: Recovering Wholeness through Body, Mind and Breath*. New York: HarperCollins, 1993. A compact collection of short meditative exercises on the breath.

Bonhoeffer, Dietrich. *Meditating on the Word*. Translated and edited by David M. Gracie. Boston: Cowley Publications, 2000. www.cowley.org/books/bonhoef.asp Exploration of biblical meditation, written by the man executed at age thirty-nine for plotting to assassinate Hitler.

Chödrön, Pema. *When Things Fall Apart*. Boston: Shambhala, 1997. Radical and compassionate advice for what to do when things go wrong from one of the first Western women to take full monastic Buddhist vows.

———. *The Wisdom of No Escape and the Path of Loving Kindness*. Boston: Shambhala, 1991. A wonderful collection of talks given by Chodron at a month-long meditation retreat at Gampo Abbey. www.shambhala.org/teachers/pema/index.html; www.gampoabbey.org

Cooper, David A. *A Heart of Stillness: A Complete Guide to Learning the Art of Meditation*. Woodstock, Vt.: Jewish Lights Publishing, 1999. A comprehensive, nonsectarian guide to meditation from a rabbi and longtime student of mysticism.

De Mello, Anthony. *Wellsprings: A Book of Spiritual Exercises*. New York: Random House, 1986. Prayerful writing that blends Eastern and Western wisdom, from a beloved Jesuit priest.

Gefen, Nan Fink. *Discussing Jewish Meditation: Instruction and Guidance for Learning Ancient Spiritual Practice*. Woodstock, Vt.: Jewish Lights Publishing, 1999.

Halifax, Joan. *The Fruitful Darkness: Reconnecting with the Body of the Earth*. San Francisco: HarperCollins, 1993. Stories from one woman's journey into the practice and ancient teachings in Buddhism and Shamanism. www.upaya.org

Hesse, Herman. *Siddhartha*. Translated by Hilda Rosner. New York: Bantam, 1951. One classic version of the story of the Buddha.

Housden, Roger. *Retreat: Time Apart for Silence and Solitude*. San Francisco: HarperCollins, 1995. A beautiful guide to retreats in many of the major religious and spiritual traditions. Includes information on retreats in meditation, yoga, art, music, nature, and silence. www.sacredamerica.com

Kabat-Zinn, John. *Wherever You Go, There You Are*. New York: Hyperion, 1994. A simple and clear guide to bringing mindfulness meditation into everyday life. Short chapters, each with a meditation exercise to try. www.mindfulness.org

Kaplan, Aryeh. *Jewish Meditation: A Practical Guide*. New York: Random House, 1995. Guide to technique by an Orthodox rabbi who died in 1983.

Kaplan, Marty. "Ambushed by Spirituality." *Time Magazine,* 24 June 1996.

Kelsey, Morton T. *The Other Side of Silence: Meditation for the Twenty First Century*. Mahwah, N.J.: Paulist Press, 1997. A classic primer on the art and science of Christian meditation.

Levine, Stephen. *Healing Unto Life and Death*. New York: Anchor Books, 1987. Like many of Levine's books, this one has great guided meditations.

Low, Albert. *An Invitation to Practice Zen*. Rutland, Vt.: Charles E. Tuttle Company, 1989. The Zen Buddhist approach to meditation, complete with background on Buddhist philosophy and detailed instructions for developing a Zen practice. www.zenmontreal.ca

Nhat Hanh, Thich. *The Miracle of Mindfulness*. Translated by Mobi Warren. Boston: Beacon Press, 1976. Thich Nhat Hanh sees every act as a meditative one and provides simple, beautiful commentary on how to lead a mindful life. www.plumvillage.org; www.iamhome.org

———. *Peace is Every Step*. New York: Bantam, 1991. How to walk the path of mindfulness in everyday life; includes commentaries, meditations, and stories.

Norris, Kathleen. *The Cloister Walk*. New York: Riverhead Books, 1996. Moving account of one woman's stay at a Benedictine monastery in Minnesota.

Otis, James. "Silent Sundays." *New York Times Magazine*, 18 January 1998.

Rahula, Walpola. *What the Buddha Taught*. New York: Grove Press, 1974. An account of the Buddha's four noble truths, written by a Buddhist monk and scholar. It includes texts, as remembered and recorded by a group of disciples shortly after the Buddha's death.

Salzberg, Sharon. *Loving-Kindness: The Revolutionary Art of Happiness*. Boston: Shambhala, 1997. Exploration of Buddhist practice from the founder of the Insight Meditation Society. www.dharma.org/ims.htm

Sarton, May. *Journal of a Solitude*. New York: W.W. Norton, 1973. The diary of one year in the life of this writer, poet, thinker, and gardener; a wonderful account of daily life spent largely alone and in silence.

Thondup, Tulku Rinpoche. *The Healing Power of the Mind: Simple Meditation Exercises for Health, Well-Being and Enlightenment.* Boston: Shambhala, 1996. Meditations and visualizations from the basic teachings of ancient Tibetan medicine.

Thurman, Howard. *Meditations of the Heart.* Boston: Beacon Press, 1953. Meditations and prayers from one of the great preachers of the twentieth century. Thurman cofounded the first interracially pastured church in the United States.

Trungpa, Chögyam. *Meditation in Action.* Boston: Shambhala, 1996. Classic teachings on meditation, wisdom, and energy from the Tibetan master who founded the Shambhala Training program and the Naropa Institute. www.shambhala.org; www.naropa.edu

Wolpe, David. *In Speech and In Silence.* New York: Henry Holt, 1992. The importance of silence and words in Jewish tradition, practice, and text. www.macgowen.org/davwollib.html

mindful practice . . . .

Arrington Chambliss

Arrington Chambliss is the founder and director of No Ordinary Time, an organization in Boston that uses contemplation and action to help artists, activists and faith-based leaders cultivate the courage, compassion, clarity, and creativity needed for a more peaceful and just world. Arrington spent twelve years working with young people doing community service through COOL (Campus Outreach Opportunity League), and gang-affiliated men through Project LEEO. She has a M.Div. from Harvard Divinity School, is in the ordination process of the Episcopal Diocese of Massachusetts, and maintains a daily yoga and meditation practice. She lives with her partner, Hez Norton, in Boston, Massachusetts.

About ten years ago, tension and intensity in my work, and my own experience of illness, catalyzed a conversation with two friends. We talked about the need for spiritual grounding. They introduced me to the *Tao Te Ching* and the *I Ching*[1] and that's when I started studying Taoist philosophy. I immediately connected with it. There was a lot of talk about change in communities and systems, but there was rarely talk about change in how we lived our individual lives and how our way of being impacted the questions we asked and the way we did our work.

> It was clear I needed to learn to sit still. The tension inside me was a mirror for the world outside in many ways. I needed to understand it.

I was fascinated that the *I Ching* told me it might not be time to move forward, that nonaction might be the best strategy, that I didn't always have to be assertive with my opinion. The best thing was to sit still. I immediately noticed an impact on my relationships in the office. I began to wonder how systemic changes would shift anything unless there was a shift in consciousness around power and love. My practice gave me a new understanding of how my way of being was connected to the way I saw the world and how systemic change was connected to spiritual change.

And so I learned to sit. That's when I learned to meditate. I had spent six years trying to understand social change, but my own internal terrain remained unexplored. As Archbishop Desmond Tutu said, "the past has a way of returning to you. It does not go and lie down quietly." The tension inside me was a mirror for the world outside in many ways. I needed to understand it. Three to four years into it, I didn't have a name for it, but I came to learn it was mindfulness

[1] The *Tao Te Ching*, written by Lao-Tzu in fifth century China, can be translated as *The Book of the Way*. It is a treatise on the art of living in harmony with the way things are. One surrenders to the tao and finds their own truths about life. The *I Ching*, or *Book of Changes*, is a book of wisdom and an oracle. The last three thousand years of Chinese culture and history have been profoundly affected and inspired by this text. It is the source of Confucianist and Taoist philosophy. There are hundreds of translations and interpretations of the *I Ching*.

practice, focusing on the breath. As I've learned more I've decided the meditation practice that best suits me right now draws from the Tibetan Buddhist tradition, primarily because it uses the material of life – the everyday material of our anger, our life circumstance – and teaches us to transform and rechannel that energy. I practice twice a day, for about thirty minutes in the morning and twenty minutes at night.

Three or four years into meditation I'd reached a plateau about what I was able to teach myself. I needed a guide, someone who knew more than I knew, to help me structure my practice so I could go deeper with it. Now I sit with a meditation group made up of activists and artists once a week to explore the connection between the practice and our lives of seeking peace and justice in the world.

The people I look to for guidance are people who can embrace justice and peace both inside themselves and outside in the world. My inner and outer work are connected. I have come to realize that the messy, inner work that I sometimes try to avoid by pouring myself into justice work needs to be dealt with so that my justice work does not come out of my unconscious anger but out of my conscious desire to create a better world.

> Figure out the practice which grounds you within yourself, whether it be meditation or movement or dance or prayer.

I've had many experiences where the integration of my inner and outer work made a significant difference. One came while I was working at the Ecumenical Community Council with twelve youth organizers in East Boston, one of the most multiethnic communities in the city. We'd spent nine weeks planning and training them how to organize a youth-led, community development planning day, paralleling a process being driven by condominium developers in the area. There was a fear that young people, working-class people, and people of color wouldn't have a voice in that planning process.

On the culminating day of our work, the youth had a list of fifty other young people who said they were coming. The event was to start at eleven-thirty and we got there at eight A.M. to set up. By eleven-forty only four young people were there. The youth organizers became disappointed. The other adult organizer and I gathered them in a group and told everyone to take a deep breath and focus on why we were all there, why we believed this was important, and how powerful was the work we'd all done.

After sitting in silence for a bit, we each talked about one thing we needed to do. There was space to reconnect, not to wallow in our hopelessness and feelings of failure but instead to focus our attention in a different place – what we'd already done well and what could still be done. After our group reflection, the young people ended up choosing to walk up the street recruiting. They brought back twenty-five young people and the day was a great success. They received press coverage and developed priorities to represent the youth perspective in the neighborhood. So while it wasn't a success in terms of our original goals, because of our reflection time together they learned that they did not need to give in to a feeling of hopelessness. They were able to choose their own agency instead. Before I started meditating, I don't know if I would have been able to lift myself out of the hopelessness so as to be able to help them place their attention on the opportunity. For the first time as an organizer, I had the experience of not taking it personally: it wasn't about me, and it also wasn't about them. Creating the space to make that shift is what I think meditation can teach us, to take the pause and see all the possibilities.

For each of us, it is useful to figure out an embodied, reflective practice that grounds us within ourselves, whether it be meditation or movement or dance or prayer. To spend time with ourselves in a regular way whether it's three minutes or an hour. And spend that kind of time with the group of people we work with, time where we are not expected to do anything but recognize our connection to one another and the common purpose. I am learning not to look outside of myself for the answer. It's the hardest lesson of all, and one that I still struggle to remember.

Arrington can be reached at racbliss@aol.com

mindful partnership . . . .

Cheryl and Jim Keen

Cheryl and Jim Keen share a professorship at Antioch College in Yellow Springs, Ohio. They also serve as Senior Research Fellows for the Bonner Foundation, where they study the impact of sustained community service in the development of undergraduates participating in the Bonner Scholars Program on twenty-four college campuses. Together they founded and ran the Governor's School of Public Issues and the Future of New Jersey for thirteen years. They have also taught at Harvard University, Lesley College, and Goddard College. In 1996 they and two others coauthored Common Fire: Leading Lives of Commitment in a Complex World. *They have been married for twenty-seven years.*

JK: I grew up being a Quaker. I studied Quakerism in college, particularly the mystical side of the Quaker tradition. Later, I journeyed to the East and spent time in an ashram where I learned to teach meditation. That whole journey to the East brought me back to my Quaker roots.

CK: When I met Jim, he took me to a Quaker meeting, and it was exactly what I had been looking for, and I hadn't even known about Quakers. The first meeting I went to I said, "This is my spiritual place to grow." I had the sense that everybody was equal and that they all waited for the spirit to move them. I was drawn to the very strong women who were there, the feeling in the room, the lack of hierarchy, the social commitments of people. It embraced everything I cared about: feminism, social action, spirituality, mysticism, and intellect.

> Quaker belief is very strong for me — trying to be loving in all of my dealings, to look to that of God in every person.

JK: It was more comfortable to stay within a tradition that I'd been nurtured in, particularly because it was a very good tradition from which to practice a spiritual or religious orientation that is not centered on one religion but is open to a variety of traditions. I've been meditating regularly for thirty years; Cheryl's been meditating regularly for almost twenty-eight. So that's something that we've been doing together.

CK: Largely because of the demands of family life, we meditate separately. I'll meditate, and he gets the dinner started. Meditating daily, twice a day, keeps me healthy and stable and energized, because I work into the evening. I don't know if it's personality or meditation, but I don't worry. I hold people in the light. If I'm worried about an individual, I hold him or her in my mind and wait for an intuitive moment about how to be of service to that person on his or her path. It might be me who sees what the next step is in someone's life, and I need to stay open to that, spend more time with that person, and listen.

Meditation helps with that. Going to Quaker meeting in a small town like Yellow Springs where other people have powerful commitments keeps me inspired and humbled. There are other people who need support. So meeting replenishes me; it doesn't always, but I'm willing to spend an hour a week to go to meeting on the chance that someone will address my condition or the experience will renew me in a powerful way. Quaker belief is very strong for me – trying to be loving in all of my dealings, to look to that of God in every person. I really try to practice that. I get razzed for always giving the other person the benefit of the doubt, which is the popular culture way of interpreting that.

I think it's important that people develop reflective habits. I try to build it into every learning environment opportunity.

JK: Cheryl creates authentic contexts in which people can practice a greater obedience to the truth. It's a very spiritual approach to education. There's always this sense of concern, not only for people but also for how people come together and support each other and become transformative agents in the world. Wherever we go, eventually she develops a flock. There's something ministerial about her, much more than me.

I've always been kind of a communal type, and while I like solitude, the solitude is in counterpoint to community, rather than being highly individuated. That's the balance for me: solitude, self-authorship, and yet doing that in a way that is highly collaborative with other people. Being able to get that into balance is almost a spiritual discipline. I'm constantly reframing and seeking balance and I've been doing that for years.

I think it's important that people develop reflective habits. I try to build it into every learning environment opportunity. For people who do it, it's a welcome thing. And for young people who have not yet learned how to do it, nothing will serve them better than becoming self-reflective – assessing what they're learning, what they know, what they're feeling, looking for connections, becoming explicit about what's surprising them. I'm always interested in seeing young people become authentic, qualitative researchers of everyday life, including their own.

CK: It's about having spaces in which people can share fragile expressions of things they care about or avenues of exploration that seem fruitful: having people keep them company in the exploration, whether it is in dialogue, or music, or poetry. To create a moment in which something just a little different is happening because someone has opened up and said something much more honest than they ever expected to hear – and to honor that. There they can see the potential of the quickening of the spirit.

JK: I'm very interested in people having experiences like internships and travel abroad, opportunities to experience the world in different ways. That's one of the reasons I think community service programs are so important; it's so bizarrely missing from the lives of many eighteen- to twenty-two-year-olds. The other key is a mentoring environment in which the mantle is passed, and people step up and start to take on the world's challenges in significant ways. Part of the opportunity of being a young adult is to find yourself in situations where you learn important stuff from older folks who have been around.

I'm not really interested in environments that do not challenge people to move across the threshold of significant difference, so that the self evolves at a wider gyration and wider increments of evolution take place. That will, from my point of view, lead to a greater chance that the person will make a larger contribution over time and that it will be on behalf of the whole human family.

Jim and Cheryl can be reached at jkeen@antioch-college.edu

the path of kindness . . . .

Lance Brunner

Lance Brunner is a professor of musicology at the University of Kentucky in Lexington, where he has taught since 1976. He has extensive experience with leadership development, as a Kellogg National Fellow (1985–88) and as the founding director of the Commonwealth Fellowship Program (1990–96), a program for emerging community leaders in the Appalachian region of Kentucky. He has served on the faculty of the UK Emerging Leader Institute since its inception in 1989. Lance has a long-standing interest in the relationship between contemplative practice and social change. His daily mindfulness practices include playing Bach at the piano, whom he considers a secret source of energy, vitality, and sheer joy.

In college I drifted away from any kind of formal religious or spiritual practice. As I became more engaged with the world outside the classroom, particularly with peace and justice issues, I realized that, if I wanted to be effective, some kind of spiritual practice was essential. In the 1980s I worked with the nuclear freeze movement, as well as against the U.S. intervention in Central America, and eventually participated in the Soviet-American citizen diplomacy movement. In the process I had opportunities to work with a number of remarkable social activists, many of whom were deeply spiritual people with religious practices. In observing many people, I realized that those who were most effective and inspiring were those who made a connection between their spiritual practice and their work in the world.

I wasn't interested in a theistic religion, because of the personal baggage I was carrying from my church-going years as a youth. I was looking for a secular practice. In 1986 I heard a talk on the Shambhala Training program (now offered at Shambhala meditation centers throughout the world) and realized that this program was exactly what I was looking for. It is a secular – but also sacred – approach to working with one's heart and mind, but with the goal of helping others and establishing an enlightened society. I recognized this as my path and it has remained so ever since.

For me, the Shambhala path strikes an essential balance between the inner work with heart and mind and the outer work in the world through action and service. Meditative and contemplative practices can provide clarity and energy for the work that needs to be done with and for others. From my involvement with the Shambhala path, I developed an interest in Buddhism, and have been working with that path as a practitioner as well. As I understand it, Buddhism is not a belief system. It is more like a science of the mind than a religion. It invites a radical and direct exploration of one's own experience.

Shambhala was introduced by Chögyam Trungpa Rinpoche, who came to this country in 1970 and began teaching Tibetan Buddhist practice. By 1975 or 1976 he began offering the Shambhala teachings, which also have their roots in Tibet. As I mentioned, an important goal of the Shambhala path is establishing enlightened society. The earliest teachings in Buddhism focused on the causes and cures of human suffering, which remain essential and common threads throughout all schools of Buddhist practice. The Shambhala approach begins from the other direction, in a sense, in suggesting that the world is infused with a quality called "basic goodness." Basic goodness is not a concept we are asked to believe in, but something that we can perceive directly, if we pay attention, which is

> I realized that those who were most effective and inspiring were those who made a connection between their spiritual practice and their work in the world.

where the actual path of meditation comes in. Through meditation we can cultivate such qualities as clarity, tranquility, and focus. Without the clouds of habitual patterns of thought and compulsive distraction, the world becomes very vivid. From this perspective, we can begin to bring the insight of contemplative practice to work on social and environmental problems facing the world today. For a warrior, by the way, problems are not considered obstacles, but are seen as inspirations to work further with a particular situation.

Shambhala Training is described as "the sacred path of the warrior." In this context the warrior's task is not to go to war, but the opposite: to make friends with ourselves, by overcoming our own aggression, our fear, our own prejudice, our own afflicted mind states. The project of Shambhala is not to change ourselves, but to look carefully and to get to know ourselves better, to approach our predicaments with a balance of gentleness and fearlessness. The opportunity just to *be* who you are is a tremendous relief and it allows us to be much kinder toward ourselves and others.

The notion that one can, or has to, save the world can be an egocentric position. I feel that we all have a responsibility to leave it a better place, but it's not up to any one individual to fix it all. It drives you crazy if you try. To work in the world requires energy – the ability to get up, to get started, to stick with it. If you let your energy be drained away by a battle inside your mind and body, that's not a very effective or sustainable way to accomplish anything. I use the slogan "you can't teach peace if you're at war" as a reminder to continue to do the inner work. If we're at war with ourselves, how can we awaken peace and loving kindness in others?

I see spiritual practice as the ground for fruitful action in the world. In ancient Chinese cosmology, it's the joining of heaven (possibility) and earth (practicality). Our job as human beings is to join vision with practicality, heaven and earth. If we're too stuck in earth, with all its details, then we have no vision. If we're fixated on heaven, and have no way of working with practicalities, then we're just dreamers. We need the balance. The sky is endless, endless possibilities. Earth is hard and real; it creates obstacles and challenges to be overcome with skillful means.

The basic practice is a simple sitting meditation that works with the breath, noticing and letting go of thoughts as they come and returning back to the breath. The breath is the object of mindfulness, our point of reference in the present. Meditation is basically just paying attention, but that means paying attention *to* something. The most common "object" is the breath because you can't really hold onto it, but it can connect you to the present moment. When thoughts of elsewhere come in, you can make a note of it and come back to the breath. This simple coming back eventually allows the mind to settle; it creates clarity and calm that is the ground for other practices. The practice by design is simplicity itself, yet it is very challenging to do. It's a gradual path, both difficult and joyful. And I haven't found any other path that works as well for me.

It's naive to look to this type of mindfulness meditation for quick changes and dramatic shifts in one's personality or behavior. Our patterns are deeply set. We continually set up expectations for ourselves, and when we don't live up to them, it is easy to consider ourselves failures. That's where the practice comes in. For example, it's very easy for me to misplace a paper – a document, a bill, a letter. How many times has this happened to me and I think, "I'm a meditator and a teacher, How could I be so mindless?" It's easy to go on and on and obsess, which I find myself doing more than I would like to admit. But it is possible to see oneself starting this process and then just dropping it, giving up on the compulsive searching and getting another copy.

> Through meditation we can cultivate such qualities as clarity, tranquility, and focus. Without the clouds of habitual patterns of thought and compulsive distraction, the world becomes very vivid.

That seems like a small thing, but actually it's symptomatic of a much broader set of expectations we have of ourselves that are the source of a great deal of anguish and wasted energy. If we don't match up to our self-image or expectations in a given situation, small or large, it is an opportunity to be either cruel or kind to ourselves, to meet the situation with a grimace or a smile. Seeing these tendencies in ourselves allows us to see how hard other people are on themselves. We can be kind to them so they can be kind to themselves. It seems much easier to be kind to others than to be merciful to myself, which is why the inner work is so important. We need kindness everywhere. It strikes me that we're all in this predicament together. The particulars are unique, but our general predicament seems to me very common. The Buddha called it *dukkha*, usually translated as "suffering" or "unsatisfactoriness." From the Shambhala point of view such irritations, in any form, are reminders to wake up to the inherent basic goodness of our existence. That's the ground for helping others – for sowing seeds for an enlightened society.

Lance can be reached at brunner@uky.edu

a journey to God

Thérèse Murdza

Thérèse Murdza is a painter and published poet who lives in Durham, North Carolina. She has worked as an organizational development consultant with Lambda Rising, a chain of independent bookstores committed to serving lesbian, gay, transgendered, and bisexual people and their allies. She has also served as a coach to start-up nonprofit organizations in Washington, D.C. and Durham, helping with strategic planning, resource development, change management, and program delivery. She has a strong commitment to working with other white people on dismantling racism in personal relationships and organizational systems.

I was raised Roman Catholic. Both of my folks had gone to Catholic schools and Catholic colleges. My sister and I went to CCD (education for Catholic youth) every Saturday, and we went to church every Sunday or Saturday night. It wasn't a question; it was just what you did. I really loved it, especially communion – the body and blood of Christ. It's not the representation of the blood and body of Christ, it *is* the blood and body of Christ! It was so dramatic and full of passion.

> For me, it's about allowing every action to turn towards God or away from God.

I remember wanting to be a priest as a child. The messages came subtly and not so subtly that it wasn't possible. It wasn't even possible at that time for girls to be altar attendants at my parish; only boys could do that. Even women lay readers were new so I felt really disheartened. I remember being told I could be a nun, and I remember thinking, "Well, that would be cool, but how come I can't be up there on the altar with God?" There was a certain disillusioning that began pretty early. What was it about me that wasn't good enough to be that close to God? How could there be something not good enough for God? Those were big questions for a little girl to be carrying around.

> There's no way
> I can undo it all,
> fix it all,
> alleviate it all,
> and that doesn't
> mean that
> I am allowed
> to go crawl
> under a rock.

Once I left for college, I never went to church. I became friends with Jews. I realized that Catholicism grew from Judaism, that Jesus was a *Jew*. I started understanding the value of where something comes from. And I learned the difference between cultural Judaism and religious Judaism. I realized some people are Jewish and yet they don't go to temple, but they have some familial connection to Judaism. I felt like I had that too. My whole ancestry is Catholic. I became interested in genealogy and how Catholicism was integrated into the very cells of our family. I got the message that Catholics were somehow better, that Catholicism is the only true religion and that we had to pray for everyone else. I never felt proud, per se, but it was something I bore as part of my cultural heritage.

Then, in my twenties I attended twelve-step meetings, and God was being spoken about right there, out loud. It was the first time outside the Catholic church that I had heard people talking about God, about their faith–their faith that things were going to pass or their faith that things were going to get better. I was in an intense period of suffering. My nose was right up against the abyss, and at that time, I felt I had two choices: death or insanity. Instead, there was a small group of us who talked about God. In those rooms you hear people who talk about being able to face a deep level of suffering because right there is also God. I started counting on something being there. Then, even when I was walking around in my daily life, it was there – a presence of something, a hum. It's the only "count-on-able" thing. It is the change. It is witness to the change. It is everything. It is in everything. I always say that if you stick your toe in the river, wow! When you listen for it, there you are. Then there are moments when you're actually *in* the river, however briefly. I think they come unexpectedly. They're windows of grace. It almost feels like God is checking in: "Just wanted to let you know, it's still here." Just when I think, "Oh, it's just a big old random mess," I realize, "Oh, it's a big old *divine* random mess."

For me, it's about allowing every action to turn towards God or away from God. I've tried to embody that and have that inform everything I do. When I get into a quandary or I want to be mean, or someone hurts me or I feel hurt, or I read or witness or hear about something really horrible – it reminds me not to act in the same way. It helps to guide me. It's a really simple thing, not a whole bunch of rules, things I have to remember.

If I don't find a way to recognize the mercy, I might as well crawl under a rock. There's so much suffering. So many people are in so much pain, and every day I participate in something that hurts somebody else. If I let all that stuff in, I couldn't hold it. It reminds me that it's bigger than I can remotely think about. There's no way I can undo it all, fix it all, alleviate it all, and that doesn't mean that I am allowed to go crawl under a rock. I feel like I'm responsible for whatever I can do. My piece of turning the tide.

I guess it all just helps me go a little further. It says, "You don't have to climb the whole mountain today. Just take one more step. Go a little bit further and then you can rest." When I can't possibly hold it all, I know that the river is way longer and bigger. There are other people along the banks. I can lay the burden down, even if it's just for a moment. And then I can pick it up and go on again.

mindfulness.

words

*I found a way to make peace with the recent past
by turning it into WORD.*
~ *Charles Johnson,* Middle Passage

what are words? . . . .

Words allow us to express our joy and our pain and they give us a medium in which we can praise. With words we can sort through all of the ideas and messages floating in our heads and get down to the truth. They allow us an opportunity to shape or discern the features of what is happening and how we're feeling about it. Words, vessels for feelings and experiences, help you admit things.

A relationship with words begins with writing, no matter the content or quality. Natalie Goldberg says, "Writers live twice." Writing provides a clearing process, a space to tell stories (true and imagined), communicate feelings, voice worries, process experiences, work through challenges, and dream big dreams. Writing can also be a tool for spiritual exploration and vocational discernment. When thoughts and feelings about spirituality, faith, God, and belief systems seem difficult to express orally, they may flow easier when pen is put to paper. Writing can lead to a new sense of clarity, insight, and healing.

The words of prayer (those we read or create ourselves) and the words of other sacred texts can change our lives in an instant. Language wrapped around inspiration by another soul may come as welcome relief or fitting challenge. And, the writing of our own poetry or prayer may free us from having to fill in all the details or stick to a sentence structure. Of course, there will always be the "unnameable" – that which cannot be spoken about easily – powerful experiences of love, of nature, and of spirit. The words of poetry and prayer do not try to express a vision of the whole word; they present an angle by which you can see, feel, hear, and touch a corner of reality.

You can become a co-creator with God.
The act of writing is magic, one word, then another.
You create a world.
You display a vision of the universe.

~ Stuart Horwitz

turning point . . . .

I was in my early twenties when I began to understand my infatuation with words. I had always been a "Dear Diary" kind of kid, interested in words and the ability to chronicle my life. When it was time to pick a major in college, English was the easy choice, given my love of reading and writing. But I had not completely understood the power words had to comb through experience and reveal truth until I was organizing a national conference in Washington, D.C. for students working on poverty issues. I was working with the National Student Campaign Against Hunger and Homelessness. For four months the conference staff worked hard to get ready for the five hundred students and administrators from around the country who were planning to attend. There were meals to arrange, speakers to attract, workshops to plan, and logistics to coordinate. This meant a lot of long days and little time for reflection.

The conference finally rolled around on a clear weekend in October, and people poured in by the carload. Friends and colleagues from across the country reconnected and we got to meet the faces of the voices we had spoken with on the telephone. Within hours, we went from a ten-person staff to a community of five hundred energized, committed young activists. The weekend was overwhelming: intense and honest discussions about poverty in this country and abroad, a hundred new program ideas to bring back to campus, and the chance to be a part of the Housing Now! rally on the mall – a gathering of over half a million low-income people, organizers, and advocates. We finished the conference with a big celebration, giving everyone a chance to let off some steam. The spirit of hope and possibility was electric.

Back home in Boston a few days later, I struggled to make sense of the whole experience. I was full of information, images, feelings, and questions. On a gray Sunday afternoon, I paced around my apartment, wondering where to put everything floating around in my head. The story of the previous week was so complex that I did not know how to begin to tell it to another person. When my roommate asked me about the weekend, I could only reply in the simplest of sentences. "It was good. Really good. I'm tired."

By the grace of God, my eyes fell on a blank notebook, bought no doubt to use for conference planning and left over, untouched. I began to write, and this act of recording took me through the rest of the afternoon and into the night. As my words, feelings, and questions tumbled onto the page, I found ways to capture the richness of the event, listing my highlights, exploring lessons, and musing about what impact this all might have on the rest of my life. It was in this writing that I understood, for the first time, that I'd made a long-term commitment to working on social change issues. It was in this telling of the story that I was able to honor my strengths as an organizer and explore some of my greatest leadership challenges. And I began to see the value of relationships in a whole new way. I wrote out the names of the twenty individuals who'd had the greatest influence on me over the previous forty-eight hours. More than just participants at a conference, they were people to whom I wanted to stay connected for a long time, companions for my journey as an activist and as a human being.

In that notebook, I found the safety of a private world, one I could shape and reshape, appreciating the many layers of experience. It didn't matter if I went on and on and on. With the sanctity and safety of the blank page, no one could criticize my idealism, talk me out of my plans, or question my passion. Putting something into words was like a green light to move forward.

? questions for reflection . . . .

How would you describe your relationship to words?

Do you keep a journal or find other ways to reflect on your life through writing?

What happens when you write? What surfaces?

How is your written voice different from your spoken voice?

℮ journals: starting to write

A journal is a record of experience and growth. . . .
Here I cannot afford to be remembering what I said or did . . .
but what I am and aspire to become.
~ Henry David Thoreau

Journals are a place to capture your story and your perspective. They make room for writing that is emotional, personal, and tentative. In a journal, you can give yourself permission to write without concern for grammar, writing style, sentence structure, or censorship. Journal keeping does not lend itself to rules. Do it whenever you want. Early in the morning and at night before bed are fruitful periods for many. Feeling like you must write every day can be death for some and a welcome discipline for others.

You can do it almost anywhere: alone at home, in a coffee shop, in the woods, on a bus or a plane, on your roof, beneath a tree. Sometimes ten or fifteen minutes is too long; other days an hour won't feel like enough. All you need is a sturdy notebook, a writing implement, and some free time. Part of the fun is choosing your materials, letting the ink color or the texture of the pages delight you. Carry a notebook around with you; you never know when the mood may strike you to write or you'll have some extra, unexpected quiet time. Small tablets work well to record key words of an experience or insight to develop at greater length in your journal.

You might use your journal to explore:

How you use your time	Favorite people/places/things
What inspires you	Lessons you've learned in your life
What you believe in	Seminal events and turning points
What you can do without in your life	Dreams you remember
Memories from your childhood	Places your soul feels at ease
Significant people in your life	Heroes and heroines

As you create a written record of life unfolding, consider including:

quotes	lists	passages
prayers	words as art	poems
photos	colors	textures and materials
things from nature	description	dialogue
words you love	artwork/collage	foreign words
maps	charts	diagrams

℮ speaking in your own voice

We live our lives forward but we can only understand them backwards.

~ Sören Kierkegaard

It's easy to go through much of our lives not knowing a lot about ourselves. Learning more makes us stronger, and more able to stand steady in the truth of who we are, rather than who we want to be or who others might expect us to be. Consider these questions slowly.

What are my strengths?	*What are my limitations?*
Who/what do I love?	*What do I mock?*
Who/what do I need?	*Who/what do I fear?*
Who/what makes me sad?	*Who/what makes me happy?*
What do I have to give?	*What am I jealous of?*
Where is my path blocked?	*What would I like to see?*

℮ awareness of spirit

Your own words can also help you better understand your relationship to spirituality. Here are some more questions to ponder in writing:

What do the words "spirit" or "spirituality" mean to you?

What is the difference between spirituality and religion for you?

How would you describe your relationship to spirit?

Barry Hopkins, an art teacher and naturalist from upstate New York, helps his students make earthbound journals, places to record their lives with personal artwork, words, and treasures from the great outdoors. They are collages that represent a moment in time or a walk in the woods. The multidimensional journals are more than just a scrapbook, though they might include items of significance: photographs, letters, dried flowers, leaves, and other items.

Hopkins suggests the following materials for those interested in making an earthbound journal:
- an artists' sketchbook, unlined, at least 7½" x 8½"
- felt tip or rollerball pens, colored pencils
- aerosol spray to attach things (it lasts longer than glue)

*Recall a moment you've experienced when spirit was present in a whole new way.
What was the experience like? How did you feel at that time?
How did you feel afterwards?*

When, if ever, do you find yourself forgetting that spirit is present?

What activities cause time to stop for you; what can you do for hours?

℮ ancient words sacred text

The first time I understood the power of scripture was in a Black Southern Baptist Church, a few days before Easter Sunday. I'd gone to hear a friend, Reverend Classy Preston, preach. Up until this point, I'd heard preaching before but it always felt foreign to me, as if I was just watching a play written and performed for someone else. I often feel uncomfortable with some of the passages from the Gospels. But this time was different. Classy preached on Matthew 26:41–42, the portion of the Easter story where Jesus is in the garden of Gethsemane. He's trying to pray and he asks his disciples to keep watch because he knows his days are numbered. But the disciples keep falling asleep, again and again and again. Three times he asks them to stay awake and three times they fail. Classy asked us, over and over again in her commanding voice and rhythmic cadence, if we'd ever fallen asleep when we should be awake. Had we given into the temptation of slumber when we should be serving? The words came alive, leaping right to me from her mouth. My relationship to text was completely transformed and a seed had been planted.

A few years later the seed began to germinate. I was spending part of the summer in residence at a monastery in the Midwest, far from home and knowing no one. Not quite the spiritual respite it was designed to be, I was lonely and depressed much of the time. Having always wanted to read the Bible, I spent many hours attempting to get through the Torah and the Gospels. I chose to read them as parallel stories, starting simultaneously with Genesis and the gospel according to Matthew. I marveled at the creation story and the Beatitudes, but my real epiphany came on the afternoon I got to Exodus, chapter 3, a story I'd known since childhood.

This is the place in the story where an angel draws Moses' attention to a bush, burning but not consumed. Moses turns to see God and God calls to him out of the bush, "Do not come near; put off your shoes from your feet, for the place on which you are standing is holy ground." God is getting ready to choose Moses in a way that he will fiercely resist. But before all of this, God is saying, wherever you are, it is good enough, it is close enough, it is holy enough. Such an old image and yet it put my struggles in a completely new light. Holiness is everywhere, and most particularly in this moment, under

Moses' own feet, so perhaps it was under my own feet as well. I stopped to consider the possibility and felt a dark cloud start to fade ever so slightly.

Shortly thereafter, God calls Moses to lead his people and Moses basically says, "No way." He realizes the magnitude of the task and he is not up for it. But God is persistent and asks again, answering all of Moses' concerns – his speech impediment, his lack of self-confidence, his fears. Six times they go back and forth, and six times God takes the time to address Moses with a thoughtful reply. This passage – this call to reluctant leadership – also resonated with me immediately. How many times had I witnessed this among the activists I'd worked with over the past fifteen years or so? How many times had I noticed it in myself?

Only through my own exploration did I realize that it is not necessary to be a scholar to enjoy these texts. Houses of worship convene people to study scripture in an effort to demystify these ancient stories and bring them to life. Even without being part of an organized religious community, it is still possible to do this kind of study on your own or with a group of friends. Stories that have survived thousands of years usually offer valuable lessons or insights into some of the most common human dilemmas. They have staying power and they deserve the lens of our own lives, our struggles, and our wisdom.

Sacred texts to consider:

Bhagavad Gita: A chapter of the Indian epic, the Mahabharata, the Gita is a dialogue between Arjuna, a hero overcome by despair in the midst of battle, and Lord Krishna. An incarnate of the Hindu god Vishnu, Krishna teaches Arjuna about self-mastery and selfless service.

Bible: The Bible is divided into two parts: the Hebrew Bible (which Jews call the Tanakh and Christians called the Old Testament) has thirty-nine books, and the Christian Bible (or New Testament) has twenty-seven books, including the Gospels. The Bible was written by more than forty human authors, inspired by the divine word of God.

Cloud of Unknowing: A manual written anonymously by a cloistered English monk around the year 1375 for a young person beginning a life of contemplation. It emphasizes the path of "apophatic" mysticism – relating to God through no created thing, not even through words or mental images.

Gnostic Gospels: Fifty-two texts discovered in Egypt, including the Gospel of Thomas. Ultimately denounced as heretical by the early church, these Gospels contain poems, teachings, and myths attributed to Jesus and his disciples, but not found in the Christian Bible.

Haftorah: Dates back to the Greek empire when Jews were banned from reading the weekly Torah portion. The Rabbis substituted readings from the prophets that captured the lessons of the weekly Torah portion, which came to be known as the Haftorah.

Holy Qu'ran: Sacred book of Islam, the Qu'ran is the last book of guidance from Allah, sent down to Muhammad through the angel Jibraeel (Gabriel). Revealed over a period of twenty-three years in the Arabic language, it contains 114 chapters and over six thousand verses. It deals with three primary ideals: the oneness of Allah, prophethood, and life after death.

Mahayana Sutras: Discourses delivered by the Buddha and his close disciples during the Buddha's forty-five-year teaching career.

Psalms: A collection of 150 hymns or poems (also known as the Psalter) that convey both praise and lamentation. Part of the Hebrew Bible, some of the Psalms were written for individual prayer and others for congregational recitation.

Tao Te Ching: Written by Lao-tzu in the fifth century B.C.E., the *Tao Te Ching* can be translated as *The Book of the Way*. It is a manual on the art of living from the perspective of "doing nondoing."

Torah: The Jewish holy book, the Torah is the five books of Moses: Genesis, Exodus, Leviticus, Numbers, and Deuteronomy. The term "Torah" is often also used to refer to the compilations of Jewish Oral Law found in the Mishna and the Talmud, texts of Jewish religious law that outlines how to follow rules set down in the Torah.

Upanishads: Written by sages of India between the eighth and fourth centuries B.C.E., the Upanishads are the final part of the Vedas, the most ancient and sacred scripture of India. The Upanishads are the teachings of the sages on mystical experience and are considered revealed scripture.

Yoga Sutras: Written by the Indian sage, Patanjali, in 100 B.C.E., these 195 sutras represent the collected wisdom of the philosophy and practice of classical yoga.

Zen Koans: Parables or anecdotes used by Zen monks to guide their students in meditation.

@ prayer: words in motion

Prayer is an invitation to God to intervene in our lives.

~ *Abraham Joshua Heschel,* Man's Quest for God

How you pray, when you pray, and why you pray is a direct reflection of your understanding of the Divine and the role that it plays in your life.

~ *Iyanla Vanzant,* One Day My Soul Just Opened Up

Prayer allows us to shift our level of consciousness. It's a way of articulating an intention, expressing gratitude, and releasing our own wisdom. Prayer enables us to reach beyond ourselves to something else. It is an opportunity to engage in a direct conversation with a higher being, to bridge the gap between our very finite, human selves and an infinite spirit. Like meditation, prayer invites us to be still and to focus. But while meditation is a practice of paying attention, prayer is a practice of voicing intention, even if the intention is simply to listen and bear witness.

Through prayer, we find ways to give up control of the outcome, allowing us to focus on the task at hand. Through prayer, we can strengthen our faith when we are scared. Through prayer, we can ask for guidance when faced with difficult situations or decisions. Reading prayers, silently or aloud, can also reconnect us with tradition. It can be a time to recall the messages of ancient stories and make them real again.

? questions for reflection . . . .

What do you know or remember about prayer?

Have you ever been moved or even forced to pray because of a situation or crisis?

Do you have any favorite prayers? What do you love about them?

What about prayer has enabled you to connect with spirit or God? What about prayer has kept you from this connection?

What kind of prayer would you like to be praying?

℮ beginning to pray

Pray according to who you are. If you are an extrovert, pray in an extroverted way.
If you are quiet, pray quietly. Pray to God, pray to Allah, pray to The One,
pray to The Only, pray to your Ancestors. It's all received. It's all acted on.
Pray with acceptance and gratitude. Pray for connection, pray for your love to be felt,
pray for the ability to show it. Pray for people you know to feel better. Pray on your bike.
Pray in the bathtub. Pray in silence. Pray in song.

~ Dr. Larry Dossey

There are many ways to talk to God. Check the library or bookstore for collected prayers, reflections, or sacred prose from one or many different religions. Read through and see what strikes you. Take a prayer you've known for a long time and recite it. You may find a deeper meaning as you say it aloud, quietly and slowly. You might just want to begin your own conversation with the spirit, the life force, God, or Christ. Consider what mode of address works best for you – to whom are you praying? Does the figure or expression of spirit seem like a friend, a parent, a lover, an element of nature, an "everything" you can't quite describe?

It might be useful to take stock in the role prayer has historically played for you and how you remember it, if at all. You may need to unlearn or adapt old styles of praying in order to fulfill your current needs. If you have not drawn strength from organized religion or the religion you practiced as a child, then prayer may have negative connotations for you, reminding you of an unfulfilling experience. You may be more comfortable exploring the prayers of other traditions, reading sacred poetry, or writing your own prayers. In time, you may find that your own tradition has some new territory for you to explore.

Consider developing a daily practice of prayer for yourself. Perhaps you'll pray in the morning, maybe when the sun is rising and you are greeting the day with hope. Maybe you will pray before going to bed in the evening, remembering what has been holy about the day, the times the spirit was present, what you are thankful for. You might find that prayer becomes something you do anytime you take time to stop and collect your thoughts. Some people keep a regular record of their prayer life: which prayers they are saying, why, and what other thoughts or feelings these prayers invoke. Writing down what comes to mind during or after prayer can capture the essence and enrich the experience.

℮ write your own prayer

There are a hundred ways to kneel and kiss the ground.

~ Rumi

Crafted over time, your own prayer can be a simple statement of what you want to remember each day. Here are some questions to get you started:

praise

What are you thankful for?
What do you hope for?
What is new in your life or your work?
Whom do you have to appreciate?

surrender

What forces surround your life or your work that are out of your control?
What fight or burden are you willing to give up for now?
What are you resisting that could be a source of energy for you?
What do you welcome into your life?

petition

What do you need?
How would you ask for it?
What are you afraid of?

guidance

Where do you feel stuck?
What additional wisdom or guidance would you like to resolve this situation?
What do you want to pledge yourself to?

I wrote my first prayer on a lazy summer day, swinging on a friend's porch.

> *Today*
> *Let me live fully and love completely.*
> *Let me honor and celebrate others and myself*
> *So that the best of what lies within might come forth*
> *And let me be present enough in the world around me*
> *To choose love over fear.*

About a year later, I needed some more specific guidance, so I added the following:

> *I give thanks for this new day of possibility that stretches out*
> *before me.*
> *Every day I make choices.*
> *Today, in grace, I choose to pray often, love as well as I can, remember*
> *everyone is a child of God, breathe deeply, work hard and work smart.*

℮ prayer offerings

Prayer is an act which enables you to become an instrument,
surrender your own will and be led by God's will.
Prayer restores whole(r) consciousness.

~ Stuart Horwitz

When he first lived in New York City, my brother would hand first-time visitors pieces of paper when they entered his apartment. People were offered the chance to write their prayers and throw them into the nonworking fireplace that was filled with candles. The pieces of paper accumulated. They were never read by anyone other than the writer. And you could offer as many prayers as you wanted; there was no limit. Your own mood or courage dictated how many prayers or how often you contributed. That felt real – no human restrictions on what is essentially a human-to-divine communication.

As the years went on, the prayers became covered in soot. (The flue was open.) Materially dirty, there was always something that remained spiritually bright about these folded-up words of prayer. When my brother moved, he took all the prayers with him and buried them in the ground outside his new place. The promise and pain of each slip was released organically back to the earth.

℮ mystics: inspiration for the journey

Mysticism is the way in which we truly understand what it means to be one with the Divine. Through a personal mystical experience we are reunited with the divine in ourselves and gets closer to the unknowable: God. Over the past two thousand years, many saints, teachers, rabbis, nuns, and monks have described the content and impact of mystical experiences. Their writings are an inspiration.

Baal Shem Tov (1700–1760), whose name means "master of the good name," spent years contemplating and studying the Kabbalah, the Jewish mystical tradition. The Baal Shem Tov preached to and inspired thousands in Poland and founded Hasidism, a Jewish tradition that emphasizes mysticism and religious zeal. The Baal Shem Tov believed that ritual is not enough for faith: that faith requires a vibrant relationship with God that can be achieved through joyful prayer.

The Desert Fathers is a term for generations of Christian monastics who left Jerusalem and other cities for more remote locations in order to live their faith. St. Antony, born in 250 B.C.E., inspired the movement. He lived as a hermit for many years before emerging in public life as a healer and preacher. Others were moved to take up a similarly monastic life in caves and cliffs throughout the Mediterranean region.

Meister Eckhart (1260–1328), a German Dominican, believed mystical experiences were possible if one emptied one's mind of all activity. Throughout his life, he was preoccupied by the relationship between divinity and humanity. He believed there was a "little spark" of God, the divine kernel, in each being's inmost self: "Where the creature stops, there God begins to be. Now God wants no more from you than that you should in creaturely fashion go out of yourself, and let God be God in you." For these and other inflammatory writings, Eckhart was condemned as a heretic.

Hildegard of Bingen (1098–1179) entered a Benedictine monastery at the age of eight. As a child, Hildegard had prophetic visions that continued throughout her life; they inspired her to write and illustrate three books. A cloistered nun, Hildegard founded two monasteries. She was also an herbalist and a scientist who catalogued medicines of her medieval era. Her liturgical chants have been redis-covered in recent years. Hildegard wrote, "For the shape of the word exists everlastingly in the knowledge of the true Love which is God: constantly circling, wonderful for human nature, and such that it is not consumed by age and cannot be increased by anything new."

Mirabai (circa 1498–1546) was an Indian noblewoman who rejected her station after her husband's death and devoted her life to the Hindu god Krishna. She wrote religious poetry and music to express her love: "Like a bee trapped for life in the closing of the sweet flower/Mira has offered herself to her Lord./She says: the single Lotus will swallow you whole."

Jelaluddin Rumi (1207–1273) was born in Persia. A scholar and teacher under royal patronage, Rumi's life was transformed when he met Shams of Tabriz, a wandering dervish. Rumi wrote: "What I had thought of before as God, I met today in person." Their relationship and shared mystical experiences sparked Rumi to write ecstatic poetry, describing his longing to be with, for, and of God. For Rumi, it is through the suffering and sacrifice of love that one finds God. His writing addresses longing and satisfaction, separation and union, the worldly and the spiritual, love and pain.

St. Teresa of Avila (1515–1582) was a Spanish Carmelite nun who detailed her visions and revelations of God. In numerous writings, she describes the various stages of a mystical life from her first meditative experiences to an almost ongoing connection with the divine through which the soul loses itself to its love for God. With a few companions, she founded an enclosed convent at Avila in Spain. It became one of the foundations for the reformation of the Carmelite order.

resources for words . . . .

Besserman, Pearl. *The Shambhala Guide to Kabbalah and Jewish Mysticism.* Boston: Shambhala, 1997. An introduction to philosophy and practice written by a descendant of the Baal Shem Tov. Includes meditation techniques.

Bly, Robert. *The Soul is Here for Its Own Joy.* Hopewell, N.J.: The Ecco Press, 1995. Sacred poems from various cultures; includes Emily Dickinson, Kabir, Mirabai, Rumi, Rilke, Sappho, Simone Weil, and more. http://ppl.nhmccd.edu/~dcox/ohenry/bly.html

Castelli, Jim, ed. *How I Pray.* New York: Ballantine Books, 1994. People of various religious traditions share information about their own prayer life. Includes Baptist, Buddhist, Catholic, Episcopal, Hindu, Jewish, Lakota Sioux, Lutheran, Mormon, Muslim, Quaker, and Presbyterian perspectives.

Dunn, Philip. *Prayer: Language of the Soul.* New York: Daybreak Books, 1997. Three thousand prayers from around the world on themes from abundance to peace. Includes locations for prayer in the United States and abroad.

Eckhart, Meister. *Meister Eckhart: A Modern Translation.* Translated by Raymond Bernard Blakney. New York: HarperCollins, 1941. www.op.org/eckhart/default.HTM

Fellowship in Prayer. *The Gift of Prayer.* New York: Continuum, 1995. A collection of personal prayers from many spiritual traditions, East to West, ancient to modern. *Fellowship in Prayer* is an interfaith journal with readership in eighty countries. Contact: Fellowship in Prayer, 291 Witherspoon Street, Princeton, N.J. 08542–3227.

Goldberg, Natalie. *Writing Down the Bones: Freeing the Writer Within.* Boston: Shambhala, 1986. For people who want to explore their own talent for writing and/or use writing as a spiritual practice. Short essays on writing and exercises to try. www.nataliegoldberg.com

———. *Wild Minds: Living the Writer's Life.* New York: Bantam Books, 1990.

Heschel, Abraham Joshua. *The Circle of the Baal Shem Tov.* Edited by Samuel H. Dresner. Chicago: University of Chicago Press, 1985. www.baalshemtov.com

Kamenetz, Rodger. *Stalking Elijah: Adventures with Today's Jewish Mystical Masters* San Francisco: HarperCollins, 1997. Story of the author's journey to seek counsel from Jewish spiritual teachers across the country. http://literati.net/Kamenetz/

Keay, Kathy. *Laughter, Silence, and Shouting: An Anthology of Women's Prayers.* London: HarperCollins, 1994. Great collection of poems about God, creation, daily life, self, relationships, work, aging, peace, justice, hope, and suffering.

Keen, Same, and Anne Valley-Fox. *Your Mythic Journey: Finding Meaning in Your Life through Writing and Storytelling.* Los Angeles: Tarcher, 1989.

Matthews, Caitlin. *Celtic Devotional Daily Prayers and Blessings.* New York: Harmony Books, 1996. A combination of traditional blessings and prayers written by the author. There are practices and prayers for morning and evening of each day of the week and they change with the seasons.

Mayers, Gregory. *Listen to the Desert.* Liguori, Mo.: Triumph Books, 1996. Writings and stories of the Desert Fathers. www.christdesert.org/noframes/fathers/introduction.html

Mitchell, Stephen, ed. *The Enlightened Mind: An Anthology of Sacred Prose.* New York: HarperCollins, 1991. Passages from an array of sacred texts and the writings of mystics, rabbis, priests, ministers, teachers, nuns, and philosophers from the sixth century B.C.E. though the modern day.

———. *Tao Te Ching: A New English Version.* New York: HarperCollins, 1988. A beautiful translation of the ancient Chinese text. www.wuwei.org/Taoism/taoteching.html

Nepo, Mark. *The Book of Awakening: Having the Life You Want by Being Present to the Life You Have.* Berkeley, Calif.: Conari Press, 2000. Powerful daily readings and reflections.

Nixon, Will. "Call of the Wild." *New Age Journal,* September/October 1996. A story about art teacher Barry Hopkins and his earthbound journals. http://members.tripod.com/~nickles/bhopkins.html

Rilke, Rainer Maria. *Rilke's Book of Hours: Love Poems to God.* Translated by Anita Barrow and Joanna Macy. New York: Riverhead Books, 1996. The simple prayers of German philosopher and poet Rainer Maria Rilke define a reciprocal relationship between the divine and the ordinary. www.geocities.com/Paris/LeftBank/4027/

Rumi. *The Essential Rumi.* Translated by Coleman Barks with John Moyne. Edison, N.J.: Castle Books, 1997. A new and definitive collection of Jelaluddin Rumi's ecstatic poetry. www.rumi.org.uk/

Saint Hildegard. *Hildegard of Bingen's Book of Divine Works: With Letters and Songs.* Edited by Matthew Fox. Sante Fe: Bear & Company, 1987. www.tweedledee.ucsb.edu/~kris/music/Hildegard.html

Saint Teresa of Avila. *The Interior Castle.* Translated by John Venard OCD. Sydney: E.J. Dwyer, 1988. This is considered the essence of St. Teresa's doctrine of prayer. www.karmel.at/eng/teresa.htm

Sewell, Marilyn, ed. *Cries of the Spirit.* Boston: Beacon Press, 1991. Poetry and prose celebrating women's spirituality, including self, intimacy, mothering, generations, death, sacredness, and spirit.

Sumrall, Amber Coverdale, and Patrice Vecchione, eds. *Storming Heaven's Gate: An Anthology of Spiritual Writings by Women.* New York: Penguin, 1997. A collection of poetry and prose, written by a diverse and powerful group of women, that addresses the search for and finding of spirit in likely and unlikely places.

Umansky, Ellen M., and Diane Ashton, eds. *Four Centuries of Jewish Women's Spirituality.* Boston: Beacon Press, 1992. An anthology of letters, prayers, speeches, rituals, poetry, and more from 1560 to today. This book brings women's voices back to the forefront of Jewish history.

Williamson, Marianne. *Illuminata: A Return to Prayer.* New York: Riverhead Books, 1994. An inspiring and useful collection of prayers on everything from the body to work to relationships. The book includes sections on prayers for the world and rites of passage ceremonies. www.marianne.com

writing with passion . . . .

Ed Chaney

After graduating from the University of North Carolina at Chapel Hill, Ed Chaney worked with the Student Coalition for Action in Literacy Education (SCALE) for four years and then was director of North Carolina Youth for Tomorrow (NCYT), an organization that builds the capacity of young people to serve as staff, volunteers, and board members in the nonprofit sector. Ed is a writer of fiction and poetry, as well as a consultant for various nonprofit organizations.

I started writing with passion and vigor when I was going through a personally hard time. When I was young, my mother began going crazy, and I needed a creative outlet to help me process what was happening. I needed to tell stories. It was a kind of therapy for me. I've kept writing throughout my life, but when I started working in literacy, I discovered another level of the power of writing: voice. And I mean that in two ways.

> **Each person's story is powerful and needs to be heard if we're going to make any progress.**

First is self-discovery. Writing can be a conversation of one, and by its nature it is honest and unfettered. When you put your uncensored self on paper, especially if it's for you and you alone, you can be really surprised about what comes out. It's unbridled emotion, unedited thought process. Because you are the only audience, you have no reason to hide or stretch the truth or be fearful of being judged. All that's left is your emotion, experience, and wisdom. It's enlightening, especially on hard, big themes like faith, spirituality, and social justice.

The other part about writing and power is sharing your voice with groups. Once you've put yourself on paper and realized your wisdom, you let others hear your words. You listen to the wisdom of *their* words. It's a powerful teaching and community-building tool, a way of sharing things that you wouldn't in a normal conversation. It lends power to each individual and whatever he or she is bringing, and it helps define and strengthen a group.

The most important thing to do is to make sure that the space is safe enough, for yourself or for the group. People put risks on the paper, and in order for those risks to make a difference in their lives or in other people's, they need to be raw and uncensored. And for *that* to happen, people need to feel comfortable enough first writing, and then sharing, and not feel like they are going to be laughed at if their language is different or not as sophisticated. People have a lot of internalized fears about their writing. From a very early age, we're taught there are only a few masters of language. Rather than question that assumption, we lock in our self-expression, fearing that it will never be adequate, when it will always be more than adequate. It will be a perfect extension of the writer. You can build up to safe space by starting with safe topics to break the ice, to get the writers used to writing and risking and sharing.

Once, I picked a free-writing topic: "I knew God when . . . ,"
and everyone in the group was supposed to go with it.
First, everyone wrote about this. Then, we made a book
from the writing; everyone had time to make a page –
collage, drawing, etc. We made a book of people's stories.
It was a powerful learning experience on a number of
levels, because I'm relatively sure no one had thought about that question before. It was a good
reflection tool to get people to think about what knowing God means. The activity also
capitalized on different learning and expression styles. Hearing the stories and seeing the end
product, it showed how brilliant and creative everyone was. And how different. Every page was
powerful. It was all about personal reflection, journey, relationship. We could have gone a lot of
places with that knowledge.

From a very early age, we're taught there are only a few masters of language.

Working for social change is not only about institutions. It's also about living and making
changing intentionally. In order to do that, you've got break past the boundaries that our
culture has set up and get to the heart of the issues you are working on. It all goes back to voice
and stories for me. The philosophy I've developed around writing, that it's important for us to
connect on an honest deep and unbridled level, transfers into my community work. Each
person's story is powerful and needs to be heard if we're going to make any progress.

the gates of prayer . . . .

Rabbi Sid Schwarz

*Rabbi Sid Schwarz is the founding director of The Washington Institute for Jewish Leadership and Values,
an educational foundation dedicated to the renewal of American Jewish life through the integration of
Jewish learning, values, and social responsibility. He is also the founding rabbi of Adat Shalom
Reconstructionist Congregation in Bethesda, Maryland.*

The sacred texts are codes that continue to reveal to me deeper and deeper layers of my own life experience.

Reflecting on it now, my relationship to prayer was
pretty nonexistent, even after I became a rabbi. I
knew the liturgy backwards and forwards – the body
of Jewish prayer was part of the air I breathed – but
it was all rote. There was never a deep spiritual
component to it. As I matured as a rabbi and as a
Jew, I found ways to pull people's spiritual journeys
out of them. I found myself automatically connecting their stories to pieces of Jewish texts and
Jewish liturgy. The whole prayer thing began to make sense to me. It was like this code had
been broken.

> Thousands of minds have pored over these texts for centuries. There's an answer in the texts to the struggles we face every day, if we can only pull it out.

I remember the first time it happened. I made a trip to Russia and we went into a synagogue in Moscow. There were twenty-five of us in the group. We had brought a lot of religious artifacts to give away to Russian Jews, which were contraband. We were told that they were eager to meet us, and that there were KGB operatives in the synagogue. The usher brought us to the dignitary box, alongside the *bimah*.[1] It dawned on me that we had been put in quarantine. He didn't want us to mix with the local Jews.

But I was desperate to make a connection. When they brought the Torah out for the service, they brought out a dozen. There were twelve tables and twelve torah readings going on at once. We all went out of our box and we began to make connections. I kept introducing myself, saying I was a Jew from New York, etcetera, and people kept moving away from me. It turns out the KGB had trained people to entrap the Jews. They would play the role of Jewish tourist to get someone to say something inflammatory. So, I was doing all the wrong things, although I didn't know it at the time.

In frustration, I started to pray and when I finished the *Amidah*,[2] I suddenly had a throng of people around me. Because the one thing they couldn't teach KGB agents how to do was to *daven*.[3] Suddenly, the local Jews knew that I could be trusted. At that moment I was powerfully struck with how the liturgy of the Jewish tradition offered a language of Jewish connection through both space and time. It was a connection that allowed me to connect to my oppressed and persecuted sisters and brothers, right under the nose of the KGB.

There's a part in the Amidah that literally says "to the informers, the tattletales, let them have no success." Suddenly that prayer just started to scream out of my head because what we were experiencing was exactly that – I was living the prayer. It began a process for me of recapturing every prayer I knew by heart and saying, "What in my life experience makes this prayer come alive?" I started doing that for myself, and now I do it for other Jews. I never considered myself to be a deeply religious person. I'm observant but the meditative mode has never worked for me, it's not who I am. But the sacred texts are codes that continue to reveal to me deeper and deeper layers of my own life experience.

I've got this group of twenty to twenty-five people who are in major political positions. We meet once a month and do Torah study. Most are not connected to Judaism but they have these continual "a-ha" experiences where they find a text that speaks to what they are wrestling with. First, they connect it to a personal struggle about how they keep to their mission. Embedded in the heritage of which they are a part is something that can give them a certain amount of comfort and support.

[1] pulpit in a synagogue where the Torah scrolls are kept
[2] a central Jewish prayer
[3] Hebrew word for prayer

Second, when they share with each other their own struggle, in the context of Pirke Avot, the Ethics of Our Fathers, they feel very connected. I don't know another way to have that conversation without putting it in the context of Jewish texts. I think the reason is that somehow I believe that there's some wisdom embedded in the text, that is more than all the wisdom of the people in the room. Thousands of minds have pored over these texts for centuries. There's an answer in the texts to the struggles we face every day, if we can only pull it out.

Sid can be reached at sids@wijlv.org

why read the Bible?

Ched Myers

Ched Myers is a fifth-generation Californian living in Los Angeles, California. He worked for five years doing disarmament and anti-military work, another five years with indigenous people in the Pacific Basin, and ten years with the American Friends Service Committee. An ecumenical theologian who has published four books and numerous articles, he also consults for non-profit organizations. His itinerant teaching ministry is based on the conviction that we need to create a pedagogy that moves between the seminary, the sanctuary, and the street.

As a teenager growing up in a household that didn't have a vision of faith, I was asking: "Why bother helping?" But I was impacted by the Vietnam War; my imagination was fired by the counterculture of the sixties and the peace movement. But in a few years I saw it peak and die. I was disillusioned. That was behind my search for a deeper vision, and there was this magnificent vision in the Bible. It made sense to struggle and work with poor people, because what *is* is not the only way it can be. I wouldn't have stayed in the church if there wasn't a political dimension to the gospel, and I would not have sustained myself in politics had I not had a deeper vision of the work.

> It's like living in a paper bag and trying to imagine the world outside the paper bag, but I have this little book I read in the paper bag that talks about the word outside the paper bag.

Different ways of reading texts are determined by what one has to lose and what one has to gain. That's a helpful dialectic through which to read American history. The idea of progress has always been a vision of the elite, shaped through enlightenment, manifest destiny. But immigrants came to America with a vision of God, not necessarily a vision of progress. So our social vision is contested. Most of America would like to have safe neighborhoods, for example, but whether people actually think it's possible, whether they have a role in bringing it about is another question. People at the top don't think it's possible.

Cornell West comments that churches may be the last institution that can engage the American public with non-market values. In fact, West says that "religion must be connected to public life in such a way that there is mutual respect, civility, and the protection of rights and liberties in our exchange." Religion ought to be robust and uninhibited, on the one hand, but equalizing – rendering accountable the most powerful and wealthy in society – on the other. West is interested in how to jump-start this process in a way that deals with patriarchy, class inequality, and homophobia. That is the fundamental challenge.

> Different ways of reading texts are determined by what one has to lose and what one has to gain.

There are very few voluntary associations left that have a language or a story that even talks about the poor, much less believes that the poor might be important or have something to teach us. The culture of merit is so relentless – whoever isn't upwardly mobile is invisible. But it's hard to read the Gospel and erase the poor, erase oppression. People ignore it, but to ignore it is not to erase it. As long as the Bible is still in our churches and synagogues, you still have the possibility. It's simple but subversive. There are not many places left where it's going to happen, not the YMCA, not the Rotary Club.

I have hope. An alternate vision of economics – Sabbath economics – is embedded in the tradition that we are still appealing to. It is a story that is increasingly anathema to the dominant story and dominant culture of capitalism. For a while there was an attempt to moralize capitalism using Judeo-Christian values but that project has disappeared so now capitalism is looking more like it did in the early stages – unrestrained. That's the challenge to our religious communities: to continue to testify to a God that's not the patron saint of the capitalist order and may not be a perfect partner in the dance of progress.

The most important thing for me in my faith life is also the most important thing in my political life: reading the Bible and always coming around to the story, trying to learn more about it. It presents such a profound alternative to the world we live in, and most of that alternative I don't grasp yet. It's like living in a paper bag and trying to imagine the world outside the paper bag, but I have this little book I read in the paper bag that talks about the world outside the paper bag. The other thing is real contact with the poor for me, both politically and spiritually – that is the bottom line. I believe the poor help us read the Bible, and the Bible teaches us to listen to the poor.

Ched can be reached at chedmyers@igc.org or www.bcm-net.org

words.

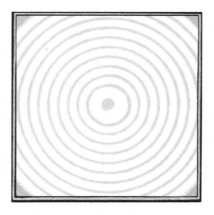

healing

When one does not get what one wants or expects
and feels trapped by obligation or economic circumstances,
one responds with a withdrawal of energy characterized as burnout.
~ Dennis T. Jaffe and Cynthia Jaffe, Self Renewal

Healing occurs when you align with the pure, positive energy that created the planet —
and that keeps your heart beating and your blood chemistry normal.
Healing occurs when you release all your resistance to well-being and allow yourself to be well.
Healing occurs when you're in harmony with your life's purpose and those who are meant
to accompany you on this path. Healing occurs when you've created a sense of safety and security
in your life. Healing is a major leap of faith in this culture.

~ Christiane Northrup, M.D.

what is healing? . . . .

Healing is the process by which we release that which no longer serves us and cultivate that which does. Healing happens when we give up a bad habit, address an addiction, or examine old patterns. It happens when we stimulate the flow of energy in our bodies or become conscious of what we put into the body, mind, and spirit.

Many people who easily muster tremendous discipline and dedication for their families, their work, or their community find it hard to set aside a fraction of that time for their own healing and transformation. We want to have a positive impact on the people and the world around us, but how can we if we don't also have a positive impact on ourselves?

We witness physical, mental, and emotional breakdowns, in ourselves and others, made manifest in any number of ways. Healing is not just about self-preservation. It is about preventive maintenance that in turn strengthens the energy, intelligence, and joy that we are able to bring to everything else in our lives. Healing comes from the same word as "whole" and "holy," just as cure comes from the same root as care. To be healed, therefore, is to be whole and holy. To care for oneself is to begin to find a cure for the world.

turning point . . . .

I was not a particularly active child. I grew up hating gym class and overeating when people weren't looking. Snacks were used as reward for a hard day and I grew up with an unhealthy relationship to nutrition. Food was a salve rather than nourishment. I struggled to make the lacrosse team in high school and played for two years before giving up. I was saddled with a negative body image that plagues many of the women I know. I continued to be sedentary throughout college, with only the occasional attempt at exercise. I loved to run, the feeling of my body in motion, but by that point my athletic confidence was so low that it was a challenge to maintain any kind of commitment.

After college I made a sporadic commitment to exercise. My first job, organizing college students to fight hunger and homelessness, mandated a grueling sixty-hour week. I operated under the theory that if I excelled at work, the rest of my life would either fall into place or not matter that much. I ate hot dogs at eleven A.M., saturated myself with chocolate and nicotine to get through the afternoon, and drank beer after work. I wasn't lazy, exactly; I was far too curious about the world for that. But I just could not devote any attention to my health, in the broadest sense of the word. When I finally left that job, I left behind some of the worst habits, but not all.

In the mid-nineties two things happened that completely changed my understanding of my own capacity for healing and how my body could function. First, I accompanied a friend to an Alcoholics Anonymous meeting and for the first time I began to understand the true nature of addiction. I realized that I had food addictions that would not easily disappear. In one way, dealing with a food addiction is tougher than something like drugs or alcohol because complete abstinence is not possible. Instead, I had to be honest with myself about which foods trigger the addictive tendency to eat without stopping. This continues to be a struggle for me, almost every day of my life. I am a healthier eater now but I still make many bad food choices and my discipline is not what I would want it to be. I try to take solace in the progress I have made. It has given me tremendous compassion for folks dealing with other kinds of addiction.

Around the same time, I took my first yoga class. I felt my entire body come alive in a way it never had before. For the first time, the aggression I had toward my physicality began to subside. I started sleeping better and easily stopped drinking caffeinated coffee in the morning. I began to realize we are all sitting on a gold mine – our bodies. We just needed teachers, time, and practices to help us tap into this treasure. After practicing yoga for five years, I decided to attend Kripalu's yoga teacher training. I was already using yoga in limited ways in my work, helping activists and change agents get back in their bodies and find a greater source of energy. Proper training seemed to be in order. Only in the back of my mind lay the other reason: the possibility that yoga might become my primary spiritual discipline.

What I found during that training and in the time since is beyond what I could have imagined or hoped for. I have never been so awed or humbled by anything. Yoga has challenged my inherent tendency toward laziness and it has been the only way I know to ease up the blatant hostility with which I had always treated my body. As I practice and teach, I watch old notions of who I am dissolve. The discipline has helped me see how weaker places can be strengthened or accepted. And it has given me a way of moving through the world with more openness and confidence than I believed I would ever have.

When I first started practicing yoga I heard teachers call it a "life science" but did not know what they were talking about. Now I have begun to understand it as a system that provides as much as the practitioner is willing to take on. Yoga is more than just a physical discipline (in the form of the postures and breath work) that can help develop a stronger spine and muscles, greater flexibility, more energy, and healthier organs and digestive system, though perhaps that alone would be enough. Yoga also offers a philosophy to govern one's behavior toward others and self. The lessons in acceptance, flexibility, nonjudgment, presence, and overcoming limitation that we learn on the mat serve us in our lives off the mat.

Yoga helped me identify some of my most basic hungers – the desire for a healthier body and a more open spirit. It has helped me to shift slowly my relationship to a number of "healing edges" in my own life, those conditions or habits that separate me from being a positive force in the world: low energy, unhealthy eating, and depression. This chapter focuses mostly on those edges that I know something about. Your edges may be very different: repeated colds, major health crises, eating disorders, alcoholism, persistent pain, disease, codependency, insomnia, abusive relationships, anxiety, or something else altogether.

Regardless of what specific issues we must face, the healing process is similar. It begins the moment we identify our healing edges. Next, we need to realize that recovery is possible, no matter what the area of need. Finally, we have to love ourselves enough to get whatever help we need. Healing can begin with a small act that simply makes us feel better: walking instead of driving, a new choice of snack food, a resolve to face some hidden physical or emotional pain. The effect of one decision ripples out to the rest of our being.

❓ questions for reflection . . . .

What activities or practices do you currently have that contribute to your own healing?

What gives you energy?

What interrupts or sabotages healing in your life? What drains you?

What type of healing do you crave?

Are you healthy enough now to sustain yourself over the next decade and beyond?

℮ the realities of stress

Even the healthiest people experience stress, and most of us experience it with some regularity. We might not be able to choose the events that trigger stress, but we can always choose our response. The sense of urgency we feel about our lives and our work may be a great motivator, but when mismanaged, it can be a negative force that limits our capacity to act with sound body, open mind, and loving heart. Our health is affected greatly by the circumstances in which we find ourselves as well as the general state of society – a fast-moving world, the need to succeed, and rising levels of violence and fear.

We can sabotage our body's ability to move through stress (with fast food, alcohol, caffeine, cigarettes, drugs, and other substances), or we can choose a different path. In the short term, we can cultivate healthy and creative responses: drinking enough water, getting plenty of rest and exercise, taking hot baths, getting enough fresh air, asking for support from those around us, making sure we eat well, and taking time for ourselves. In the long term, we must come to terms with the fact that stress-related symptoms are a sure sign that whatever demands life is making on you are too much. Healing and renewal do not lend themselves to the quick fix. They require a daily commitment. A spiritual practice that engenders a daily commitment to healing and rest is one of the most effective ways both to prevent and face stress.

℮ your energy flow

How familiar are you with your own energy flow? Becoming conscious of the peaks and valleys of your day is a vital aspect of the healing process. Spend a few days monitoring yourself throughout the day. On a scale of one to ten, write down how much energy you feel you have once each hour. One means you're ready for a nap; ten is the best you've ever felt. Write down what you were doing that hour (working, reading, eating, driving to work, playing with your kids) and record anything else that may have contributed to that energy level (not feeling well, being hungry, feeling nervous about presentation at work). Don't change or add anything to your daily routine. Do this for at least three days, a week if you can. Then, looking at the data you've collected, answer the following questions:

What are your most energetic times of the day, those you rated seven to ten?

What were you doing during those times? List the activities. Is there a pattern?

What were your least energetic times of the day, those you rated one to four?

What were you doing during those times? List the activities. Is there a pattern?

What can you learn from this?

Movement of any kind is a great antidote to slumps. For example, if you always hit a low just after lunch, which is common, use some of your lunch hour to take a walk. If late afternoons tend to be a black hole, maybe you can figure out a way to exercise during those times. If you know evenings are when you're most awake, save what requires your greatest attention for that time. It may mean finding or asking for some flexibility in your workday. Once you're familiar with your own patterns, you can help others around you to gain more energy awareness as well. You might consider charting your eating habits as well (see the activity "your relationship with food" toward the end of the chapter), because nutrition will also impact your energy level.

Note: If you're consistently rating most of your day at five and under, it may be a sign that you need to take a closer look at your sleeping patterns, eating habits, stress level, or other health-related issues. This would be a good time to see a doctor or alternative health practitioner.

healing the physical self

When we are disconnected from the wisdom of our bodies, we're at risk of separating ourselves from its needs and rhythms, and the messages about what it needs to function. Children intuitively are not content to stay in one place for very long. They want to move. Healing movement is any movement that deepens your connection to your physical body and unleashes energy.

Even moderate activity, twenty to thirty minutes three times a week, can result in significant benefits for mind, body, and spirit. Physical activity strengthens the heart and the circulatory system, which increases our stamina. It improves our muscle power, our bones, our flexibility, and our joint mobility. In a 1997 report on physical activity, the U.S. Surgeon General also found that physical fitness also improves one's mood, self-esteem, confidence, and cognitive functioning. Inactive people were twice as likely to have symptoms of depression as active people.

℮ walking

*I suggest a time apart or a time alone with God, walking in receptive silence
amid the beauties of God's nature. From the beauty of nature you get your
inspiration, from the silent receptiveness you get your meditation, from the walking
you get not only exercise but breathing – all in one lovely experience.*

~ Peace Pilgrim

This is by far the easiest — most of us do it every day. If you're not
used to exercising a lot, have problems with your joints, or just love
to walk, this is a great way to start moving. It is also a way to spend
time quietly with someone else. Many soulful conversations happen
while in motion on the sidewalk, through the woods, around the
park, or along the beach. Often moving side by side allows for greater
intimacy than sitting across a table. Walking is also a good way to
explore new places. Like most forms of exercise, walking aids
digestion, reduces anxiety, and increases your stamina, circulation,
and muscle tone.

Get out a map that includes your street and figure out one
point that is a mile from your house. Use that to approximate a circle
with a mile radius, the center of the circle being your home. If you
have a protractor lying around, it will double your fun and your
accuracy. If not, a pencil tied to a piece of string will work. Do the
same thing for a half-mile radius. Now look at the areas contained
within each of these concentric circles. What's there? What can you
easily walk to: parks, friends' houses, school, library, work, post
office, restaurants, stores? What is your usual mode of transport to
these places?

℮ aerobic exercise

During aerobic exercise, the cardiovascular system works at a rate
that demands large amounts of oxygen, much more than usual. This
forces the heart to beat faster as it pumps this additional oxygen-
enriched blood to the muscles. So aerobic exercise, in addition to
building stronger muscles and reducing body fat, strengthens our
heart and makes our lungs more efficient. More oxygen means more
deep breathing, and therefore more resource to handle situations and
process feelings. Aerobic exercise includes, but isn't limited to running, cycling, swimming, many team sports, and exercise equipment
– bikes, treadmills, and StairMasters. Cycling is non-weightbearing,
so it's particularly good for the joints; and swimming is practically
stress-free for the body.

Acupuncture is used for both acute and chronic conditions.

Ayurveda: This healing system recognizes three main body types, each of which require different diets. Ayurvedic medicine has been practiced in India for more than five thousand years.

Chiropractic: Chiropractors correct misalignments in the spine, which in turn impact posture, the nervous system, and overall body health.

Herbalism: Natural plants are transformed into compounds and tinctures to treat a wide array of ailments.

Homeopathy: A minute amount of a natural substance is chosen to treat illness based on a series of biological and environmental factors. This substance stimulates the body's immune system.

Naturopathy: Naturopathic practitioners use nutrition, herbs, homeopathy, and other techniques to stimulate the body's ability to heal.

chakras

The *chakras* are the seven energy centers in the body, according to Kundalini yoga. Each one, represented by a different color, corresponds to a point in the body and the realm that it governs. There are specific practices to free or strengthen the energy in each *chakra*.

1. Root chakra (red) governs survival, grounding, and security.

2. Genitals/abdomen (orange) governs sexuality, pleasure, emotions, and creativity.

3. Solar plexus (yellow) governs power, will, transformation, and energy.

4. Heart chakra (green) governs love, unity, balance, and relationship.

5. Throat chakra (blue) governs communication, judgment, and choices.

6. Third eye (violet) governs intuition, visualization, light.

7. Crown chakra (white) governs transcendence, knowing, enlightenment.

℮ t'ai chi and qigong

Over four thousand years old, the Chinese arts of t'ai chi (pronounced *tie-chee*) and qigong (pronounced *chee-gong*) have their roots in the philosophy of Taoism. Both are based on the cultivation and direction of *chi* – the Chinese concept of life force or life energy. It is *chi* that awakens and enlivens the body. These practices can prevent illness, provide relaxation, build muscle strength, promote circulation, increase stamina and vitality, and fight disease. Many gyms, martial arts studios, and yoga studios now offer both t'ai chi and qigong.

Qigong is a series of stretching exercises that lead *chi* to various parts of the body, in addition to breathing techniques and concentration exercises that strengthen the spirit. All three of these – body, breath, and spirit – work in tandem. A derivation of qigong, t'ai chi is a full-body movement meditation. Technically a martial art (*t'ai chi ch'uan* literally means "supreme ultimate boxing"), t'ai chi is a series of flowing movements. During t'ai chi, your legs and arms are in constant, fluid motion, but the movement is almost effortless. Millions of Chinese, and now others around the globe, practice t'ai chi at dawn and at dusk.

℮ yoga

The word "yoga" actually means yoke, or union. Yoga goes beyond the physical discipline that we normally think of when we hear the word; it includes selfless service (*karma yoga*), breathing exercises (*pranayama*), and meditation. "Hatha yoga" is the term used to describe the actual physical postures, or *asanas*. Each posture is designed to increase body flexibility (including the health of the spine), stimulate various organs, and increase circulation. Without putting any strain on the body, yoga stimulates energy. And it is practiced with constant attention to the breath. It induces a state of meditation and concentration, allowing our bodies to come into a state of true physical relaxation. You can take classes at a local yoga or dance studio, check out video or audio tapes from your local library, or find books with photographs of the postures. Taking a class will give you the best sense of how to do the postures for maximum effectiveness. The benefits of yoga are immeasurable and can be felt in as little as ten to fifteen minutes a day.

ℯ invigorating stretches

What follows is a combination of stretches and gentle yoga postures that flow together. These are easy to learn. Attending some yoga or stretching classes will give you more background. Wear loose clothing and pay attention to your body. If anything starts to hurt or feel strained in any way, ease up on the stretch immediately. Every time you see ". . . ," pause for three to five seconds and just breathe.

Head rolls. Start by standing with feet placed hip distance apart, arms at your sides. Close your eyes . . . Let your head drop slowly forward, so your chin moves to your chest but without straining any muscles in your neck . . . Then, again very slowly, bring your head back to center and tilt it slowly back so your neck stretches slightly but without any strain . . . Let the head move all the way forward and then back a second time . . . Next, tilt the head to the right so the right ear moves toward the right shoulder . . . Do this to the left side . . . Repeat once more in each direction . . . Do a couple of very slow full head rolls . . . It's important to do these movements very slowly so as not to pull the neck too much in any one direction.

Shoulder rolls. Hunch your shoulders up to your ears and slowly roll them back, giving the shoulder blades a slight squeeze as you do so . . . Repeat this five times . . . Then roll the shoulders forward five times . . . Next, breathe in as you hunch your shoulders up to your ears and let them drop back down as you exhale with an audible, "Ha!" This is a great release of energy and tension . . . Do this five times.
What weight do you carry in your shoulders?

Center of Gravity. In this same standing position, rock forward and backward, slowly. Find your center of gravity in the middle . . . Stop and feel what it is to be in this place . . . Then, rock slowly side to side and return to the place in the center again . . .
How do you find your center in the world?
How do you regain a sense of balance?

The Mountain. Standing straight, raise your arms to shoulder level, turn palms so they are facing upward, and then continue raising your arms until they form a V shape with your head in the middle . . . Feel your feet planted firmly on the ground . . . Stretch your fingers up and drop your shoulders so they're not hunched up . . . Stand tall in this position for as long as you can . . .
This is a posture of strength and stability. What do you need to be strong for today?
Let your arms slowly float back down to your sides.

Half-moon. When you're ready, slowly bring your arms up again as in the mountain and then together overhead so you can clasp your hands, leaving your two index fingers straight out and touching . . . Slowly, breathing in, stretch over to the right so your head, arms, and waist are all bending in the same direction. Stretch out as far as is comfortable and then, breathing out, return to the center position . . . Do the same thing to the left . . . Repeat one to two more times on each side . . . Let arms float to the sides of your body . . . Rest . . .

Body twist. Begin slowly twisting your body from side to side, letting your arms wrap around your body on each twist . . . Twist slowly for a couple minutes . . . then hold the twist on one side so you are looking behind you over one shoulder and your hands are on your waist . . . Do the same on the other side . . .
What helps you gain a new perspective?

Rag doll. Drop your chin to your chest. Very slowly let your whole body begin to roll forward, as if you were going to touch your toes . . . Instead just let your arms hang loosely, fingers a few inches above the floor . . . If you want you can sway gently from side to side . . . When you've had enough, begin to roll up very slowly, taking ten breaths to return to a standing position . . . Leave your chin on your chest until the end . . . Let the head be the last thing to come up . . .

℗ your relationship with food

How would you characterize your relationship with food? Do you remember what you ate yesterday? Do you know, in general, what you eat and how much? Food means different things to us at different times. One meal might be a family or social event, another might be a cure for boredom, still another simply fuel for the day. Cooking is a great way to become familiar with ingredients, to control what goes into your food and to honor being nourished. Conversely, going out to eat can create a feeling of choice, a slower pace, and food as celebration rather than escape. Keep track of your relationship to food for seven days. Every time you put food in your mouth, write down:

- What you ate and how much
- When you ate, how long it took, where you were, and with whom
- Why you eat and how you felt afterwards
- Your level of hunger before eating, on a scale of one to ten

If you do this, you will be able to notice many of the patterns in your relationship with food:

When do you eat and how often? How long does it take?

Where do you eat? Are you sitting down, standing up, or in motion? Are you able to relax?

Why do you eat?

What do you eat? Which foods would you consider healthy? Unhealthy?

℮ healing the emotional self

depression

Depression is more common than most of us care to admit. Healing from depression is a chance to focus inward, to stop and pay attention, and to take better care of ourselves. There are many forms of emotional ill health, ranging from the not-so-serious blues to depression and more serious illnesses. Some forms of depression may require the attention of a medical professional.

There are signs to watch for. In his book *Undoing Depression*, Dr. Richard O'Connor describes major depression as "a depressed mood or loss of interest or pleasure in ordinary activities for at least two weeks." This mood is usually accompanied by a number of symptoms, including significant weight loss or gain (without dieting), frequent insomnia, significant slowing of activity levels, fatigue or energy loss, feelings of worthlessness or excessive guilt, diminished ability to think or make decisions, and recurring thoughts of death or suicide.

If you notice these, consult a health practitioner, local health department, or community mental health clinic as soon as possible. Many treatments for depression are available, including counseling, psychotherapy, antidepressant medication, herbal compounds, and alternative therapies. Dealing with less severe depression can also be an important part of a spiritual journey. This level of pain calls us to turn inward, to stay present to the lows, and to remember the inevitability of change in everything, including our mental states.

addiction: a call for healing

We indulge to excess for a variety of reasons: to forget about problems, to become someone else or a version of ourselves we like better, to shift what is happening in the present or how we feel about it, to get something we want that we don't currently have, to get back to a peak instead of struggling through a valley, or to avoid a truth that we don't want to deal with. All of these boil down to one thing: *Addiction is a denial of the present moment.* It is a visible manifestation of a need to escape whatever is going on.

We have all sorts of addictions in this country: sugar, alcohol, work, food, television, drugs, shopping/spending money, nicotine, complaining, sex, caffeine; the list goes. Some have the potential to be much more destructive than others, but all forms of addiction cause pain, not just in our own lives but in the lives of others around us. There are few addictions that do not alter our personality or our judgment in some way. The irony is that while we often turn to an addiction to *gain* some kind of control, addiction is something over which we have very *little* control. Once we start, it's not clear if, when, and how we are going to stop. One person can eat a helping of desert while another will eat hordes of sugar in search of a satiation that isn't possible. One person can leave work behind on vacation while another obsessively checks voice mail and E-mail. One person can enjoy a glass of wine with dinner while another needs most of the bottle to feel good. Getting a handle on addiction is a big step toward healing and increasing your energy level. The first step of many addiction programs (including twelve-step programs) is admitting you have a problem. Once you do this, you open the door of possible solutions. Facing an addiction can be one of the most spiritual and energy-giving transitions of a lifetime.

resources for healing

Benson, Herbert, M. D. *The Relaxation Response.* New York: Morrow, 1975. www.green-river.com/assign34.htm

———. *Timeless Healing: The Power and Biology of Belief.* New York: Fireside, 1997. Examines the role that spirituality and belief play in the healing process.

Borysenko, Joan. *Fire in the Soul: A New Psychology of Spiritual Optimism.* New York: Warner Books, 1993. Stories of the spiritual growth that arises from the darkness of fear, illness, and tragedy. Practical exercises and resources for meditation, prayer, and healing. www.joanborysenko.com

Christensen, Alice. *The American Yoga Association Beginner's Manual.* New York: Fireside, 1987. Easy-to-follow series of three, ten-week yoga sessions. Photos of each posture and very explicit instructions. www.americanyogaassociation.org/

Epstein, Mark, M.D. *Going to Pieces Without Falling Apart: A Buddhist Perspective on Wholeness.* New York: Broadway Books, 1998. Perspective from a Buddhist psychiatrist on how weaving Buddhism and psychotherapy can allow us to experience the happiness that comes from letting go. www.human-nature.com/interviews/epstein.html

Farhi, Donna. *Yoga Mind, Body and Spirit: A Return to Wholeness.* New York: Henry Holt, 2000. Comprehensive guide to the principles of yoga, with careful descriptions of the postures, overview of philosophical precepts, and home practice sessions. www.donnafarhi.co.nz/

Fluegelman, Andrew, ed. *The New Games Book.* New York: Doubleday, 1976. A guide with photographs to physical games for pairs, small groups, and large groups. www.mcn.org/a/newgames/page1.html

Huber, Cherie. *The Depression Book: Depression as an Opportunity for Spiritual Practice.* Mountain View, Calif.: A Center for the Practice of Zen Buddhist Meditation, 1991. A look at depression as part of a spiritual journey and an opportunity to cultivate self-compassion. Written in a manner that is readable and accessible.

Jaffe, Dennis T., and Cynthia D. Scott. *Self Renewal: A Workbook for Achieving High Performance and Health in a High Stress Environment.* New York: Fireside/Simon & Schuster, 1984.

Judith, Anodea. *Wheels of Life: A User's Guide to the Chakra System.* St. Paul, Minn.: Llewellyn Publications, 1997. A practical guide to working with the seven "chakras," or energy centers in the body. www.sacredcenters.com/

Kripalu Center for Yoga and Health, P. O. Box 793, Lenox, Mass. 01240. (413) 448-3400. www.kripalu.org

Liu, Qingshan. *Chinese Fitness, A Mind/Body Approach: Qigong for Healthy and Joyful Living.* Jamaica Plain, Mass.: YMAA Publication Center, 1997.

Murray, Michael T., and Joseph Pizzorno. *Encyclopedia of Natural Medicine.* Rocklin, Calif.: Prima, 1991. Covers the use of herbs, diet, and vitamins for the treatment of various diseases.

Northrup, Christiane, M.D. *Women's Bodies, Women's Wisdom: Creating Physical and Emotional Health and Healing.* New York: Bantam, 1994. A comprehensive guide. www.drnorthrup.com/

O'Connor, Richard. *Undoing Depression: What Therapy Doesn't Teach You and Medication Can't Give You.* Boston: Little, Brown, 1997. www.undoingdepression.com/

Page, Linda. *Healthy Healing: A Guide to Self-Healing for Everyone.* 10th ed. Carmel Valley, Calif.: Healthy Healing Publications, 1997. Covers diet, herbal, and lifestyle suggestions for two hundred common ailments; provides an overview of alternative health systems with a special section on herbal healing. www.healthyhealing.com/

Porter, Phil, and Cynthia Winton-Henry. *The Wisdom of the Body: The InterPlay Philosophy and Technique.* Oakland, Calif.: WING IT! Press, 1995. Contact: WING IT!, 669A 24th Street, Oakland, Calif. 94612. (510) 814-9584.

Rosen, David. *Transforming Depression: Healing the Soul through Creativity.* New York: Penguin, 1996. Case studies from a Jungian psychiatrist who helps patients use creativity to transcend ego and transform depression.

Roth, Gabrielle. *Sweat Your Prayers: Movement as Spiritual Practice.* Los Angeles: Tarcher, 1998. Roth looks at movement as a medium for awakening. Through personal stories and interactive exercises, she discusses the body's five natural rhythms: flowing, staccato, chaos, lyrical, and stillness. www.ravenrecording.com/gabrielle.html

Sivananda Yoga Vedanta Center. *The Sivananda Yoga Training Manual.* New York: Sivananda Yoga Vedanta Center, 1991. Pocket-size book with overview of the five points of yoga (exercise, breathing, relaxation, diet, and meditation) and full explanations of the twelve basic postures, their variations, and mental and physical benefits. www.sivananda.org/

———. *101 Essential Yoga Tips.* New York: Dorling Kindersley, 1995. Photos of the basic postures and good supplementary information; good for travel.

Thorne, Julia, with Larry Rothstein. *You Are Not Alone: Words of Experience and Hope for the Journey through Depression.* New York: HarperCollins, 1993. The author is the director of the Depression Initiative; this book gathers the words of people who are suffering and healing from depression.

Weil, Andrew, M.D. *8 Weeks to Optimum Health.* New York: Knopf, 1997. Weil marries Western medical training with traditional medicine. He also publishes a monthly newsletter with information on a broad scope of health issues and answers to frequently asked questions. Contact: Self-Healing, P.O. Box 2057, Marion, Ohio 43305-2057. (800) 523-3296. www.drweilselfhealing.com/

body wisdom . . . .

Martha Abbott

Martha Abbott teaches Kripalu Yoga, Danskinetics, and Movement Therapy at Kripalu Center for Yoga and Health in Lenox, Massachusetts. She is a director of Kripalu Yoga Basic Teacher Training as well as other programs at Kripalu. Her own body of work uses the modalities of Movement Therapy[1] and Motional Processing which supports students to accept responsibility and vitality, and live lives of personal integrity. Martha spends most of her time in Lenox and maintains a connection with the islands of Martha's Vineyard, Massachusetts and Maui, Hawaii.

My body has always been real learning ground for me. I learned about discipline from running. I saw that if I did it consistently that I felt much, much better. I met yoga formally through a school I attended to become a personal fitness trainer.[2] During our weekly yoga classes, I was drawn inside my body to find that place where body, mind, and spirit converge. I loved the environment of self-discovery. As I continued my training, I realized that I wanted to work with people in a spiritual realm, using the vehicle of the body for exploration and growth. I was led to Kripalu Yoga because it has a clear methodology of working with the body through breath, postures, and meditation. It cultivates personal discipline, sensitivity, and awareness – all within the strong and loving container of Kripalu's spiritual philosophy. Yoga created an atmosphere of safety.

The difference is about will and surrender. Physical training works on the willful level. You have an intention and you powerhouse the body towards that intention. There is a goal and it can be wonderful to get in better physical shape. I was very good at setting my mind to a task and overriding my body. I think in America we are called to do that again and again and again. We keep to certain time schedules. That's where stress comes from – people are constantly overriding their natural rhythms. With the body-mind-spirit, you get to observe the interplay of those things. You're asked to move into a posture, exert your will by moving into a particular form and then you're asked to notice the spirit in it, notice where your awareness is drawn in your body, notice the emotions. You're bringing your consciousness to the fact that spirit is there.

> When we are disconnected from how we're feeling, we cannot and do not accept personal responsibility for being fully present. We're not able to act from a place of authenticity.

---

[1] Motional Processing is a form of Movement Therapy developed by Alice Rutkowski, Ph.D., RMT, with roots in Anna Halprin's work.

[2] Strong, Stretched, and Centered on Maui, HI.

As I continued to work with people in this way, I saw the role of creative expression as a vital part of the healing and self-actualization process so I began to study movement therapy.[3] The body provides such a beautiful framework for people to orient themselves. It is a practical way to understand where your boundaries are. We can feel empowered through this physical form that we have and also notice where that power isn't being accessed – where we've been wounded, where our physical form is protecting ourselves rather than standing up fully in our power. The process is individual, personal, and goes as deep into self-discovery as a person is willing and able to go. My role is to create a safe and sacred environment for the work and to offer a form for the journey.

I believe that so much dis-ease is caused by people judging themselves harshly, overriding their natural rhythms and instincts, and not being in touch with the reality of who they are. When we are disconnected from how we're feeling, for whatever reason, we cannot and do not accept personal responsibility for being fully present. We're not able to act from a place of authenticity. Our behavior – how we treat ourselves and others – comes from a place of confusion or illusion. The quality of our communication, instead of being clear and effective, is unclear and indirect, which produces discord.

I lead people in gentle, fluid movement. They are encouraged to be conscious of how their breath is moving and how they are feeling as they move. In a safe and supportive environment people can begin to relax and allow themselves to feel more than they may have in a long time. I believe that we can all find that safety in the body. I haven't met anyone who hasn't been able to find that place within themselves. I have watched people discover exhaustion, inflexibility, deep relaxation, peace, playfulness, joy, and sorrow.

> Entering the environment of the body with consciousness leads one to their personal truth. If we do this regularly, there is a chance to examine all we've circumvented before, all that we have ignored through learned and habitual behavior.

Entering the environment of the body with consciousness leads one to their personal truth. If we do this regularly, there is a chance to examine all we've circumvented before, all that we have ignored through learned and habitual behavior. There is an opportunity for healing. As people begin to discover who they are, their participation in their lives and community is more direct and open. They are able to act from a place of authenticity and integrity. The reward for this is immediate; it promotes health and honesty within the individual and the community. In our bodies we have everything we need to live a rich and beautiful life.

My path claimed me. There came for me a dark night of the soul, a metaphoric night that lasted a few years when I felt that my internal landscape was shed, viscerally torn out of me. What once

[3] These studies included a Danskinetics Training Certification and Movement Therapy Training Certification through In-Motion, both taught by Gale Turner and Daniel Levin, as well as a Motional Processing Training Certification taught by Alice Rutkowski, Ph.D., RMT.

had given me a sense of security, a sense of self, was no longer there. All of the familiar internal landmarks were gone and in their place was a wasteland. I had a visual image of the set for *Waiting for Godot.* I continued to be present, in my body, in my feelings. I got in touch with excruciating emotional pain as well as deep and beautiful moments of spiritual connection. I continued to be true to myself, to be honest. During this wasteland period, my faith grew. Though I was feeling hopeless and uncomfortable in my own skin, I knew I had to keep walking my path with integrity no matter how emotionally painful and solitary it was. It was during that time that my path was made clear.

I define my personal practice broadly: to the best of my ability being true to myself, maintaining a life of honesty, integrity, and compassion for myself and others with humor and humility. My work is an important part of living my path. When I teach, I pray that I will be a channel for the message of love. I open up to being aware of my students to the best of my ability. That's where the teacher becomes the student all the time in the process. Because spirit is brought in, it is a transformational territory. The students and the teacher have the opportunity to reflect things to each other, to offer insight.

It's important to find ways of being in your body consciously on a regular basis so that you don't get disconnected from who you are and what you are feeling. Support your practice by moving through gentle stretches while being conscious of your breath, free-form dancing, finding a physical way to play in your body. Get outside to be aware of other natural forces – the sun, wind, water, trees, and plants. Spend time with animals, cultivating your powers of observation and sensitivity as you interact with them. Find a way to create a network of supportive friends, people with whom you can honestly and comfortably talk about your spiritual journey. My path continues to grow me, opening me to greater awareness of myself, and all that surrounds me. My hope is that we all feel blessed with the honesty, open-mindedness, courage, and love to walk our path with integrity.

healing hand . . . .

Lori Fendell

Lori Fendell has been a traditional acupuncturist for eight years. She is also trained as a Chinese herbalist, Western herbalist, and a physician's assistant. She has a master's degree in international public health from the University of Hawaii. In the early eighties, she spent a year running an outpatient clinic and helped train midlevel health care workers in a Cambodian refugee camp. She and her partner, Walton, are committed to creating intentional community with other like-minded people.

My spiritual life is evolving; there's nothing stagnant. It's like walking into new rooms and thinking, "Oh! I never considered that before." When I let go of my own will and planning and allow life to happen, I trust that I will be carried along with the life force. Each time I can drop deeper into that awareness, I get supported, always. It's like breathing. Sometimes you're taking a breath in, you contract and forget to really breathe. As soon as you remember, there's the opportunity again. Life can be a breath of a reminder. Something wakes you up, and you have a choice again.

"The master never plans for greatness, or the one great big thing. She just pays attention. She is just with what's right in front of her." That's from *Tao Te Ching*.[1] I never could have known that I wanted to be an herbalist and an acupuncturist because those things didn't exist. I knew I wanted to take chemistry, because I wanted to learn about the world. In high school, I was making good decisions for where I am now, but I didn't know why. I wasn't attracted to working with sickness and drugs, the drama of severe illness. But, I worked in a hospital for four years and applied to a physician's assistant program.

> Acupuncture demands that I be present with every encounter, beyond how I even *know* how to be present . . . And that's what I'm asking of my patients, too — to become present to their own lives.

Years later, I was doing research on AIDS, and a small group of various health practitioners were writing a grant for alternative approaches to treatment. We met and the one person who couldn't come was the acupuncturist. Later, he invited me to his office to observe treatment of an AIDS patient. When I got into his office, I felt something totally different than anything I had experienced in medicine. It was healing, and it was simple, and it was elegant. When I left his office, I had the phone number to an acupuncture school. I applied and I got in, all in an instant. My friends looked at me and said, "What are you doing, career suicide?" I had a very good, professional position. I was getting all kinds of promotions, recommendations, status. It was great, but it wasn't what I loved. There's another quote from the Tao about that: "When a wise person hears the Tao, they run to it. When somebody in the middle hears the Tao, they ask questions. When a skeptic hears it, they laugh at it."[2]

Acupuncture demands that I be present with every encounter, beyond how I even *know* how to be present. And there's nothing else in life other than learning how to be present. So I'm getting the best teaching of my life. And that's what I'm asking of my patients, too – to become present to their own lives. Now, to do that in a way that resonates for each person, fresh, that's the part I love. I don't always succeed. I am at a growing edge with it.

I am the life force when I'm doing the work. I am the representative of it, rather than just my own personal will. I'm just settling into it as I am able. The more I do it, the more it's a mystery, how profound it is. I'm just a conduit. It's phenomenal. It's just about paying attention at deeper and deeper levels. Chi, the life force, is not as mysterious as the tao. Chi animates all of life, not just people or the animals or the trees. It's the wind, the movement of the rivers, the tide of the ocean, the pull of gravity. We receive our chi from our breath; it comes into the lungs. And the

[1] *Tao Te Ching: A New English Version*. Stephen Mitchell. New York: HarperCollins, 1988.
[2] Ibid.

> **Society says you're a good person if you get up early, work hard, push through. I like people to have permission to get ten hours of sleep, plus a nap, if they need it.**

food we eat is filled with chi, if it's good food. Another more subtle spiritual level of chi is the surrounding in which you place yourself. You can elevate your chi. If you're on the path that resonates for your heart, then you will be bringing about healing for the life force, in whatever modality it is for you.

I like to do gentle, steady change rather than anything to shock the body, because I think those are the lasting changes. You know people will say, "Get off the coffee, get off the cigarettes." People don't change like that, really. But I might hold a huge vision for where I know they could go over time. I've seen some people come in, just off chemo, drugged up, sick, entrenched in the medical model, weak through their illness, and I can't tell them to get off all their drugs. It's a slow education process of good nutrition with foods that have vitality, getting enough rest, having permission to have all the rest your body wants – going for a nap, not the coffee – and following your heart in your line of work, which includes lots of time off. Sometimes this is the only time people hear about it. Society says you're a good person if you get up early, work hard, push through. I like people to have permission to get ten hours of sleep, plus a nap, if they need it.

I find that some people, when they're young, won't consider paying attention to their health, so I don't push it. I encourage them to live a joyful, creative life and follow their heart with their work, not their pocketbook. Some people reaching forty or fifty are furious that they have to pay so much attention to their health. They don't want to learn about nutrition. They want their arthritis to go away. People can realize that the body is always changing. I have compassion for them, but there's no way around it but being with it. We may be here to do our external work and we can be present to our physical bodies, too. It is the vehicle for our work, the temple for our spirituality, and we have an opportunity to clean up the temple.

moving into play . . . .

Ginny Going and Tom Henderson

Tom and Ginny are community artists, teachers, performers, organizational consultants, and self-described "recovering serious people." They teach InterPlay, a system of ideas and practices that promote fullness of life through movement, story, voice, and stillness for individuals and groups. They are co-directors of Off the Deep End Ensemble, an InterPlay performance group.

Tom is a Ph.D. organic chemist with twenty-five years experience in the pharmaceutical industry (research, development, and management). Ginny has thirty years of business management experience and was the Executive Director of Triangle AIDS Interfaith Network for five years. She is an ordained deacon in the Episcopal Church. Tom and Ginny have been married for twelve years and have four married daughters and three grandsons.

GG: I was always kind of looking for opportunities to have dance and movement in my life regularly. I got introduced to modern dance by a gym teacher and then used baby-sitting money to take dance lessons in my late teens and early twenties. I always had this pull toward dance but never did it enough to satisfy myself.

TH: For me it started in third grade. The class was doing *Peer Gynt*, a play, and I was a goblin and had to do a goblin dance. I was having a great time. But the day before we were to perform for the parents, the teacher said, "Now, don't get stage fright on me," and I immediately felt something go "clench" inside me. Of course I was terrified the next day. Ever since then, I've had this angst about dancing, and I went through high school knowing I couldn't dance. I learned to play music, so I could be in the dance band and not have to dance.

GG: The beginnings of what we're doing now happened early in our marriage. We had been married for six months, and I had retired from my thirty-year career. To celebrate, we went to a workshop on "Sexuality and Spirituality: The Travail of Integration." That was the mountaintop experience for us. We were introduced to improvisational movement, dance, and art in a very gentle, invitational way. And we came down from the mountain saying, "Wow."

> It's occurred to me why movement works so quickly: we don't lie as easily with our bodies. It's harder to put on the usual masks.

TH: It was a gradual integration. By the end of the week, we were all running and leaping and dancing with each other. I found an inner dancer. I think everybody did. That was the first time I really allowed myself to believe that my sexuality and my spirituality were intimately connected.

GG: We met in small groups every evening. People took forty-five minutes to share their sexual-spiritual story. I don't think I would have dreamed of being able to do that with such honesty. In retrospect, I was learning about the power of movement and the experiential arts inspire individuals in a group to much more honesty and depth of sharing around whatever it is they're doing together. The movement is a metaphor for what you're doing as a group.

TH: Movement seems to build community very quickly. Other ways of community-building take time and energy and they're heavy. It's occurred to me why movement works so quickly: we don't lie as easily with our bodies. It's harder to put on the usual masks. What we say is more honest, and it is about a yearning for connection. Our stories come across.

GG: Movement raises up every interpersonal issue in the world. Last night, we were introducing our class to contact, and most hadn't done this type of movement. We said the simplest thing: "When you feel your partner's touch, move into it." Then we said, "When you feel your partner's touch, move away." In that one little exercise is the tension of the coming together and the distancing that goes on between people.

TH: And questions about who's going to control that . . .

GG: But we're doing it in a light, playful way, with a light spirit. I emphasize that it builds confidence in our bodies. I always say, "I know we're all sitting here with messages we've internalized about our bodies. They're somehow inadequate, not enough." I'll have folks make a full-page list of "My ___ is too ___." We've been taught to hate our bodies. We haven't been taught anything about loving our bodies, which means we haven't been taught anything about loving ourselves.

> **There's something about the joy and fear and terror of being seen alive and changing.**

Then, we saw the InterPlay materials, and it seemed to circle back to where we had started at Kirkridge: movement and experiential arts as powerful tools on the spiritual journey. The philosophy was a way to be in my body every day, not just when we're doing movement. The fruits of it are worrying less, going for more, deciding you can have more. Moving from a place of judgment to one of affirmation. Noticing choices and exercising them. Going from a stance of scarcity to one of plenty. Wanting to see the people around you in all their fullness.

TH: One of the tenets of InterPlay is an ethic of play. We're all familiar with the work ethic. After I recognized that I was in a midlife crisis, I realized I wanted more play in my life, but I'd forgotten how to play. So for the next few years, I worked really hard at playing. An aerobic dance class helped save my life, literally. But it wasn't until I started doing improvisational dance that I remembered how easy and natural it is to play.

GG: We went to San Francisco and did the InterPlay "Wisdom of the Body" workshop. We loved InterPlay; it seemed like the natural next thing for us. We met Phil Porter and Cynthia Winton-Henry, the co-creators of InterPlay, who have been bridging the world of dance and the world of religion for twenty years.

We got introduced to improv performance by seeing WING IT!, their dance company, perform. They had the audience give them words and phrases, and they did two hours of dance, storytelling, and singing, making up lyrics and tunes on the spot. I was in disbelief. There's something about the joy and fear and terror of being seen alive and changing in improv performance. Before, if I had a presentation to do, every word had to be on paper, and perfect. Now, I get up in front of an audience, trusting that something will come and we'll connect with each other.

TH: We got to perform that week in California. We didn't sign up, but at one point near the end of the performance, Cynthia said, "Tom and Ginny: following and leading," one of the forms they use. You just don't say no to Cynthia, certainly not in front of a whole room of people. That was our plunge. Cynthia has a habit of drawing people into a new place.

GG: And now we have our own InterPlay performance group now, Off the Deep End.

TH: For the first three years of our involvement in InterPlay, I said that I wasn't in this to perform, that it was for myself and for helping men and women relate to each other better, engage in conflict better. I still think those things are true.

GG: If you're interested, find someone in your area that's doing creative movement and just start with whatever you can find.

TH: And find someone who will tell you there's no wrong way to do this, because lots of people think there's a right way.

GG: And I would say, dance at home, move at home. Put on some music and just do what feels good.

Ginny and Tom can be reached at interplaync@nc.rr.com or www.interplaync.org

healing.

Part Two

Union
Reaching Out at Home and at Work

We search for the holy at home and at work. We want relationships with family, friends, and colleagues that feed and inspire, that stimulate and challenge, that support and nurture. We tend to marginalize the sacred to the realm of our spiritual practice or faith communities when it already exists in our primary realities: family, marriage and partnership, friendship, work.

How we treat other human beings reveals a lot about where we are on the journey, what lessons we still need to learn, and how readily we can find the best within ourselves and make it available to another. One of the ways we live out the spiritual, godlike pieces of ourselves is through companionship; it is the place where the heart opens or closes in the most telling ways.

Sometimes it is only our inability to see what is already there – the magic and the mystery – that keeps these interactions from thriving. Day to day, we experience disappointment, disconnection, and miscommunication. Unchecked, these feelings become more severe – mistrust, anger, fear, and abuse. In their most potent forms, these emotions fuel oppression and violence.

How do we transform the darkness we see in ourselves and in others we care about? By developing authentic relationships, creating ritual to mark time together, sharing our stories, and exploring the power of images. Reaching out to those around us in the context of spirit creates an ethos of shared power, the base of healthier and more engaged relationships. Strong and lasting unions are a vital building block at real and lasting change. A healthier, more just world depends on relationships of mutuality, honor, and love.

relationships

Finally it all boils down to human relationship . . .
whether I shall go on living in isolation or whether there shall be a we . . .
love alone is radical.

~ Howard Zinn

The heartbeat of true love is the willingness to reflect on one's actions,
and to process and communicate this reflection with the loved one.

~ *bell hooks*, All About Love

what are relationships? . . . .

Relationships give us an opportunity to *be* whatever change we are seeking in the world. It is in relationship with other people that we begin to notice how present we are, how well we listen, how we judge people, how well we see what *is* as opposed to how *we'd like it to be*. Relationships expose our limitations and our possibilities; our most significant life lessons, however painful, come through our relationships. Sometimes it is not until years later that we see why we needed to be in a relationship with or meet a certain person at a certain time. Since some of our own search for consciousness involves others, we need to think well about who exactly these others are, and who we want them to be. It's good to ask questions now and then: What is the purpose of this union? Why are we here together? What are we supposed to be learning?

Ultimately we must decide what kind of relationships we are going to have. Will they be based on ego or compassion, on our need to protect our own power, or our desire to love people more fully? We may treat people well when things are running smoothly, but the minute our life gets hard, compassion goes out the window, and suddenly we're acting from a different place. Whether a relationship seems easy or hard, enriching or draining, or all of the above, spirit is always present. With attention, we can become more aware of how we cultivate the presence of harmony and goodwill.

turning point . . . .

As a grown woman or man, you make a break with your family of origin, the kind of separation that is necessary to establish your independence. You begin to wonder who you belong to, and who belongs to you, not in the sense of possession but in the sense of connection that will be last an entire lifetime. The web of relationships in my life, personal and professional, is rich and wide. There is a group of people, spread around the country, that I consider home – people who seem to understand me when I cannot understand me. They celebrate the moments of blessing and walk with me through the messy stuff. We grow together and apart and somehow, usually, together again.

When two of these friends, Julia and Brian, were expecting a baby, they asked me to be a birth partner. This meant being present to help out during the birth, along with each of their sisters. I'd never seen a live birth before, and I can be a bit squeamish at times, but I knew I wanted to be a part of this child's entry to the world. When they found out the baby was a girl, her proud parents disclosed to the birth partners that her name would be Frances. With the naming, this character, still deep within the womb, took on a fuller identity. I began to wonder what she would look like, which books would be her favorites, what activities she would love and hate, what colors would draw her in. I grew impatient for her arrival. I talked to her through Julia's stomach and began envisioning the house full of toys. Over the course of nine months we talked through the birth plan: what kinds of breathing Julia might do when, what music she wanted playing during labor, even stimulating the wave of a contraction by holding ice in the palm of our hands for two minutes.

During a long labor, we took turns making Julia comfortable with massage, juice, and those all-too-frequent reminders to breathe. We sang James Taylor songs, caught a few hours of sleep in the hospital waiting room, and eagerly awaited the last stages of birth. When Frances finally appeared on the night of October 7, she appeared to me as essence of perfection, from her wide eyes to her tiny toes. It was impossible to hold back tears as we took turns holding her and then watched Julia take her first crack at breast-feeding. Over those first two months I began to understand the clichés of parenthood, as I found myself wishing she'd stay this age forever and never tiring of discussing her latest feat.

Having been with Frances since the inception of her life, it was easy to say yes to the honor of serving as a godparent. On the morning of January 24, 2000, we gathered as an icy snowstorm began to form. Brian talked about the importance of baptism in the Catholic Church, and how it symbolized, for him, the beginning of Frances's relationship with Jesus Christ. The mass that followed was one of the highlights of my life. The priest talked about the need to respect people of all faiths and all the many routes to God. When it came time to bring Frances up to the altar, he held her up so that all the children in the congregation could come give their blessings, in the form of the sign of the cross on her forehead.

Then he handed the baby to me and we walked over to the baptismal font. He prayed over her and then I dipped her down toward the water. Holding her in my arms as Father David splashed water over her head, I gazed at the slight smile on Frances's face and realized that what was happening here was something I could never fully understand. In that instant, there was some kind of mystical triangulation of relationship. I recalled a rabbi I heard describe all partnerships as having a third presence and how the partnership would thrive if that presence was God or another manifestation of spirit. Suddenly, I understood the weight of my role as friend, guardian, and spiritual supporter all at once.

The sacrament had plucked me out of normal experience and given me a responsibility I'd never had before. I was the primary witness as this child began to form a relationship with God, uniquely her own and yet so much in the context of a church community and the beauty of Catholicism. And I began to feel the weight and strength of my vow to her – that for as long as I lived I would somehow be both committed to and responsible for her.

? questions for reflection . . . .

What different kinds of relationships do you have?

Which relationships are most significant to you? Do you know why?

What is hard about being in relationships with others? What is holy about it?

℮ your own footing: examining relationships

*Relationships are assignments. They are part of a vast plan for our enlightenment,
the Holy Spirit's blueprint by which each individual soul is led to
greater awareness and expanded love.*

~ Marianne Williamson, A Return to Love

Polly Guthrie introduced this activity to me as a way to take stock of one's
relationships and reorient oneself to what is most nurturing and challenging.
Make a list of categories that describe the various relationships in your life.
Here are some to get you started: work, home/family, community, friends.
Draw two concentric circles (one inside the other) for each of these categories.
In the inner circle, write the names of the people with whom you have
primary relationships. In the outer circle, write the names of others who are
important in one way or another. Do this intuitively. There may be only one
person in the inner circle, or there may be ten.

- What, if anything, surprises you about the names you wrote down?
- What are your expectations of those relationships? Are these ever
  voiced? How?

Put a star next to the people who feed your spirit the most, the people you
genuinely love to be with.

- How do you nurture these relationships?
- When do you realize you are consciously paying attention to them?

Underline the people you spend the most time with.

- Are they mostly family members, coworkers, friends, others?

Circle the people you'd like to spend *more* time with.

- What keeps this from happening?

Draw a line through the people you'd like to spend *less* time with.

- Why? What is hard about these relationships? What do you learn from them?

Notice which circles should overlap; that is, where there is a lot of crossover in certain arenas of your life.

- What effect do these overlaps have on your relationships?

ℯ reaching out to others: tools for relationship-building

To be effective in human relations requires both skill and "feel"; it demands the use of head and heart.

~ *Howard Thurman,* Meditations of the Heart

In the best of relationships, we stand in the truth of our experience, our own particularity, and from there we are better able to explore the differences and similarities between ourselves and others. In space made sacred by the presence of spirit, we begin to see each other in fuller dimensions, hear each other more completely, and sense the connections to one another that exist on a deeper level. Even a small amount of this kind of attention can alter our work and our lives considerably, making us more available for the people and issues we care about.

In many vocations, attention is paid to the skills needed to do the job well. Formally or informally, we learn a set of skills that, in the best of circumstances, will help us succeed at what we're doing. So much of work and life is relational, and yet it is rare that we specifically learn the skills for healthy relationships until a crisis ensues. We argue with a loved one and we realize we want to become better listeners. We have a miscommunication with a coworker and it seems time to speak more openly about our perspective. We begin to uncover some unhealthy patterns in an ongoing conflict we have with a sibling or parent and we commit to changing the dance. The following three tools can assist us in building sustainable, joyful relationships: listening with reverence, speaking from the heart, and dealing with conflict.

℮ listening with reverence

The time we spent together – whatever it was, twenty minutes, two hours, an evening –
began to have a shape we filled better each time we met.
It wasn't only that I listened to Rhoda, it was that we listened to each other.
I saw after a while that each of us was concentrated on what the other had to say.
It was the concentration that was so striking: I'd never before been conscious of its
presence in conversation. It made me sing inside. It wasn't that I came away thinking
my words brilliant; it was only that I came away feeling I had been fully heard,
and because I was being fully heard I was saying everything I had to say.
It seemed to me, then, that ever since I could remember I'd been fighting for someone's
undivided attention in conversation. Now I had it. I could breathe easy.

~ *Vivian Gornick*, Approaching Eye Level

Listening with reverence is one of the most important building blocks in any relationship – the ability to listen well and with compassion, without a lot of unnecessary responses. At first we think that our feedback as a listener is vital. We have been socialized to nod our heads in agreement, laugh in the appropriate places, tell our own stories to demonstrate our understanding, come up with solutions, and give great advice. In all of these cases, the usual result is that the person speaking does so for our benefit and not just her own, conscious of our reactions and what impact their words are having. The focus subtly shifts from whatever she was speaking about to a conversation about something slightly, somewhat, or entirely different.

Listening with reverence, not reaction, gives the other person more space to tell a story without having to worry about how it will be received. The speaker actually becomes empowered to follow her own path rather than taking the direction(s) offered by the listener's questions or comments. She continues speaking in her own language, from her own frame of reference.

This is a rather simple technique, but not an easy one. It means listening fully to another person in order to best hear and understand what they are attempting to communicate. It's great when this attention is reciprocated. For example, two people can agree just to listen to one another for a set amount of time. This is a great way to support someone who is facing a tough situation or difficult decision – give them the time to speak without necessarily having to respond to questions or comments from the listener unless they really want that. It's also useful when two people are in the midst of a disagreement or misunderstanding. Knowing that each of you will have a certain amount of time just to talk can really take the pressure off of having to make sure you are able to express your perspective.

@ speaking from the heart

Honest, clear, heartfelt communication is another key to successful relation-ships. And it is easier said than done. Speaking from the heart means speaking your truth. It happens when we open up to the power and reality of the present moment and take a risk to say what is real for us. Being connected to your breath and your body helps a great deal. When we can stop, breathe and check in with our physical being, we gather energy and strength for the words to come. It takes courage to get down to what is really going on for you, where you are coming from. It might take a while, but the essence of spirited speech is the ability to be where you are.

A friend once told me about something she calls the "ten-second rule." If someone says something to her that is hard to hear – because it is painful, too sarcastic, or rude – she waits ten seconds before responding. This has two benefits. First, she does not force herself into a response that she might regret later. Second, the words of the speaker linger in the air for a little while, and more often than not, the speaker begins to recognize the negativity in his or her speech.

@ dealing with conflict

In most relationships, conflict is inevitable. Often a conflict arises because an old hurt or memory is triggered. We can't change the past, but we can use the information to inform our reactions and decisions in the present. The first step is getting clear on why something feels particularly hard. This might entail answering some tough questions, such as: Who does this person remind me of? What does this situation remind me of, and how could it be different this time?

We get angry, frustrated, or impatient, and the tension builds. The stronger the relationship, the easier it should be to address conflict with respect and openness. In the weakest relationships, conflict is avoided or ignored. Many of our relationships are somewhere in between: we may deal with the conflict, but we may not deal with it very well. The more strength we can find to face conflict, the stronger our relationships will be.

There is a simple conflict resolution technique called X-Y-Z. For it to work, two (or more) people use the following framework, substituting their own words for X, Y, and Z:

> When you do X
> I feel Y
> Because of Z
> And what I need from you is . . .

(continued on next page)

Then the listener responds to the request being made in one of three ways: (1) yes, I can give you what you need or do what you are asking me to do; (2) no, I don't think I can do that; or (3) I'm not sure if I can do what you are asking, but I will try. In the case of no or maybe, it's helpful if the listener explains his or her response.

The formula may seem awkward at first, but it helps people concentrate on what they need to say, without worrying about the best way to say it. Key information is conveyed in a way that gives the listener specific and useful data: "This is what you do and this is how it makes me feel." It facilitates assertiveness, rather than passive or aggressive communication. All of this makes it easier for people to take greater risks in their communication, which in turn creates opportunities for strengthening relationships. Here are some examples:

When you interrupt me, especially in front of other people, I feel angry and insecure, because it makes it seem like I have nothing important to say. What I need is for you to let me finish my sentence and not assume you know what I'm going to say.

When you schedule meetings (or plans with friends) without telling me, I feel frustrated, because it often means I can't attend, and I would like to be present. What I need is for you to write me a quick note or leave me a message when you schedule something.

When you monopolize the conversation in this group, I feel sad, because I feel like we are missing out on a lot of other perspectives in the room. What I need from you is a commitment to talk less and encourage other folks to talk.

When I learned this tool, I was living with my brother, who was not quite as committed to kitchen cleanliness as me. One day I came home to find many dishes in the sink. Instead of getting uptight, I calmly walked into the living room and said, "Stu, when you leave dishes in the sink, I feel frustrated, because I think you don't care about the state of our apartment or my feelings. What I really need from you is to make a more concentrated effort or for us to create a job chart, so you have other responsibilities instead of washing dishes."

At first, he seemed surprised. Up until this point my standard reactions to his negligence moved between scathing silence and exasperation. Now here I was, fairly calm, making a request that seemed reasonable. He was able to say that while he hated doing the dishes, he was more than willing to take on other chores around the apartment. In the end, I did more dishes (a job I've always enjoyed), and he took the tasks I don't like as much, like taking out the garbage and cleaning the bathroom.

@ strengthening our intentions

One powerful way both to deepen a relationship and add value to your own life is by enlisting specific support from people to strengthen your own intentions and plans. This also creates streams of accountability. For example, goals are often easier to reach when we share them with someone else and set up a system to keep them informed of our progress.

One friend and I kept a daily log of progress around one specific goal we each had. We'd check in every two weeks to see how it was going, what was getting in the way. I wanted to clean up my eating habits and she wanted to be writing on a regular basis. After sharing specifics, we'd help each other brainstorm ways to overcome the barriers that were making it hard for us to reach our goal.

I've also done larger, life-dreaming with other people. One Saturday in January, a few years back, a close friend and I decided to spend some time thinking about our futures. We headed to my office where we turned on music and spread out large pieces of paper on the floor. We took time in silence, working individually to map out possibilities. I looked at my entire life by the decade. This was astounding because I'd never been able to see beyond a six-month corner in my entire life, but the support of another person made it easier to dwell in possibility. After a half an hour, we shared our work with each other, asking questions and probing deeper.

Finally, it is useful to build a support system when large events loom on the horizon. I know many people who have done this in anticipation of weddings, births, and job changes; there may be other, less obvious moments that warrant similar strength. When I decided to go abroad to see a spiritual teacher for the first time, I only wanted a handful of people to know. I carefully chose the six people whom I thought would be most supportive and ask the least number of questions. While I was gone, I thought about each of them on a daily basis. Their love and encouragement made a significant difference in my comfort level and ability to open up to the moment.

@ clearness sessions

From the Quaker tradition, a clearness session is a way for people to assist each other in discerning life choices. A small group of people (four to eight) comes together to help one person clarify a present reality or determine a future direction. They do this through compassionate listening and strategic questioning.

It's useful if the individual convening the clearness session gives the group information ahead of time. For example, he might write a page or two about different possibilities he is considering and the questions he has been asking himself. Then, the group gathers for a time, say two hours. It's great to have someone facilitate the discussion and another person take notes so the person convening the session can just listen. Their role is to:
1. Listen carefully to the individual's story and central challenge;
2. Reflect on what they have seen, heard, and felt; and
3. Ask strategic questions.
Strategic questions are those that:

- Identify ideals, vision, dreams, goals: *I hear you saying that you want to initiate a new program.*
- Consider obstacles: *What gets in the way of taking six months to work overseas?*
- Uncover strategies for change and hidden solutions: *Have you talked to your boss about partnering on that project?*
- Ask the unaskable: *Are you wanting to leave this current job or relationship or city?*
- Consider consequences: *What would happen if you cut your hours back to make space for something else?*

If desired by the individual, the group can also suggest possible directions, options, possibilities; offer wisdom, ideas, and challenges; and point out false assumptions or other elements that seem limiting.

@ mentors and coaches

Mentoring and coaching are two ways we can formalize relationships with individuals who enhance our lives through their experience and strength. We are drawn to people because we feel they know or understand something that we don't. A good mentor shares their experience when it is relevant to what we are going through, and they share it in a way that is useful to us – a story, a suggestion, or a thoughtful question. So, being a mentor is an opportunity to pass on your own wisdom to another person, perhaps in a more formalized way than normal. Mentoring tends to imply a difference in age or experience, as well as a commitment to a long-term relationship.

Coaching, on the other hand, can mean more hands-on attention and assistance with a specific issue or problem. Mentors and coaches can easily overlap. A good coach provides support and assistance, often asking the questions others would not ask. More reciprocal, peer coaching may simply involve two people who are willing to listen to each other as they explore a new direction in their lives, deepen an existing commitment, or overcome a difficult situation. Mentoring and coaching relationships work best when expectations are clearly laid out by both individuals. Pay attention to how much time you are spending together and who is benefiting.

Mentoring, being mentored, and coaching make us stronger, in our work and in our lives. Sometimes it means lending encouragement and support during rough times. Sometimes it means telling us the truth when no one else will. Sometimes it means asking a dreaded question, because we fear the truth that lies in the answer. Above all, intentional relationships like these hold out hope for the best that we can be, a vision of possibility. They remind us of what that is, what we're good at, and where we were headed before we got off track or sat down to rest.

℮ a company of solitude

As your own spiritual practice deepens, you might find it helpful to cultivate relationships that support your practice and your solitude. This might mean starting a group with friends, neighbors, or coworkers that convenes weekly to sit in meditation. Even if you are all beginners, you can gain a lot from practicing with other people. You can sit for fifteen to twenty minutes and then spend some time allowing each person to check in about how he or she is doing. Similarly, you might gather with coworkers to do yoga once a week in your conference room, using a videotape.

If you live with family, a partner, or in a group housing situation, you may want to try a shared silent retreat. A weekend is the perfect time for this. Begin with a meal or ritual together – a chance to set any intentions you each have for the period. Agree that you will not engage with each other for twenty-four or forty-eight hours. Reconnect for a meal at the end, giving everyone an opportunity to share their experiences and tell the stories of their silence, or just enjoy the quiet of each other's company.

In their multiyear study of over one hundred people who have sustained a commitment to the common good, Larry Parks Daloz, Sharon Parks, Cheryl Keen, and James Keen, the authors of *Common Fire: Living Lives of Commitment in a Complex World,* found that "the single most important pattern we have found . . . is what we have come to call a *constructive, enlarging engagement with the other."* This goes beyond the day-to-day encounters with otherness that we all have. Rather, it is the encounters that give rise to "a recognition of shared capacity for the feelings that lie at the core of our essential humanity." It is through inspired encounter with the "other" that we grow the most in how we see ourselves and the rest of the world.

℮ honoring each other

This comes from the Institute for Conservation Leadership. It is a great exercise for a family gathering, a work team that has just completed a big project, or a group whose time together is ending. Write down each person's name on a piece of paper and put them in a hat. Have each person draw one piece of paper out. Explain that at your last gathering each person will have the opportunity to honor the person whose name they drew out of the hat. It's optimal to give everyone twenty-four hours to prepare; less time will work if necessary. You will need an evening to do this ceremony. You'll find written instructions, like those below, will have the greatest impact.

WRITTEN INSTRUCTIONS FOR THE GROUP:
(Hand out a copy of the following instructions on paper when explaining them.)

HONORING CEREMONY

You can honor this person in any way you see fit. Think about the following:

1. *What have you learned from the person over the course of your time together?*

2. *What has struck you about this person?*

3. *What does he or she bring to the group, and to the world, that is unique and special?*

Tangible representations have lasting impact. You can use any materials already available to you in this process, but no purchasing is allowed.

Please don't reveal whom you are honoring until the time comes.

---

resources for relationships

Chetanananda, Swami. *The Logic of Love.* Portland, Ore.: Rudra Press, 1992. Beautiful discussions of what it means to live a life of inner mastery and authentic love. www.nityanandainstitute.org/

Covey, Stephen R. *Seven Habits of Highly Effective People: Powerful Lessons in Personal Change.* New York: Fireside, 1989. A principle-centered approach for solving personal and professional problems. www.franklincovey.com

Daloz, Laurent, A. Parks, Cheryl H. Keen, James P. Keen, and Sharon Daloz Parks. *Common Fire: Leading Lives of Commitment in a Complex World.* Boston: Beacon Press, 1996. www.futurenet.org/11powerofone/daloz.htm

Drener, Henry. "Why did the People of Roseto Live So Long?" *Natural Health,* September/October 1993, 72–79, 130, 131–133. Explores the miracle of a small town in Pennsylvania famous for low death rates as a result of close-knit families and communities.

Fox, Matthew. *The Reinvention of Work: A New Livelihood for Our Time.* San Francisco: HarperCollins, 1994. Draws on a rich spiritual tradition to make greater connections between inner and outer work.

Green, Tova, and Peter Woodrow. *Insight in Action.* With Fran Peavy. Philadelphia: New Society Publishers, 1994. Explanation and stories of three tools for supporting a life of commitment: support groups, clearness, and strategic questioning.

hooks, bell. *All About Love: New Visions.* New York: HarperCollins, 2000. A personal, social, and political look at the question, "What is love?" Exploring community, spirituality, loss, and justice.

Lerner, Harriet Goldhor. *The Dance of Anger.* New York: Harper & Row, 1985. Written for women, this book offers a look at how to channel anger constructively and change unhealthy patterns of relationships. www.readinggroupguides.com/guides/dance_of_anger.html

Levine, Stephen and Ondrea. *Embracing the Beloved: Relationship as a Path of Awakening.* Two Harbors, Mass.; Anchor Books, 1996. A look at how familial and love relationships can be an opportunity for growth and healing.

Tannen, Deborah. *You Just Don't Understand: Women and Men in Conversation.* New York: Ballantine Books, 1990. Groundbreaking for many, this book explores the differences in communication between men and women. www.georgetown.edu/tannen/

Williamson, Marianne. *A Return to Love: Reflections on the Principles of A Course in Miracles.* New York: HarperCollins, 1992.

mentoring relationships . . . .

Lisa Sullivan

Lisa Sullivan was the founding director of LISTEN, Inc., a nonprofit organization that identifies, prepares, and supports youth leadership in urban neighborhoods and communities. While pursuing a master's degree in political science at Yale University, Lisa also organized students and young people in New Haven. She then served as the director of the field division at the Children's Defense Fund and a consultant for the Rockefeller Foundation's Next Generation Leadership program. Her work began there in 1991, when she cofounded the Black Student Leadership Network. Lisa died on October 1, 2001 at the age of forty, leaving behind a network of friends and colleagues who continue the legacy of her work.

I believe that a good mentoring relationship is beneficial for both partners. I've got several strong mentoring relationships. The one that I've been in the longest is with a young woman, Deirdre, who is now twenty-seven. I've been her mentor since she was fourteen.

> **I am one of those people born to support the underdog.**

The first two years of the relationship were about me gaining her trust. I was doing community organizing in New Haven, and she was a high school student. A counselor pointed her in my direction. When you're dealing with young people of color from communities where the infrastructure has broken down – the family or the school or the neighborhood – they are used to bad things happening. They've been abandoned so many times, that to them, a mentor is just another adult who's going to let them down.

It was consistency that broke the ice. In a moment of crisis, I became the person to come to. She recognized something genuine was happening. This was a young woman who was the youngest of twelve. She had raised herself and didn't know how to trust. She found herself wanting to build a relationship with me and didn't quite know how to do it. Suddenly, I had this sixteen-year-old ringing my buzzer every day, coming to my house, taking over my bedroom, talking on the phone, giving out my phone number. She was integrating herself into my life.

Then came the second phase: making commitments, being there through thick and thin. Together, we got her out of high school and into Spelman College in Atlanta. I had to raise Deirdre's tuition, and buy her plane tickets home for Thanksgiving and Christmas. When I took her shopping before college we actually had our first major disagreement. I had my functional "we're-going-to-college" list, and she had her "we're-going-to-Spelman-I-need-fly-gear" list. It was like parenting.

When she got to Spelman, she felt out of place, because everyone was middle class and here she was from the ghetto, the first one to go to college. I went to Family Day and I connected her to my support system in Atlanta. As we've grown, the relationship has gone through several changes. Now we interact as peers, though I'm ten years older. I'm providing information and perspective, but of course she doesn't have to do what I say, and I'm okay with that. All of my roommates from grad school feel like they have helped to raise her. She's in law school now at Villanova, and she gets pampered by all of the women in my life as if she's my child.

There's probably a significant number of young people who claim me as a mentor. That means being accessible and responsive to them, within reason. I try to keep up with them on a quarterly basis, see what's on their radar screen. As things come across my desk, I try to make connections between them and those opportunities.

And then there's another tier – the people who have been explicit in asking me to be a mentor. Right now, that's probably eight to ten people. We've actually explored what it is they need from me, and it is clearly a mentoring relationship. It gives me an opportunity to assess what is going on in my life, whether I can show up for them. Interestingly, half of them are men. It's been my experience – and I've talked to other Black women about this – that the older Black men get, the harder it is for them to relate to Black women as mentors. It's easier when they're younger, because it's a mommy or sister kind of thing. There's a bit of truth to this whole thing about Black women *raising* daughters and *loving* boys. But there are several Black men who call and E-mail me on a regular basis seeking advice and support around their life decisions.

> I'm providing information and perspective, but of course she doesn't have to do what I say, and I'm okay with that.

I'm the oldest and I was raised to be the big sister. We were typical latchkey kids. I had the responsibility of getting my sister from the baby-sitter, fixing her snack, and basically taking care of her. I grew up knowing that you take care of people younger than yourself. Another piece of why I'm drawn to mentoring is just who I am. I am one of those people born to support the underdog. I believe so much in young people; I feel passionately about young people who have been abandoned. And I realize I've been incredibly blessed in my life with parents who have been very supportive of me and have given me a lot. Out of five other Black women with whom I was housed in college, I was the only one whose father was present in her life and who had a positive relationship with him.

Every step of the way I could say there have been people who have significantly influenced my development. Some of them have been peers; there's the traditional litany of teachers. Through age eighteen, it was definitely parents, godparents, and people in the neighborhood. And then from ages eighteen to twenty-two, being in Atlanta at Clark University, it was definitely faculty. In New Haven, my best friend in graduate school, who is deceased, was a guy named Tony Thomas. I can honestly say that if Tony had not come into my life, I'm not sure I would have hit the level of leadership that I've hit. He saw me through Yale. He was my guardian angel, helped me demystify the place, put it in perspective. He convinced me that the world was my oyster. He was hugely significant and influential to me when I was in my twenties.

The other person is Dr. Susan Lincoln. She is extraordinary. By the time she was twenty, she had four children, was on welfare, and had dropped out of school. She refused to give up. She got her GED, her bachelor's degree, her master's degree, and her Ph.D. in education. Before retiring as dean of students, she was the bedrock of the community college in New Haven and very active in the community, politically and socially. She's amazing – very well-known and respected by her community in New Haven, fiercely independent, and a quiet person of substance – not a lot of fanfare. When she makes up her mind to do something, it's done.

Right now in my office I'm looking at a photograph of Ella Baker on one wall. On another wall is Fannie Lou Hamer. Over my desk are Septima Clark, Langston Hughes, Mary McLeod Bethune, Althea Gibson, Frederick Douglas, and my friend Tony Thomas. For a while now I have known that my energy, my passion, and my commitment are all things that are flowing through me. It's the spirit of these other people that lives in me. I may be tired as shit, but I go home, I get a good night's sleep, I wake up at 6:45 A.M., and I get to it. And I can't explain that. I can't explain my energy level. It's not about me.

LISTEN can be reached through www.LISN.org

coaching relationships . . . .

Julia Scatliff O'Grady

Julia Scatliff O'Grady runs TimeShape, an organization that helps people reflect upon and manage their lives more boldly. Through Southern Community Partners, a project she initiated and directed, Julia provided funds, technical assistance, and coaching for thirty-four young people throughout the Southeast, all of whom founded community-based programs. She lives with her husband, Brian, and her two children, Frances and James Trygve, in Durham, North Carolina.

Coaching is the only way people can actually reach their potential – to have someone who can challenge them, nurture them, and remember what they said they'd do. You expect to learn from a podium but you don't embrace learning until you build a relationship with someone.

One of the hardest parts of my decision to be an active coach is that I don't always know the impact I'm making in people's lives. So it's lonely, because I'm not sure if I've been a pest or if I've been useful. At times it's hard for me to know what I've actually done when I'm not the creator; I'm the champion of the creator.

> Peer-to-peer coaching challenges the assumption that you have to hire a consultant from five hundred miles away for your every need and pay him or her a lot of money.

In being with a peer, I'm vulnerable, too. That's where I grow more, because I have to put myself on the line, and I have to be open to critique from the other person as well. That's the only way the peer relationship will grow. I have loved being more deliberate, seeking out conversations with people who have what I need. I really want to see people of all different backgrounds, not flying across the country for the big answer but getting it at home. Peer-to-peer coaching challenges the assumption that you have to hire a consultant from five hundred miles away for your every need and pay him or her a lot of money.

> I think people think it's corny to be deliberate; it goes against the grain.

I think people think it's corny to be deliberate; it goes against the grain. There's our planned work time, and then there's our relaxed, free time, and this coaching relationship bridges the two. It's a kind of code shifting that most of us haven't learned to do very well. Even some of your closest friends will think you're weird when you approach them with this idea of coaching each other, because custom says wisdom comes from the elders only. But don't stay there too long. Create a list of dreams, small to big, that you hope to see and then think of whom you know and how they can help you. People of all ages are so afraid to ask for help of any kind. Coaching each other helps you get over the fear.

What's key is being honest about whether you feel competitive at that moment, or sad, or frustrated. In a typical friendship, you let most of that stay inside your body. It doesn't feel so bad when it comes out into the air. Peers have a similar history and day-to-day framework, so the power dynamic is not swinging in either direction, in the best of circumstances. A lot of times the traditional relationship doesn't transform into a peer-to-peer coaching one because you're not observant. You don't see that your closest friends and colleagues have certain talents. Once you pick up on that talent, you can push it. I'm really stunned by how little it takes to inspire someone to do great things.

Julia can be reached at Julia@timeshape.org or www.timeshape.org

right relationship . . . .

Polly Guthrie

Polly Guthrie, a native North Carolinian, has worked in women's organizations and philanthropy for eight years, most recently with the Triangle Community Foundation. She has a master's degree in business administration and is currently working as a strategic advisor to a group vice president at SAS, a global software company. She is active with her church, St. Philips Episcopal, and the Food Bank of North Carolina, and lives in Durham with her partner of over ten years.

I had a seminal experience when I was fifteen and I went to Haiti with my church. Seeing poverty of that magnitude really affected my lens on the world. Four days after I got back from Haiti, I went to the beach with a couple for whom I used to baby-sit. Their eleven-month-old infant had died. Even though they had all the money in the world, they couldn't save him. And I knew if I went back to Haiti in six months, most of those babies I'd seen wouldn't be there, either. Those two events, so close together, set into motion a whole new way of thinking. It made me ask, What's the purpose or meaning of life? Why do people suffer?

To me, "right relationship" is similar to a Buddhist concept of relationship – it's a way that makes manifest between humans the love that God chose for us. In order to move God's love from a static thing to an active presence, we can relate to other people in a just and meaningful way.

> I try to manifest my relationship with God in the way I treat other people.

That means being intentional, which means that you sometimes choose to do the hard thing because it's the right and just thing to do. It might mean holding someone accountable or loving someone who's hard to love, or at a time when they're hard to love. It means seeing relationships as God's work. It means acting in such a way that it's clear you believe relationships are sacred and holy and deserve to be conducted befitting that holiness. Being in relationship is an integral part of being a person of faith.

There is a passage from Micah, "Act justly, love mercy, and walk humbly with our God." Acting justly and loving mercy are about how you treat other people, and walking humbly with your God is certainly about how you conduct yourself. If I had to distill my faith down to a few sentences, that would be one of them. The other one would be where Jesus says, "Thou shall love thy Lord, your God, with all thy heart, soul, body, and mind. This is the first and greatest commandment, and the second is like unto it; thou shalt love thy neighbor as thyself. On these two commandments hang all the law and the prophets."

Both those phrases are about relationships: my relationship with God and my relationship with other people. I try to manifest my relationship with God in the way I treat other people. It's about nurturing people – writing notes to people I hear won an award or remembering to commend someone at my office who's just completed some task really well. It also means challenging assumptions or statements when they concern me. I think about it more when particular challenges arise – someone has said something that really bothers me, and I call them on it instead of just sweeping it under the rug.

Faith for me is not about "Did Jesus really rise again?" or the doctrines of the Episcopal Church. It's what I believe and how I try to live my life accordingly. I just sort of assume that everyone thinks about these things. It's such a part of how I am and how I live that it's sort of like trying to describe how you breathe.

relationships.

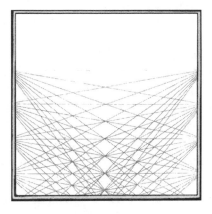

ritual

Ritual is the way culture enacts and affirms its values.

~ *Starhawk*, Truth or Dare

A man without ritual cannot live;
an undertaking without ritual cannot come to completion;
and a state without ritual cannot attain peace.

~ *Hsun Tzu (298–238 B.C.E.)*

what is ritual?

Ritual is an act that brings us to a new level of awareness. By focusing our energy in a purposeful way, rituals allow us to recognize the uniqueness or specialness of an event, a person, a time, or an idea that we might not have otherwise noticed. Spiritual lessons are often acted out in rituals and many are universal, transcending the boundaries of time, culture, and place:

- All over the world, birth is celebrated with namings and blessings, both symbolizing entrance into the community.
- All over the world, adolescents mark their journey from puberty to manhood and womanhood, either through rituals of their own devising, or through those conducted by elders.
- All over the world, the loving union of two people is celebrated with feasting, dancing, elaborate costuming, and the witnessing of vows.
- All over the world, death is commemorated by returning the physical body to the earth and a period of mourning or remembrance.

But rituals do more than mark significant life transitions or the passing of time. They build community, offering an opportunity to gather people in ways that break out of more familiar forms. Ritual is a way to honor people, outside of the more traditional context of big life events. Finally, rituals help us honor God, the presence of spirit in our lives.

Rituals that repeat themselves give our lives a sense of continuity. A parent making a favorite dish, a couple's regular return to the place where they met, even wearing a favorite shirt for an interview: these are all rituals. Team huddles, candles on a birthday cake, dressing up for a special event – some rituals have been around in our lives for so long, we take them for granted. Going to synagogue on Shabbat, attending confession, or going to church on Sunday – these are all rituals, too. The need for ritual lives deep within us and if we pay attention, we can sense this need as well as the fitting response.

turning point

One of the best and still evolving rituals in my life began out of fear. It was during the the fall of 1998, thirteen months before Y2K would come to pass. A couple of friends began expressing their extensive concerns about the possible danger. I blew it off at first but their words of caution crept into my brain. Then I began to hear about other people stock-piling food, buying expensive water filters, and passing around survival guides. I refused to get caught up in the panic, and I began to wonder how this could be an opportunity to strengthen community. In early 1999, I started thinking about where I wanted to be when the world ushered in a new millennium. I knew I wanted to stay in North Carolina, to travel by car (if at all), and to be at the beach.

Soon after, my friend Tony asked what I thought of getting a group of people together to spend New Year's at Topsail Beach, a three-hour drive from where we lived. It was the perfect idea and I got excited about it right away. We started to invite people. Ten friends committed to coming, and we rented a house. When we arrived at Topsail on December 27, the list had grown to sixteen, and by New Year's Eve we numbered twenty-two.

The days leading up to New Year's Eve were restful and fun. People did their own thing, together and separately: kayaking, art projects, long beach runs. There was some structured time to reflect on the highlights of 1999 and the upcoming transition. Nightly feasts were prepared by teams of people and we even pulled off a hilarious talent show. On the afternoon of December 31, 1999, just before sundown, I gathered with two close friends, Maura and Arrington, on the beach. We voiced the anxiety that had been building and said some prayers for whatever might happen in the next twelve to twenty-four hours. We returned to the house in time to watch some of the first celebrations in Sydney, then Rome, Paris, and London. As I saw fireworks exploding over the Eiffel Tower, something inside me began to relax. Then we started to cook.

When we sat down to a tremendous meal, an evening of ritual was set in motion, planned by a few people, with input from the rest of us. It started with creating group poems, later read aloud, and then each person wrote three resolutions. These were put in a hat and passed around the table, to be drawn out randomly by someone else. Somehow, the resolutions each person received were quite apropos.

Two people had collected stones and tiny pieces of driftwood from the beach for everyone. We were asked to envision what we were ready to let go of from the year ending, represented by the stone, and our hopes for the new year about to begin, symbolized by the driftwood. Around eleven P.M., we headed out to the beach where we joined our voices by chanting the word *namo* which means "life force" in Swahili. One by one, folks broke away to throw their stones into the ocean.

Just before midnight we were back at the deck of the house, champagne glasses in hand, ready for the countdown. Staring up at the stars, listening for the ocean right in front of me, I had to laugh out loud. Y2K seemed very far away, almost a joke. To this ocean and these lights in the sky, what could the number 2000 possibly mean? My very ability to laugh, to know that everything was going to be okay somehow, was in part a result of this deep connection with the natural world, older than time. But it was also a function of the energy and goodwill that we'd cultivated as a group. The time spent together and the rituals we'd done allowed us to look within and to deepen our connections to each other.

❓ questions for reflection . . . .

What rituals were important to you growing up? Which are still important today?

How do you mark transitions in your life?

What rituals, if any, have you created for yourself?

ℰ your own footing: rituals for daily living

Some of the best rituals are those that celebrate an action we do every day and make it more special. You can create rituals for yourself simply by thinking through your day and identifying which aspects might be more meaningful with some recognition or ceremony. For example:

the beginning and ending of your day

Many of us wake up and get going immediately, and by the time the end of day comes, we fall into bed, tired and ready for rest. Writer Annie Dillard says that "the way we live our days is the way we live our lives." How do you acknowledge this very simple, basic, vital unit of your life? One way is to begin by giving thanks for the day that stretches out before you. Another way might be setting an intention for the day before you even get out of bed. A spiritual practice can also serve as a morning ritual. Similarly, how do you end the day? Consider a ritual of remembering or even record the highlights of the day, or what you learned. Some people write down five things for which they are grateful at the end of every day.

marking the work day

Whether we work in or out of the home, many of us tend to screech into our workdays with a thud, and fly out at the end of the day. It's all too easy to bring work into the rest of our lives if we don't find conscious ways to leave it behind or to resist bringing our full selves to work if we are still caught up in other matters. How do you begin your workday, or work periods, if your schedule is less structured? Is there an act or set of actions that lets you know you're starting anew? While working on this book, I had a short ritual that I used to begin each writing period – just a short prayer and three deep breaths. What would help you leave your work behind at the end of a day? One friend has a three-step process for leaving the office each day: turn off the computer, turn off the light, turn off the work part of the brain. Another likes to clear her desk completely, think through her schedule for the next day, and then lay out what she'll need for the morning.

connecting with others

There are daily opportunities to connect in meaningful ways with those around us. We can pause as we begin our meals, taking the opportunity to give thanks for the food and those responsible for gathering and preparing it. You might create a ritual for the time when your kids leave for school or day care, and then return again at the end of the day. You can even ritualize the way you share news of your day with family, housemates, or others.

@ rituals for mourning

In death and in grief, we do not need as much protection
from painful experiences as we need the boldness to face them.
We do not need as much tranquilization from pain as we need the strength to conquer it.
If we choose to love, we must also have the courage to grieve.

~ Roy and Jane Nichols

A young and powerful activist I knew in Philadelphia was tragically killed by a drunk driver just a few days before Easter. At her memorial service, people wrote messages on a huge white sheet and listened to the music of the Indigo Girls. The minister, who knew of her work, recalled her beauty, her strength, and her imperfections. There were tulips everywhere. Many of us took the flowers home with us. A month later I planted the bulbs in a community garden near my house in North Carolina. I gathered five friends for the planting. I spoke for a few minutes about this woman's life and her death, but mostly about her life. I asked each person to say something even though they had never met her. I can remember feeling less alone in my grieving.

How does death take its rightful place in your life? At the core, grief is really a form of praise. Grief carries with it the seeds of strength and hope, but if grief goes unrecognized, those seeds never grow. We are fearful of grief and reluctant to find our own ways of dealing with the pain, let alone sharing it with others. When one experiences loss, all things begin to feel unreal. There is a period of disbelief and denial, which then leads to anger and pain. When we lose someone (family, friend, or colleague) or even something (a job or relationship) we need ways to mark and express the loss. Only after these are expressed can true healing begin.

We tend to be fearful of people in mourning, not always knowing what to say or do. It is a gift to make space where people have permission to mourn. Ask people what they need, what they remember, and what stories they'd like to share.

rituals for transition

Life is full of transitions, large and small. Many of these go unnoticed or marked with routine, in part because they take so long or overlap or their boundaries are unclear. This is exactly why we need rituals, to mark out a major shift within the more minor grind of routine.

leaving home

A couple I know made the decision to leave the house and community they'd shared for years to move across the country. On the night before their departure, I was their witness as they said their good-byes to their house. Together we went from room to room; in each they took time to remember experiences associated with that room and what about the room was particularly sacred. At the end, they lit candles to honor a house of love and caring. The ritual helped them celebrate the walls that heard their voices, the floors that grounded them to the earth, and the ceilings that protected them. They were able to recognize the fullness of the lives that had been lived there.

How do you leave spaces that have been important to you, in a way in which you can remember what transpired there with respect and ease?

honoring ancestors

My friend Billie is raising her nine-year-old son Che with many rituals from Yoruba, a religious and cultural tradition of Nigeria that is also practiced by people of African descent in Brazil, Cuba, and the United States. Che has participated in and understood this tradition since before he began to read. On the first Mother's Day after Billie's mother passed away, the three of us had dinner. After the meal, Che asked us to close our eyes and share a memory of his grandmother. Then he had us stand in front of the ancestor altar. We were instructed to put our hands on an object on the altar that spoke to us. Then we lit some incense and said our own silent prayers. This series of actions, created intuitively by a child who trusts and honors the power of ritual, was the perfect way to pay tribute to his grandmother.

How do you remember those who have passed on?

What role do they play in your life?

a new decade

A few months before I turned thirty, I planned a gathering with family and close friends I rarely got to see. Two friends graciously opened up their home for the event and a small group helped me prepare a delicious dinner. Before the party, I had chosen a poem for each individual. After dinner, we gathered in a circle. I gave out the poems and spoke about what each person meant to my life. In turn, they each shared something about our friendship. For one evening, my very scattered tribe became whole. I felt less alone in the world, less worried about the implications of growing older, more excited about the time I had left on the planet. Suddenly, thirty felt like liberation; all things were possible.

How do you mark the passing of years in your own life?

Do some years feel more important than others?

What has been similar about these celebrations? What has been different?

signs of friendship

The day before my friend Julia got married, a group of women friends and family members gathered for lunch. Each woman brought with her a bead and a wish for the bride. As we went around the circle, each woman shared a wish, a prayer, or a poem, and the beads were strung. We shared stories of our varied relationships with Julia, the role she has played in our lives, and our desires to continue supporting her in this new phase of life. After the luncheon, her soon-to-be sisters-in-law took the necklace to be restrung. She wore it to the party after the wedding and on many occasions afterwards. It is still a tangible reminder of a supportive circle of women.

How do you let someone know how much you care about them?

How can you make this tangible in time and space?

alternative thanksgiving

My friend Maura took Thanksgiving into her own hands recently, creating an experience for friends before the actual holiday. Here's how she described it:

Thanksgiving was last night at my house. It didn't matter that it was two weeks before the rest of America celebrated it. The house was filled with twenty friends, a fifteen-pound turkey, sweet potatoes hiding under a blanket of marshmallows, two big bowls of stuffing, and more pumpkin pie than any of us could eat.

A couple of months back I agreed to spend Thanksgiving weekend with the guy I've been seeing. Since I booked the ticket, the relationship has been preparing for a crash landing. Needless to say, I was having massive second thoughts so I decided to take the pressure off the holiday by having it ahead of time. I got on the phone, called a bunch of friends, and told them to bring their favorite Thanksgiving dish and show up at five o'clock. Unfortunately, the turkey stayed too long in the oven and ended up severely overcooked.

(continued on next page)

supporting partnerships

When two friends of mine, Meredith and Galia, decided to celebrate eleven years of commitment to one another, they gathered their community to help them. Each guest was sent a two-by-two-foot square of cloth to decorate as part of their *chuppa*. A Jewish wedding custom, the *chuppa* is a cloth supported by four poles that covers the couple. Erected that morning by friends, this *chuppa* covered the entire group assembled for the ceremony. Prayers were read, songs were sung, and the couple exchanged their own vows. Then, one by one, people stood to offer their own wishes and prayers for the couple.

How do you mark your commitments?

How do you do invite others in as part of this?

going home

Manju, a young woman who was born in India but has lived much of her life in the United States, began making plans to return there for an extended period of time. Over the course of eight months, she raised over $5,000 from community events, feasts, and friends. A few nights before she left on her trip, much of this community gathered, packed into the small, screened-in space behind her house. One by one, people shared their goodwill – wishes for her journey, memories of their first meeting, lessons she had taught them. In the act of galvanizing support for her voyage, she had engaged her entire community and made them a part of it.

How do you marshal support for an idea or dream?

How do you invite others in to help you?

℮ holidays as ritual

Holidays can be tougher than we like to admit. We know rates of suicide and domestic abuse go up during Thanksgiving and Christmas; drug and alcohol use often intensifies as well. We may have thoughts of what holidays should be like as well as some painful memories to contend with. Just because you had one great Fourth of July, complete with family reunion, cookout, and fireworks doesn't mean they'll all be like that. It takes guts to take a holiday into your own hands and recreate it, so it can be easier if you do it with someone else.

℮ a new year's ritual

If you are planning a gathering for the new year, ask each person to bring two objects. One should symbolize the year just ending, and the other hopes for the coming year. For this activity, you will need paper, writing implements, and a special table or cloth. Make sure you have room for everyone to sit in a circle and space in the middle to place the objects that people bring.

Give everyone five minutes to answer a couple or all of the following questions in writing. (See the Appendix or information on freewriting.)

What were the highlights of this past year for you?

What were one or two rough spots?

What have you learned over the past year?

What are some of your hopes and dreams for the coming year?

What might hold you back from these? What will help you fulfill them?

After the writing, people can share what they wrote, perhaps with one or two other people if the group is large. Then, ask everyone to talk about the two objects they brought and why. Ask everyone to lay their objects on the cloth as they speak.

alternative thanksgiving (continued)

The best part of the night was that I got to experience the pleasure of being a complete failure as a turkey chef without feeling the pressure of my mom or some guy to worry about. I could just drink red wine while laughing at the fact that I needed ten minutes to chew every time I put a piece of turkey in my mouth!

℮ word of the week

This is a great ritual to do with any group you work or volunteer with. Pick one of the words below or choose one of your own. Think ahead about what the word means to you.

gratitude	humility	communication
forgiveness	discipline	listening
patience	wisdom	purpose
simplicity	cooperation	belief
clarity	courage	acceptance
camaraderie	openness	understanding
service		

Ask everyone to think (or write) about how this concept is currently manifesting itself in their lives *outside* of work. Ask everyone to share something with the group. Then, ask everyone to think (or write) about how this concept is currently manifesting itself in their lives *at* work and again share. Finally, you might even invite people to share positive things they've noticed about others in the room, in relationship to this word. You can model this by saying, for example, "I've noticed that you often wait before answering a tough question, and this has been a great lesson in patience for me." The idea is to highlight the positive and reinforce that.

resources for ritual

"Charmed, I'm Sure: In Praise of Ritual." *Ms. Magazine,* October/November, 1999, 55–67.

Cohen, David, ed. *The Circle of Life: Rituals from the Human Family Album.* San Francisco: HarperCollins, 1991. An exquisite book of photographs and text that chronicles the rituals of birth and childhood, initiation and adolescence, marriage and adulthood, and death in cultures across the globe.

Eiker, Diane, and Sapphire, eds. *Keep Simple Ceremonies.* Portland, Maine: Astarte Shell Press, 1993. Hand-written guide to the home-grown rituals from the Feminist Spiritual Community of Portland, Maine. Includes rituals for life cycle events, personal milestones, and community celebration.

Estes, Clarissa Pinkola. *Women Who Run With the Wolves: Myths and Stories of the Wild Woman Archetype.* New York: Ballantine Books, 1992. A classic collection of old tales, infused with new meaning.

Getty, Adele. *A Sense of the Sacred.* Dallas: Taylor Publishing, 1997. Blends personal, historical, and cultural approaches to finding spiritual life through ceremony.

Greenberg, Irving. *The Jewish Way: Living the Holidays.* New York: Simon and Schuster, 1993. An interpretation of the Jewish holidays, including one chapter on Shabbat.

Somé, Malidoma. *Ritual: Power, Healing and Community.* Portland, Ore.: Swan Raven & Company, 1993. Somé describes the use of ritual in his native West African community, illustrating a powerful relationship between nature, people, and the spirit world. www.malidoma.com/Malidoma/

Starhawk. *Truth or Dare.* San Francisco: Harper & Row, 1988. Starhawk offers ritual, myth, and story as tools for resisting domination and structuring groups and leadership to maximize empowerment. www.starhawk.org/

Stein, Diane, ed. *The Goddess Celebrates: An Anthology of Women's Rituals.* Freedom, Calif.: The Crossing Press, 1991. Writings on ritual from women reclaiming goddess-centered spirituality. Includes essays on ritual planning and creating sacred space, as well as ideas for specific rituals. www.dianestein.com/

Teish, Luisah. *Jambalaya: The Natural Woman's Book of Personal Charms and Rituals.* San Francisco: HarperCollins, 1988. www.jambalayaspirit.org/

ritual time . . . .

Taquiena Boston

Taquiena Boston is an African American woman who was born, educated, and still resides in the District of Columbia. She has worked more than twenty years for a variety of community-based and national nonprofit organizations, and is currently employed as an anti-racism trainer and consultant by the Unitarian Universalist Association. Taquiena views the arts and ritual as tools to empower and transform individuals and communities.

When you enter ritual time, you're stepping out of your day-to-day concerns. It's a way of looking at life and trying to get in touch with a greater purpose and meaning. It's giving people a gift of time and attention, which to me is the most valuable thing we can give each other – that's what love is. So when we engage in ritual, we're saying that we're intent on making a connection, whether it's with God or with spirit or with other people.

Ritual prepares us for spirit to enter, even though it may not enter every time. It's like when you're a performer. You practice so that one day you will hit the peak. You don't hit it every time, but if the muscles are primed, when it does enter, you're ready for it.

When I was thirty-nine, I did a rite of passage for myself, because I had not gone through rites of passage that I thought I would have. I wasn't married; I wasn't a mother. I knew a transformation was taking place in me, and I wanted to mark it, so I invited a group of close women friends over. I started us in a circle, with a story from *Women Who Run with the Wolves* called "Sealskin, Soulskin." I talked about being someone who'd been living without her skin for so many years that I had to go home. In the process of telling the story, other women saw themselves. They began to say things that I'd never heard them say before. The hope is that people begin to see ritual as a work of art that expresses their values.

> When you enter ritual time, you're stepping out of your day-to-day concerns. It's a way of looking at life and trying to get in touch with a greater purpose and meaning . . . when we engage in ritual, we're saying that we're intent on making a connection, whether it's with God or with spirit or with other people.

A friend introduced me to a book by Stephen Levine, *A Year to Live: How to Live This Year As if It Were Your Last*. Working with that idea makes me pause many times in my day and really look and experience the moment I'm in: how green things are or the pattern of birds flying or looking at a child's face and seeing what the adult is going to look like or looking at someone who's homeless and wondering, "What is this person's story?" I also think about giving the gift of time and attention to people. I see people struggling a lot to get attention. We call it status, we call it recognition, and I think that's why people do everything that they do. It's like, "Acknowledge me, I'm here." I go back to *The Color Purple* where I think it's Celie that says, "I may be black, I may be poor, but I'm *here*." And when Shug says to her about God, "It does everything it can to please us."

Time and attention are how people say that they love us. Even though my mother worked outside of the home, I always had total access to her. If I was having a problem, I knew I could talk to her. It takes a long time to really know people, and you can't know them if you're not paying attention to all the messages they're giving you –

> By stepping out of normal time, we're able to focus in a way that we don't focus if we're thinking about paying bills, washing the dishes, picking someone up, going to the store.

with their bodies, their eyes, and the inflections in their voices. We can't know each other without time and attention. When I do diversity work with youth, they are so thrilled that for once, somebody wants to know their opinion, what they think and why. I find that small, simple things work best, to give them space to express themselves.

When we step into ritual time, we step out of normal time. And by stepping out of normal time, we're able to focus in a way that we don't focus if we're thinking about paying bills, washing the dishes, picking someone up, going to the store. I remember Joseph Campbell, and Martha Graham in a similar vein, saying that people want a feeling of being alive. Ritual is a means by which we get to that feeling of being alive, because it makes us step out of our ordinary time, consciousness, and relationships in order to experience them at a deeper level. Through ritual, we can give each other the gift of time and attention. It is also a gift we give to our perception of the Divine and to life itself.

Ritual says: Pay attention to life – see it whole.

keeping Shabbat . . . .

Jason and Devora Kimelman-Block

Jason and Devora Kimelman-Block live in New York City with their daughter, Esther. Jason is a rabbinical student at the Jewish Theological Seminary and has worked on numerous educational projects linking political activism with religion, including Columbia University's Tzedek Hillel program. Devora is an educator integrating technology into classroom curricula in Manhattan and Bronx middle schools. She previously served as a Program Officer for the D.C. Commission for National and Community Service. They recently returned from a year of study in Jerusalem.

JKB: Before college, I spent a year in Israel and during that time I spent two months living on a farm with a family that observed Shabbat. I realized I had an impression of traditional Shabbat observance as something that was restricted. Living with this family made me realize how much it enhanced their lives. It was moving from a distance but I didn't think it was something I would do.

I first started observing the Shabbat according to a traditional interpretation when I was in college. I found college and the workload very intense and I wanted some way to make sure I gave myself time to relax and to spend time with people. There were other people who were experimenting with Shabbat observance and we all started hanging out together on Friday nights, sitting in each other's apartment and talking.

Now I observe Shabbat by getting together with friends and family and having big, long meals. We sing traditional songs and melodies, there is a certain amount of prayer, and there is lazy time. There is no more specific purpose, nothing more to accomplish than just enjoying the food and company. There's an aspect of it that's just taking in the world as it is, and doing the things you enjoy the most, like going for long walks and spending lots of time with people you like.

> Shabbat provides the space to get a different perspective on my life . . . I can't imagine not having this refuge to go to. I know that whatever's going on and however crazy things get, there will be this day. Shabbat gives me permission to take the downtime.

Observing Shabbat also means ceasing from any kind of creative work, which in Jewish text ends up getting fleshed out in a million different directions. What it means for my life in the United States is not shopping, driving a car, using electronic equipment or computers, writing, or playing musical instruments. Those are the most noticeable things.

Shabbat structures my life in terms of a very clear rhythm of time passing. We all live in weeklong chunks; that's how our calendars are set up. But it feels more deep and intense than that since I started keeping Shabbat. It becomes the benchmark. You find yourself planning for it several days beforehand, and thinking about it several days after. Midweek becomes a turning point. Shabbat provides the space to get a different perspective on my life. The world is so hectic; I can't imagine wanting to continue doing that all week. I can't imagine not having this refuge to go to. I know that whatever's going on and however crazy things get, there will be this day. Shabbat gives me permission to take the downtime. I don't feel like you should be doing something else.

It's ultimately a Jewish institution, and despite the psychological benefits and advantages, it can be burdensome. It's a sacrifice to do it on a continual basis the way I do it. But it's a time to remember the creation of the world. It's a time to study Jewish texts you might not have time to study during the week; it's a time to be in the Jewish community. There's also a feeling of being connected to Jewish history because it is such an ancient tradition. It goes way, way back.

Ahad Ha-Am, an early Zionist thinker, said that more than the Jews have kept the Sabbath, the Sabbath has kept the Jews. Around the world, this is the day – it's Shabbat everywhere. When I read text from the Middle Ages and they're talking about Shabbat and describing some of the same rituals and ceremonies that I practice, it gives me a sense of being a part of something much bigger than myself.

Actually, I'm not sure it's a ritual. I think of a ritual as a symbolic act and in a sense it is that, but it's so big, it's almost like a metaritual. It contains so many rituals within it, like the blessings over candles, wine, and bread. It's hard to think of the whole day as one ritual, but in a sense it is. It's a symbolic act that takes concepts – namely the creation of the world and our reliance on God, our small place in the universe, our connection to creation – and concretizes them. A lot of the rituals and rules around Shabbat are the means to create this atmosphere.

It's very much a discipline and it's not an easy discipline. It's part of a wider rubric of how certain aspects of the Jewish religion express themselves. The idea is to make a commitment to something and continue with it. To me it's also a statement of who I am. Hopefully, it's training me to be a person who is committed to something and who will follow through; someone who is reliable and willing to put something else above my own needs. It's like a marriage – there are certain moments where it can be burdensome but ultimately you're committed to the whole thing.

There are two somewhat contradictory notions of Shabbat. One is that it's a day of perfection and a taste of the world to come, a taste of heaven. The other is that it's a day that you just let go and take the world as it is, in its brokenness. The concept of it being perfect is part of the building of the atmosphere – you do what you most enjoy doing. Part of the reason why creative work is forbidden is that you assume the world has already been perfected. You train yourself to think like that for one day a week. It's not that work is forbidden, it's that there's nothing left to do.

> A lot of the other stuff, you've got to question: What were these guys thinking? . . . But Shabbat is very natural. It's a day of connection with family, connection with myself, connection with God. These are things that a lot of people want. These are things that I want.

But then there's this other aspect (and they're interrelated for sure) of just letting go. You work so hard during the week, hopefully making the world better. You need space to say, I just need to take the world as it is and I need to stop trying to make everything perfect. You wouldn't want to surrender like that seven days a week or else you'd become completely complacent.

Shabbat creates the space for the vision of a world perfected to be kept alive during the week. People are taking the world as it is and working for incremental change within that world. Rabbi Irving "Yitz" Greenberg says that Judaism is a conservative means toward radical ends. Shabbat keeps this dream of a perfected world alive so you're energized to go back the next six days and work in the world, with all its brokenness.

To me, the whole institution of Shabbat is exactly what overworked folks need. It's the opposite of where our culture tends to place its value. In New York City, there is this competing with each other as to who worked harder or later hours. The idea of putting value on downtime and on doing nothing – I think it goes against the grain of our culture. But I think it's something that's really needed. It gives us permission to do things we would do anyway but in a healthier, more deliberate manner.

DKB: Growing up, we always did something on Shabbat, though it wouldn't fall under what Jason would call keeping Shabbat. My family always had Friday night dinner together in the dining room, which was a big deal for us. For a while, my brother would do a weekly commentary on a Torah portion. We would light candles and say blessings and my parents still do that. On Saturdays, sometimes they'd go to synagogue but not all that often.

Observing Shabbat connects me with Judaism. I'm in a very secular environment during the week. I don't work in a Jewish environment. On Shabbat I make the time to pray and it's really the only time I have for that. And we bless Esther, our daughter. We don't do that in a formal sense any other time during the week. When I was pregnant, I had a pregnancy prayer that I did every week. (I couldn't handle having to do it every day, but once a week, I could handle.) The blessing you do over your child is the same blessing the priests do over their congregation. It's very mystical – we believe that people are conduits for God. Congregants are getting blessed in the same way that I bless Esther. And that affects how I see the blessing in the synagogue.

> Rabbi Irving "Yitz" Greenberg says that Judaism is a conservative means toward radical ends. Shabbat keeps this dream of a perfected world alive so you're energized to go back the next six days and work in the world, with all its brokenness.

In general, I have a lot of problems with the strictness of the Jewish system of code, law, and ritual. But I don't have problems with Shabbat. It's not an all-or-nothing thing. People shouldn't be afraid of religion because they don't think they can take it all on. Shabbat has always come easier to me than a lot of other things. There's much more logic to it. It feels right. A lot of the other stuff, you've got to question: What were these guys thinking? And do I agree with what these guys were thinking? But Shabbat is very natural. It's a day of connection with family, connection with myself, connection with God. These are things that a lot of people want. These are things that I want.

ritual.

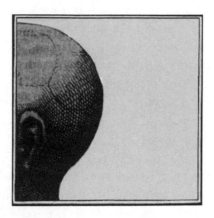

stories

I have my own story, and increasingly in my old age it weighs on me . . .
We can only speak of the things we carried with us,
and the things we took away.

~ *Barbara Kingsolver*, The Poisonwood Bible

[Myles] Horton believed that for people to see their own lives and struggles in a new light,
they need to set themselves apart for at least one full day, from rising to sleeping,
and tell each other their stories. Out of the tales of victories and defeats,
he learned, an almost religious faith is forged: an assurance that however mighty are the forces
arrayed against you, they can be overcome.

~ *Carol Polsgrove*

Crucial to finding the way is this: there is no beginning or end.
You must make your own map.

~ *Joy Harjo*, A Map to the Next World

what are stories? . . . .

Stories are one way we begin to speak the truth about our lives, who we are, and what has happened to us. When we begin to tell our stories, either out loud or on paper, we invite others to be witnesses. Being seen may initially make us vulnerable, but in the end it makes us stronger. To share the truth is revolutionary and liberating. Reading the testimony of others' lives reveals new layers of reality previously unknown, avoided, denied, or misunderstood. Throughout history, people have left their stories as legacies, extraordinary accounts of stirring times that open a door for others to walk through. Examples include Martin Luther King Jr.'s "Letter from a Birmingham Jail," *The Diary of Anne Frank,* and Nelson Mandela's *Long Walk to Freedom.*

In telling stories, we begin to convey to people what we want them to know and understand about us, our people, our community, our vocation, our loves, our struggles, and our joys. And, our willingness invites others to do the same. The impact of violence, the shame of failure, the feeling of weakness, the fear of mistakes – the details are intensely personal, but there is a universal quality about the feelings that result. We close the gap between ourselves and others. We need to create spaces for people to speak truth aloud to other people, both to share the joy and to break the isolation of the pain, which can be as damaging as the pain itself. In addition to the content our stories, the very telling of them can help ground and energize us. We begin to see patterns – certain people and types of events repeat – and by gaining insight into our own symbols, we develop a greater understanding of the meaning of our own lives.

turning point . . . .

I first read *The Autobiography of Malcolm X* one summer during college. I was helping a friend move, and his roommate had a stack of books he was ready to give away or sell back to the bookstore. This book was on the top. Without knowing why, I took it off the stack and slipped it in my backpack.

What I knew about Malcolm X up until that point would have fit on a postcard. I suspect this is true for too many white children growing up in the United States. I could remember childhood nightmares about the assassination of Martin Luther King Jr., the realization that even in this country someone could be murdered for speaking the truth. What meager understanding of racism I had came from isolated incidents, rather than from a broad-sweeping worldview. When four guys in my high school burned a cross on the lawn of a white girl who was dating an African American guy, it was dismissed as a joke. Even with a population of 15 percent students of color, the school system did nothing to foster dialogue about race or ethnicity. Because my peer group was somewhat mixed racially, I lulled myself into two erroneous assumptions: that all teenage years unfolded similarly and that people generally get along with each other, regardless of race. At college both assumptions were quickly dismantled. I noticed a much greater degree of separation; students of color created support mechanisms in the residence halls, in the classroom, and socially that may have seemed isolating to white people, but were the only things that allowed them to survive the experience of a white-dominated university.

So here I was, attending a large, urban university and becoming more curious about the dynamics of racism and the way they affected the lives of real people, beyond the newspapers and the television documentaries. I had begun to make a greater commitment to community service and was developing relationships with folks in the neighborhoods adjacent to the university. These residents, most of whom were African American, had no influence over the decisions made by the university's largely white power structure, decisions that continually affected their lives and livelihood. Could the story of Malcolm X help me start to unravel the threads of confusion and anger that were balled up in my mind?

I quickly became consumed by the story. What I'd begun to suspect about the way things worked in this country, the intuitive but unexplained hunches about injustice, were confirmed in these pages. The level of my own ignorance was becoming more and more apparent. My eyes opened to the violence and pain associated with oppression and a truth formed that I knew I could never again ignore.

Here I was, twenty years old, and trying to make sense of race in America with Malcolm X as my guide. I devoured the story, reading some parts three and four times. The book, a cheap paperback, began to fall apart in my hands and I kept the pages together with a rubber band. I started having dreams about Malcolm X, and found myself picturing what kind of statesman or activist he'd be like if he'd lived into his sixties. I began to revisit events and perceptions of my youth. I started to view interactions between strangers differently, considering the implications of power and privilege in a way I never had before. Reading the newspaper became a political act.

From the moment Malcolm is told at age fourteen by a white school-teacher that he will never be a lawyer because "you've got to be realistic about being a n_____ [expletive]" to the time he visited Mecca and experienced a kind of universal love he had never felt before, I began to see *The Autobiography of Malcolm X* as a microcosm of the struggle for love and justice in the world. It helped me to define two vital needs: the need to work for justice in the material world by owning the particularities of oppression and the need to foster a kind of love that is most present on the spiritual plane. How do we do these two things at once? It is the central question that continues to consume my energy and attention. I continue to give thanks for that act of providence, that book on the top of the stack.

？ questions for reflection . . . .

When do you find yourself telling which parts of your story?

What is easy about telling your story? What is difficult?

How do you learn someone else's story?

What stories have inspired you most?

Have you ever told a lie about who you are or where you come from? What do think you were actually trying to say?

℮ your own footing: writing your story

Take some time, through writing, to get a handle on your own story. Sit with the ideas and questions below over time; begin to notice what rises to the surface and which patterns emerge. Here are some topics to start with:

- Every life has a handful of key turning points. What event(s) in your life would help someone best understand you?
- What times in your life did you feel like you were truly on your own, forging your own path?
- Describe a rough time you've had in the past year or two.
- What have been the five greatest influences on the person you are today?
- How satisfied do you feel about your life right now? What are you doing that you shouldn't be doing? Not doing that you should be? What are you doing now that you always wanted to but somehow never thought it would happen?

℮ story as testimony

[These] testimonies are life histories of women whose political engagement represents the core of their self-identity. Through their words, readers can at least partly understand the experiences of these activists absorbed in the politics of protest and resistance . . . The evocative power of Latin American women's testimonial literature is great in that the women reveal themselves as the central actors in their own stories. They become producers of knowledge.

~ Kathleen Logan, "Personal Testimony: Latin American Women Telling Their Lives"

Throughout time there are stories that serve as testimony, a window into something we might otherwise never truly understand. Because one person has the ability and the inclination to put his or her life experience into words, those of us who read their work are forever changed by it. Rigoberta Menchú received the Nobel Peace Prize in 1992 at the age of thirty-three for her work in bringing the abuses of the Indian people in Guatemala to light. While helping peasants resist the oppressive Guatemalan military regime, Menchú's brother, father, and mother were tortured and killed by the Guatemalan army. Menchú, a Quiche Indian, has devoted her life to overthrowing colonialism in her country, working through the Comite de Unidad Campesina (United Peasant Committee). Menchú learned to read and write in Spanish so that her story might be told more widely. The passage below is from her autobiography, *I, Rigoberta Menchú: An Indian Woman in Guatemala:*

> *My name is Rigoberta Menchú. I am 23 years old. This is my testimony. I didn't learn it from a book and I didn't learn it alone. I'd like to stress that it's not only my life, it's also the testimony of my people. It's hard for me to remember everything that's happened to me in my life since there have been very bad times, but, yes, moments of joy as well. The important thing is that what has happened to me has happened to many other people too: My story is the story of all poor Guatemalans. My personal experience is the reality of a whole people.*

Here are some other individuals who have lived powerful lives of faith and action; their testimony is a gift that can help us understand both personal journeys and universal truths.

Dorothy Day (1897–1980) founded the Catholic Worker Movement with Peter Maurin in 1933 on the principles of nonviolence, communal sharing of possessions, solidarity with the poor, and resistance of coercive state power. There are now 150 Catholic Worker "houses of hospitality" in communities of need across the United States and Canada and around the world. The movement also includes community forums and newspapers. Day was called the "soul of the American left" and the "saint of the common ground." For further reading: *The Long Loneliness.*

Fannie Lou Hamer (1917–1977) grew up a plantation worker in the Mississippi Delta. She lost her livelihood after attempting to register

Minds Stayed on Freedom: The Civil Rights Struggle in the Rural South, an Oral History by Youth of the Rural Organizing and Cultural Center is a collection of fifteen oral histories of older folks in Holmes County, Mississippi. The histories were collected in interviews conducted by eighth and ninth graders. With so much written about the big-name leaders and organizations involved in the Civil Rights Movement, this book offers a different account. It provides the stories of men and women who built the Civil Rights Movement one voter registration drive at a time. The book also describes the impact of these interviews on both the young people and the interviewees themselves.

to vote. After working with SNCC (Student Nonviolent Coordinating Committee) and serving as a state representative for the progressive Mississippi Freedom Democratic Party, she organized the Freedom Farm Cooperative. She became a national spokesperson on issues of hunger and poverty in the South and helped leverage federal funding to improve housing in rural Mississippi. For further reading: *This Little Light of Mine: The Life of Fannie Lou Hamer.*

Rabbi Dr. Abraham Joshua Heschel (1907–1972) was born in Poland and raised in a Hasidic community. Escaping Poland just six weeks before the Nazi invasion, he eventually moved to the United States where he became a preeminent scholar, author, activist, and theologian. His teachings have influenced many to develop a more personal relationship with God. Heschel marched with Dr. Martin Luther King Jr. in Selma, Alabama in 1965 and later formed an organization to opposed the war in Vietnam. He is also remembered for his writing, including *The Sabbath.* For further reading: *Moral Grandeur and Spiritual Audacity.*

His Holiness, the fourteenth Dalai Lama (1935–) is both the religious and political leader of the Tibetan people. When the country was invaded by the Chinese in 1950, many Tibetans fled to India. The Dalai Lama now leads an exiled community there. He has seen his religion labeled a "disease" by the Chinese; one million monks and citizens have been killed, and six thousand monasteries been have destroyed. But still the Dalai Lama preaches a message of non-violence and compassion toward the Chinese. He has spent many years raising awareness worldwide about the plight of Tibet. For further reading: *Freedom in Exile: The Autobiography of the Dalai Lama.*

Nelson Mandela (1918–) was one of the primary forces behind the dismantling of apartheid in South Africa. A leader of the African National Congress, he spent twenty-seven years in prison on Robben Island. After finally winning his freedom in 1990 he became president of South Africa after his country's first truly democratic, multiracial election. He won the Nobel Peace Prize in 1993. His autobiography was written during his jail sentence and smuggled out in pieces. For further reading: *Long Walk to Freedom.*

Thomas Merton (1915–1968) was a Trappist monk, peace activist, and prolific writer. A committed Christian, Merton also felt a deep connection to the monks of Hindu and Buddhist traditions. One of the most important spiritual writers of the twentieth century, Merton spent the second half of his life at Our Lady of Gethsemani, a Trappist monastery in Kentucky. A committed pacifist, Merton was a keen witness of social change on a global scale and maintained relationships and correspondence with many of the most powerful, faith-based activists of his time. For further reading: *The Intimate Merton: His Life from His Journals.*

Peace Pilgrim (unknown–1981) walked twenty-five thousand miles for peace over three decades. With only a comb, toothbrush, pen, and copies of her message, she crossed America, speaking to groups and individuals along the way about peace. She believed that when enough individuals found inner peace, war would no longer be necessary. She began living a life of voluntary simplicity and started her pilgrimage on January 1, 1953, giving up "home, possessions, age, and name." She spoke about peace on television and radio, in university classrooms, from the pulpit of churches, and to people she met along the way. For further reading: *Peace Pilgrim: Her Life and Work in Her Own Words.*

℮ oral history

Oral history is the oldest history and the way we can best learn the stories of those who have gone before us. It is a great way to record details of history from those whose stories often go unheard. Usually, oral history is a well-constructed conversation (or series of conversations) between two people that is recorded and usually transcribed so it can be shared more broadly. You could even say the stories in this book are oral histories, as they grew out of interviews and a desire to record peoples' experience of spirit.

Think of someone whose story you'd like to capture. It might be an elder in your family or community. It might be someone who lives their faith daily. You might choose someone who is working actively to better your neighborhood, town, or city; a religious figure you know; or a young person whose life has touched your own in some way.

Discuss the possibility of doing an interview or a series of interviews with the person. Explain that you will be asking him or her questions and that the interviews will be taped. If you want to transcribe the interview so it can be read on paper, let the interviewee know that as well. To do an oral history, you will need recording equipment (which you may be able to borrow or rent from a local library or university), blank tapes, a quiet space, and some questions prepared ahead of time.

Think about this person's life and what you are most interested in knowing more about. Spend the early part of the interview getting to know each other.

For a full year, from May 1998 through May 1999, the Interfaith Pilgrimage of the Middle Passage retraced over four hundred years of the slave trade. Initiated by the Buddhist order Nipponzan Myohoji, the pilgrimage was organized by a diverse group and endorsed by people from numerous faith backgrounds, including Christian, Jewish, Muslim, Baha'i, Unitarian Universalist, and Native American spiritual traditions. The transatlantic voyage retraced the route of the slave trade from the east coast of North America, through the Caribbean and Central America, to Brazil, and finally to West and South Africa.

The pilgrimage was an opportunity to offer prayers for the spirits of African ancestors and their descendants; to give people of European descent an opportunity to take responsibility, breaking patterns of fear and denial; and to reverse historical patterns by showing respect for the African continent. Along the way, the pilgrimage visited sites of suffering and courage, including stops on the Underground Railroad. Ceremonies allowed for healing,

(continued on next page)

Trust is a key ingredient of a successful oral history. You want to ask your interviewee open-ended questions; if a question doesn't seem to resonate with the person you're interviewing, move on to another question or ask it in a different way. You can make some notes while the person is speaking. This will allow you to remember various high points on the tape and doing something else makes people feel less self-conscious and able to speak more freely. Give yourself permission to be spontaneous. Things may occur to you and you want to follow your own excitement, as well as the cues you receive from your subject. Some colleges and universities have oral history programs that can provide you with more information on how to conduct and transcribe a successful interview.

℮ storytelling

You can initiate storytelling in any corner or aspect of your life. You might try it with your family and watch it evolve into a regular practice. You might suggest it to a group you volunteer with, as a chance to get to know each other better. You might even bring it into your workplace, your classroom, or even a sports team – anywhere people might be yearning for ways to connect with each other outside of the normal modes. Storytelling can deepen the experience of a faith or spiritual community as well. The activities below can be done easily in groups of four to twelve.

name stories

One way for a group to begin telling stories is by telling a story about their name. Most names have a story attached to them. Ask each person in the group to share something significant about their first, last, or full name.

Where did your name come from?

Do you like it? Why or why not?

If you had the opportunity to choose your own name, what would you pick?

Do you have a nickname? How did you get it?

spiritual stories

One of my mentors, David Sawyer, reminds people that our spiritual and faith traditions are full of stories, but we do not always have the opportunity to unravel our own. This is a chance for each person to tell their own spiritual story. If you want to do this in a group larger than six or seven, divide people into groups of three or four.

Give each person five minutes to tell something of his or her spiritual story to his or her group. Let everyone know you will tell them when the five minutes are up. (It's important to keep time because it allows people to relax into the telling or listening each time.) Remind people that listening itself is a sacred act and that this is not a group discussion, but rather a chance for each person to speak truthfully about her or his own journey and have others listen with an open heart. You might even choose to have a minute of silence between each story.

When the group is finished, ask people to share how they felt about the experience and what touched them in the stories they heard.

our collective history

This is a great activity to do with people who are interested in learning more about each other's life experiences. It's particularly illuminating with an intergenerational group. First, give everyone twenty minutes to do an individual time line of their own life. Don't give any further instructions than this; it's important that each person interpret this for himself or herself.

Then ask the group to create a group time line on a large piece of mural paper. First, the group must establish some "landmarks" to create a beginning, middle, and end. People can begin to transfer things from their personal time lines to this larger time line. Make sure to suggest that everyone adds at least three to five things from their individual time lines to this larger one.

Leave time at the end to explore the lessons learned from collective knowledge. Some relevant questions:

- What seem to be the most powerful points in history? Why?
- What are the common denominators, if any?
- Did someone write down something that others had never heard of?
- What else do you notice about the time line? What does it say about spirit? About power? About change?

the middle passage (continued)

learning, and the building of community. In the words of Archbishop Desmond Tutu, honorary chairman, "If we do not acknowledge our history we cannot learn from it . . . The road they tread will be an inspiration and a means of healing for many of us who follow them by proxy in intercession and meditation."

Located in Whitesburg, Kentucky, Appalshop acts on the belief that the people of Appalachia and other cultures can tell their own stories and control their own images. They produce films on issues of critical importance to Appalachia; run WMMT-FM, a non-commercial radio station that broadcasts mountain music, storytelling, and reporting on the region; and operate Roadside Theater, a traveling ensemble that has developed plays from the rich culture and history of Appalachia. They also run June Appal Recordings, featuring both traditional and contemporary mountain music, and the Appalachian Media Institute, which trains students in media production and leadership. Their building in Whitesburg houses all of the above projects, as well as a gallery and theater, and hosts numerous concerts, plays, art exhibits, and forums.

stories of struggle, stories of courage

Communities have vital and intricate stories to tell about their own realities. Talk is a critical prelude to, and even a piece of, action. You're worried about something – a planned development, a polluted stream or the relationship between police and youth in your community. How do you begin to let others know what's going on? How do you start fighting for what you know is right? By telling a compelling story about what is going on. You talk to the press, to policy makers, to politicians, and to other people who are being impacted by the same thing. Sometimes survival depends on the ability to tell a story well, to the right audience, at the right time.

If you are working with a group in your community that is trying to bring about change, you might begin by fleshing out the story of this effort. Gather for an evening and have people talk about the following:

- How would we want to tell someone from another part of the country or the world what has been going on here?
- What picture do we want other people to see?
- Who are the main characters of this story?
- Can we think of one particular moment, image, or experience that illustrates what we are doing?

resources for stories

Appalshop, 306 Madison Street, Whitesburg, Ky. 41858. (606) 633-0108.
www.appalshop.org

Dalai Lama XIV. *Freedom in Exile: The Autobiography of the Dalai Lama*. New York:
HarperCollins, 1990. www.tibet.com/DL/

Day, Dorothy. *The Long Loneliness: The Autobiography of Dorothy Day*. New York:
Harper & Row, 1997. www.catholicworker.org/

Davis, Donald. *Telling Your Own Stories: For Family and Classroom Storytelling, Public
Speaking, and Personal Journaling*. Little Rock, Ark.: August House, 1993.
www.ddavisstoryteller.com/

Dinan, Stephen, ed. *Radical Spirit: Spiritual Writings from the Voices of Tomorrow*.
Novato, Calif.: New World Library, 2002. www.radicalspirit.com

Feldman, Christina, and Jack Kornfield, eds. *Stories of the Spirit, Stories of the Heart*.
San Francisco: HarperCollins, 1991. Parables of the spiritual path from around the
world.

Freire, Paolo. *Pedagogy of the Oppressed*. New York: Continuum, 1992. Written by a
Brazilian educator who was exiled in 1964, this book is a classic on popular
education, power, and how change happens.

Gandhi, Mohandas K. *Gandhi, An Autobiography: The Story of My Experiments with
Truth*. Boston: Beacon Press, 1957. http://web.mahatma.org.in/

Harjo, Joy. *A Map to the Next World: Poems and Tales*. New York: W.W. Norton, 2000.

Heschel, Abraham Joshua. *Moral Grandeur and Spiritual Audacity*. Edited by
Susannah Heschel. New York: Farrar, Straus & Giroux, 1996. A collection of
Heschel's greatest essays, edited by his daughter. www.socialaction.com/
heschelexcerpts

Interfaith Pilgrimage for the Middle Passage, First Congregational Church, Room
11, 165 Main Street, Amherst, Mass. 01002. (413) 256-6698.
www.interfaithpilgrimage.com

Ives, Dr. Edward D. *An Oral Historian's Work*. Bucksport, Maine: Northeast Historic
Film, 1998. An instructional videotape about checking equipment, researching,
interviewing, and transcribing.

King, Martin Luther, Jr. "Letter from a Birmingham Jail." *Why We Can't Wait*. New
York: Harper & Row, 1963. www.thekingcenter.org

Logan, Kathleen. "Personal testimony: Latin American Women Telling Their Lives." *Latin American Research Review* 32 (1997).

Mandela, Nelson. *Long Walk to Freedom.* Boston: Little, Brown, 1994. www.anc.org.za/people/mandela/

Menchú, Rigoberta. *I, Rigoberta Menchú: An Indian Woman in Guatemala.* Edited by Elisabeth Burgos-Debray. Translated by Ann Wright. London: Verso, 1984.

Merton, Thomas. *The Intimate Merton: His Life from His Journals.* Edited by Patrick Hart and Jonathan Moltado. San Francisco: HarperCollins, 2001. www.merton.org

Mills, Kay. *This Little Light of Mine: The Life of Fannie Lou Hamer.* New York: Penguin, 1993.

National Storytelling Network sponsors a festival every October that attracts thousands of storytellers from all over the country. Contact: P.O. Box 309, Jonesborough, Tenn. 37659. (615) 753-2171. www.storynet.org/

The Oral History Review. Buffalo: SUNY Buffalo. www.ucpress.edu/journals/ohr/

Peace Pilgrim. *Peace Pilgrim: Her Life and Work in Her Own Words.* Compiled by some of her friends. Santa Fe: Ocean Tree, 1991.

Shoah Visual History Foundation. www.vhf.org

Southern Oral History Program, University of North Carolina at Chapel Hill. www.sohp.org

Spretnak, Charlene, ed. *The Politics of Women's Spirituality: Essays by Founding Mothers of the Movement.* New York: Anchor Books, 1994. A chorus of feminist voices explore spirituality and its role in transforming politics.

Wallis, Jim, and Joyce Hollyday. *Clouds of Witnesses.* Maryknoll, N.Y.: Orbis Books/ Sojourners, 1994. Short biographies and personal testimony of Christian peacemakers, martyrs, and saints.

Youth of the Rural Organizing and Cultural Center. *Minds Stayed on Freedom: The Civil Rights Struggle in the Rural South.* Boulder: Westview Press, 1991.

X, Malcolm. *The Autobiography of Malcolm X.* With Alex Haley. New York: Grove Press, 1964. www.brothermalcolm.net/

where we come from . . . .

Rebecca Reyes and Sue Gilbertson

Sue Gilbertson, MSW, CCSW is the regional director of Catholic Social Ministries for the Piedmont region of the South, which covers nine counties. Raised in the Presbyterian Church, she has been influenced by both the Presbyterian and Catholic traditions. Rebecca Reyes is an ordained Presbyterian minister who grew up in Corpus Christi, Texas. She is currently working with the Latino Health Project at Duke University Hospital, coordinating delivery service for Latino patients. Rebecca and Sue have been comadres for twelve years.

SG: I was raised in Kent, Ohio. I was very influenced by the antiwar movement, and the shootings at Kent State were a formative event for me. It was at the height of the Vietnam War, and there was a possibility my brother was going to be drafted. The shootings and the turmoil around the burning of the ROTC building were really visible in our town, in our church, and even in our family. Our church provided a forum for the town to talk about the situation. People came and talked about things like: "In light of the gospel, what do we do with the situation that's happening in our town? How do we look at the Vietnam War? What we do with that?" That was really powerful for me. There were two or three ministers from the South who had been involved in the Civil Rights Movement, and they talked about Vietnam in terms of "gospel values," taking a stand about what you believe even if it's not popular.

> I think of Jesus not only as a savior or a teacher, but also as an incredible revolutionary. He went up against the powers that be and took a stand on the side of the poor and vulnerable.

At an early age, I felt a longing to know what was important in life. I remember being impressed that the church took a stand to open the doors and to invite people in to talk during May of 1970, just after the Kent State shootings. It was a brave move on their part. People in town whose windows were smashed and cars turned over were really angry with the students, and it was a volatile time. The church was willing to open the door to the chaos.

One of my ministers talked about what an amazing impact the church could have on the world if we really lived the gospel, if we took our faith seriously. I've always worked through religious institutions. I worked at Lutheran Family Services in Wisconsin, and I volunteered at a church organization in Mexico. Now I'm working with Catholic Social Ministries. I like to be in an atmosphere where questions of faith and issues of faith are part of the dialogue. Personally, I get a lot out of that. It's an accepted part of the culture of my workplace; our work comes out of a vision of faith.

I think of Jesus not only as a savior or a teacher, but also as an incredible revolutionary. He went up against the powers that be and took a stand on the side of the poor and vulnerable. He talked to the woman at the well when that was unheard of and related to people who were shunned and frowned upon: prostitutes, tax collectors. Using that life as a model is the ultimate liberation but it also gives me a constant sense of swimming upstream, against the tide, and putting my hopes in a different place. And it's hard. Through Catholic Social Ministries, I'm constantly working with people who don't have enough to eat, can't pay their light bills, and are struggling to make it financially.

If I begin to think that it's just me doing this and if I lose track of the connection I have to God through prayer, then things get out of balance, and I start to feel overwhelmed. I get a visceral feeling in my gut when things are off. Usually that means I need to take some space and have some quiet time so I can remember who the Creator is and get things back in balance.

> I was taught the gospel is about celebrating life to the fullest, and to me that means every aspect.

I believe there's a space in our hearts that only God can fill. It can only happen out of an individual longing for God. You have to get to a certain point in your life before you get to that longing, and I'm not sure some people ever do. The poet Rumi wrote, "When I try to talk about God the words turn to dust in my mouth." My vision of God feels bigger than words, and I certainly wouldn't offer it unless I was specifically asked. I think that discussion about spirituality is easily misinterpreted, seen as proselytizing or trying to save souls or judgmental. But I also love a conversation like this.

RR: My sense of God is more environmental. I grew up in a Hispanic home. It was religious, but it was also very spiritual. I think it was ingrained in me, especially by my grandmothers who were living close to the earth, using herbs, and recognizing the mystery of the earth. In the summer, I'd be watering the grass, and if I was playing with the water, my grandmother would say, "Be sure and get some water and put it on top of your head." Water was a force, and it wasn't just meant for playing. It was protection. That spoke to me, that my family believed in mystery.

My parents have been married for fifty-three years now, and they raised a family that was together all the time. We went to church all day on Sundays and Wednesday evenings. It was an understanding that that was what the family was going to do. We were products of missionaries. The white people came and told the brown people to let go of Catholicism, because to believe in saints and icons was bad. We became Protestants. And the Presbyterian Church is the most demystified. The missionaries did a great job of making sure we didn't have any of that in church – incense, candles, statues. Their mission was to save souls. But the Presbyterians gave me education, one thing my parents would never have been able to give me then. Few families could afford to send their child to school. When you're poor and your parents have minimal formal schooling, education is great. My mom went to a Presbyterian school, which was a rare thing. My uncles and my mother learned trades. My parents graduated from high school, and all of their children graduated from high school, and college, got graduate degrees.

When I was a graduate student working in environmental issues back in the seventies, oil companies and the ecological movement were just starting to blossom. I was struggling with what the church had to say about taking care of the earth. I was also taking leadership in the church. Someone asked me if would consider going to seminary. I applied and that's what I did.

> At an early age, I felt a longing to know what was important in life.

Because I happened to be one of two Hispanic women in seminary, I had access to a lot of prominent scholars that broadened my theology. I never planned on being ordained. I didn't see going to seminary as a spiritual decision; I saw it as a need for more education. But for my parents it was a call, a spiritual decision. I was ordained in the first Presbyterian Hispanic church that had ever been established, and I was being ordained to be the pastor of that church.

It was an historic moment – the first Hispanic woman being ordained in the first Presbyterian Hispanic church in this country. I didn't put all that together. Of course, the Hispanic community had a huge celebration. I never liked big celebrations, so I was trying not to pay attention. In the midst of it, my sister says, " Your grandmother wants to talk to you in private, in the back of the church." I go and my grandmother gives me this blessing: "God be with you, and God give you all the strength." She did this anointing ritual, and it clicked that even in my ordination that wasn't permitted. I hadn't even thought of including a blessing in the service or thought my grandmother would want to give me a blessing. For her, it was really a setting apart.

I've had to be more personal and deliberate about my faith. When I was working in the church, I was there because of my faith. I have had to remind myself that I am here at the hospital because of my faith and not because it's also a calling. I've had to be more deliberate in my prayer life. When I'm going to work, I say thank you to God for the blessings I have, and I ask God to prepare me for the work I'm going to do. Every day faith for every day living.

Rebecca can be reached at reyes004@mc.duke.edu and Sue can be reached at csmpie@raldioc.org

knowing your history. . . . .

Delia Gamble

Delia Gamble is currently pursuing a master's degree in African American Studies at Ohio State University. When I spoke with her, she was directing the Community Stories project at the Center for Documentary Studies in Durham, North Carolina. Community Stories is a community-based oral history project that uses young people to document their own stories and allows them to take ownership of the places in which they live. It is about the power to represent and define yourself. Originally from Washington, D.C., Delia is a graduate of North Carolina Agricultural and Technical College in Greensboro, North Carolina.

I've always loved history, but in high school it was a means of escape. I knew everything by heart, because I was dreaming about being those people – kings, queens. I did not have Black history until I got to college, especially African-American history. It was eye opening. If you're a Black person and you go from a state of not knowing your history to knowing your history in six months, your whole perception of yourself has to change, and it did for me. With white culture, we know that you have your culture in front of you from day one. But to begin to know who you are as an African American is amazing. I got excited and began to understand the possibilities. Then it stopped being a means of escape and started being something that empowered me. I love history when it's visual and oral; it becomes experiential for me.

> If you're a Black person, and you go from a state of not knowing your history to knowing your history in six months, your whole perception of yourself has to change, and it did for me.

In the Community Stories program, I did an exercise with the young people to help them understand their history better. We asked them to imagine that the Civil War has just ended, and the slaves are free. We put them into three groups: ex-slaves, ex-slaveholders, and abolitionists. They had to make up new laws for Black people, present them, and debate them. We talked about knowledge and power and what the slave codes meant in terms of control, what slaves could and couldn't do. They really began to get it. That's why history is exciting. I think that facts and what actually happened are important, but it matters more if they get the themes, if they begin to understand racism and how it works – what the possibilities are for them, and how to get there. I'm trying to give them a foot up in many ways. History exposes them to what is possible and gives them a better understanding of who they are in the context of the world.

stories of faith-based organizing . . . .

Scott Cooper

Scott Cooper, originally from Jackson, Tennessee, is the Southeast regional organizing director with UNITE, the Union of Needletrades, Industrial, and Textile Employees. After graduating from Duke University in 1994, Scott coordinated summer programs for college students to work with grassroots organizations; worked with the Southern Rural Development Institute (SRDI); and then as an organizer for the Industrial Areas Foundation - BUILD, Baltimoreans United in Leadership Development.

I grew up in the United Methodist church; my father is a minister. I didn't have much choice in my faith growing up. My mother explained that was what put food on the table. As a minister's child you learn to relate to all kinds of people. Unlike most kids who leave immediately after the service, we were always the last to leave. You end up talking with people, ranging from two-year-olds to eighty-year-olds, all class backgrounds.

Growing up in the church and in southern communities I had a pretty good vision of what community could be for people. As a member of a minister's family, I moved in and out of many worlds – rich, poor, middle class, black and white. As I grew older, I began to realize there was real disparity in the world. In college, I spent time volunteering at schools or doing service projects but it didn't get at the core of what was wrong. I really struggled to find the answer to that question. It was a natural thing, to want to work like this. It wasn't a radical shift from the path I was on.

Having grown up in church, in moderate, white Protestant denominations, there was a lot of talk but there wasn't much real action. It seemed somewhat self-absorbed. It's a failure on the part of the church not to be active in the political realm, not just electoral politics, but having a voice and being a witness in public debate. Instead of being more of a place where people find a community seeking to make this world more loving, many times the church is, as Walter Brueggeman says, "an opiate for people's pain." This is not to say we shouldn't be able to find comfort in the church, but as people of faith who believe in God, we are somewhat lax in the standards that we hold one another accountable to. It shouldn't be that easy to be a Christian or person of faith. It should be something people struggle with. Look at the life of Jesus, or the life of any holy figure for that matter, and look at our own lives. We're imperfect beings but if we're seeking to imitate the life of Jesus, that should be something that keeps us up at night considering the profane reality that we live in now.

> You can't just organize people around an issue because politics gets boring after awhile. You have to organize people around their values. Faith adds a depth to the work ... To have a common story — the old and new testament for people who grew up in the church — is really amazing.

Someone gave me a quote and I think it's from Ernest Hemingway: "The world breaks everyone and out of the broken places, some grow stronger." That really resonates for me. My understanding of the story of Christ as being someone broken by this world and the story of the resurrection is being able to grow stronger and more powerful through it.

Organizing works to build power out of institutions that share common values and that have been central to people's lives and the lives of families. In Baltimore, it wasn't until people began to talk to one another that they realized that many were only finding part-time, minimum wage jobs, jobs that used to be full-time. At the same time, many churches were angry about how much public money was being used to develop the Inner Harbor in Baltimore. The church agreed with the idea of redeveloping downtown, as long as good jobs were created for people. Since that promise was never fulfilled, the church began talking with the union about the idea of a living wage bill. And the bill was signed in 1994.

It's the first of its kind in the country. It forced the city of Baltimore to create standards. If they were going to sign contracts with private companies to provide services (cleaning, food service, transportation), they needed to be at a wage above the poverty line – then $7.70/hour. It affected the whole labor market in the city because other companies now have to compete with those paying a decent wage. It's basic economics of supply and demand. Since we did it, thirty other cities across the country have followed our lead.

But, you can't just organize people around an issue because politics gets boring after awhile. You have to organize people around their values. Faith adds a depth to the work. You're not just agitating someone around the need for better wages or better benefits. To have a common story – the old and new testament for people who grew up in the church – is really amazing.

For example, I've discussed collective leadership using the story in the Book of Numbers when Moses has led the Israelites into the wilderness after leaving Mount Sinai. They have these new rules – the Ten Commandments – they're lugging around. Everyone comes to Moses saying they're hungry for meat, they're tired of manna. Moses says he can't bear this burden alone and God instructs him to call together seventy of the elders. It's a great lesson of leadership, delegation, and not looking for one central figure. It should be a community of people that bears the burden of sustaining life for a community.

Or, there is the story of the feeding of the five thousand. People have gathered and they want to break bread together but they only have five loaves and a couple of fish. At that time, people carried food with them while traveling but weren't accustomed to sharing. By having them sit together and offer these loaves and fishes, people began to break out of their isolation. Whether or not Christ made food appear out of nothing is secondary to the miracle of people sharing with one another in community. You can take that to another level. People have a lot of ideas in their head but don't always have a chance to sit face-to-face with one another and commune.

I'm not actively involved in a church. My concept of God is a God of free will that gives us the opportunity to explore and struggle in this world and struggle with our relationship with God. My concept is that God is love. On a certain level there is a connection that goes beyond a single issue or value. This work is scary in a lot of ways. There's something very comforting about knowing there is a higher power, It reminds me not to take myself so seriously, that I can't fulfill every need for every individual. For me, having grown up in the church and being able to reconnect with that experience in my day-to-day work is really exciting.

stories.

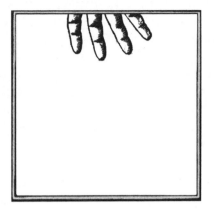

images

Imagination is more important than knowledge.

~ Albert Einstein

To live, to love, and to create are one. In living, loving, and creativity
we move in mystery, alert to possibility, bereft of models for the past and
without hint of one to come.
In the absence of models we experience absolute freedom,
and in freedom, risk, responsibility,
and the joy of being opened to whatever the moment may bring forth to us.

~ Mary Giles, "Sisters of the Yam"

Art establishes the basic human truths
which must serve as the touchstone of our judgment.

~ John F. Kennedy

what are images?. . . . .

Created or remembered out of necessity or desire, images give us a taste of what is real and a vision of what is possible. As human beings we are born with imagination, but then we are asked, in one way or another, to limit this potential. We're told to color inside the lines. To stay on the trail. To play the notes that are written. To spit back the right answers on the test. To follow the recipe. To follow the leader. Creative muscles atrophy when not used. Creating or capturing images allows us explore – and trust – our intuitive side. We are reminded of the value of the process itself and the energy that creation brings into our lives. This is a great exercise in risk taking, in recognizing that you do not have to wait for special training, and in noticing that you have gifts yet untapped. And it is a wonderful act of resistance to the prevailing cultural bias toward product. In creating imagery, we are simultaneously invited to explore mystery and reality.

Images also help us portray our own identity, giving voice to our despair, ecstasy, angst, joy, and fear. This freedom may enable us to come to terms with our surroundings, circumstances, frustrations, and dreams. Too often, images are misused or misappropriated. When we can determine how our lives are represented, we create culture. It is a means for people to define and represent their own identity, and highlight their own strengths.

turning point. . . . .

In January 1991, I attended a retreat for young people doing community service. The United States was about to bomb Iraq. War was imminent but somehow not in the forefront of my mind. I had just begun to help create Empty the Shelters, a student group that supported the organizing that poor people were already doing. I was immersed in relationship-building, recruiting participants, and training design.

On the second day of the retreat, a participant and friend named Katrina Browne reminded all of us of the disaster about to strike. A bit tentatively, she said, "I don't know if you pray, or how you pray, but you might want to pray for Butros-Butros Gali (then Secretary-General of the United Nations) who is on his way to try to bring peace to the Iraqi crisis." Suddenly everyone was silent for a few minutes. I didn't know who was praying, who was wringing their hands or who was thinking, but we were all lost momentarily in our own personal response to the situation. I sat there, wondering exactly how to "do it." I was used to praying in synagogue: reading words in unison in Hebrew and in English with the rest of the congregation. I stumbled around with some words in my mind. At some point, I looked up to find that others were making similar attempts. It didn't appear that any of us were too adept, but we were buoyed by the support around us, and somehow that was enough.

Many years and experiences later, I was working as a mentor for E Pluribus Unum, a program that brought together high school students from different faiths to explore social justice issues. About halfway through the three-week program, issues of race began to surface. As faculty, we weren't comfortable with the honesty or constructiveness of the dialogue that the students were having. The seven mentors, including myself, met to determine our next steps. We were all in our twenties and thirties, ethnically diverse, and Catholic, Jewish, and Protestant like the students themselves. We had a long and difficult conversation about our expectations for the students and for ourselves. Had we failed to give them adequate space and assistance to talk about these issues? How could some be so naïve? What did they need from us? Where did we go from here?

Our conversation went on for a while; we were going in circles. Suddenly, I remembered Katrina's bold call for prayer years earlier, and the image of a group responding. I was hesitant. It was a religious program, but praying in an interfaith context, without the benefit of a preordained liturgy, was still new territory for all of us. Finally I was able to just say quietly, "Why don't we take a few minutes of silence so we can each pray about this?" To my surprise, everyone readily agreed.

I closed my eyes and fell into a meditative space, focusing first on my breath and then bringing a mindful awareness to the situation. I didn't come up with any answers, but I was able to bring a different attitude to what was happening. I focused on cultivating compassion for all involved, beginning with myself and the other mentors and then the students. What happened next was one of the most beautiful moments of my working life. When I felt like I was ready to reconnect with everyone, I opened my eyes. Everyone had found their own place in the room, and was lost in their own form of prayer. Liz was kneeling before a chair not far from me and I could hear her praying in Spanish. Jason seemed to be davening, a Jewish form of standing prayer, near the window. Others were sitting or lying or standing up. The energy in the room had shifted profoundly.

Gradually we came back together, without anyone saying a word. We sat and smiled and looked around the circle. Someone began with an idea. Then another idea came, then an observation, a revelation. We began to talk again, but it was very different this time. We were all listening more intently to each other and we knew what needed to happen. Within a half hour we'd fleshed out a plan of action for that evening. Together we came up with the idea that we would have our own conversation about race – a conversation the students would first watch and then join. I was grateful for my own courage, which came forward only because I was able to connect with an image of bravery from long before.

? questions for reflection . . . .

Which images have power for you, either positive or negative?

What images do you find yourself using? What images, if any, have you ever created?

What are your first memories of being creative? When have you felt creative recently?

What are the things, places, experiences, and people in your life that have led you to see new possibilities?

℮ your own footing: images of inspiration

It takes practice for us to recover this ability to see, or before that, the gift of wanting to see.
~ *Corita Kent,* Learning by Heart

On one of my kitchen cabinets I keep a photo of the Guggenheim Museum in Bilbao, an industrial city in the Basque region of Spain that was once a center of steel making. Built in 1997, the museum is like no other. Step back from a photo of it, and the physical structure looks like crumpled pieces of aluminum foil thrown together. Step closer and the beauty of the space is unparalleled, the originality undeniable. Made of limestone and titanium, the museum presents a drastically different and striking view from every angle. The windows slant in crazy directions, forms thrust at you almost from nowhere, and the curves are as graceful as architecture can be. Built on an old river site, architect Frank Gehry paid homage to the museum's location, interfacing directly with a set of railroad tracks and a suspension bridge that are both still in use. Every time I look at it I am reminded of what it means to think outside of the box with great attention to the context of place and no limitation on beauty.

Images of inspiration can come through an infinite number of sources: people, experiences, places, words, music, movement, or prayer. It may come in an instant, a sudden flash of something powerful unfolding before us, or within us. Inspiration can hide in the corners of what might seem like an "ordinary" conversation or in the pairing of unlikely things.

Spend a week or a month cutting out images that appeal to you. Put them in a notebook, sketchbook, or file folder. You might even cover part of a wall in your house, apartment or office with large paper to serve as an ongoing canvas for what you collect. If you like an image you can't keep or easily extract, make a color Xerox of it. Keep your eyes open everywhere:

photographs
logos
magazines and newspapers
objects you find
wrapping paper
paint/fabric swatches

food boxes/packaging
drawings/paintings
catalogues
book/CD/cassette covers
cards you receive

You can also start by brainstorming lists of your sources of inspiration. Gather different colored pens, magic markers, paints, or colored pencils and one sheet of 8½" x 11" paper. Draw your favorite shape so that it fills the entire space. Then, figure out a way to divide it into five different parts, any way that you want. Be creative. In each of the parts put one of the following words: *words* (books, poetry, magazines), *sound* (music, stories, nature), *visual* (art, movies, video, color), *places*, and *people*. Slowly fill in each section with the relevant sources of inspiration. Brainstorm possibilities. Create other categories and add to the shape to make room for them. Notice any patterns or themes. What images came to mind while you were making your lists?

@ mapping your inner life

Another way to begin working with images is by drawing a map of your inner or spiritual life. You will need large pieces of paper (flip chart or newsprint size works best) and drawing materials such as crayons, markers, or pastels. The idea is to visually map out your journey with faith or spirit, starting with the first relevant experience you can remember and moving to the present. Consider the following questions:

- What are the highlights of your faith or spiritual journey? What are the hard times?
- Who were key figures along the way?
- What places or spaces figure prominently in this journey?
- Where are you now? In what directions might you be going?

When you're finished, take a look at the various images you have drawn. Do you notice any patterns? Does anything surprise you?

murals of a people

Diego Rivera (1886–1957) fused radical art and revolutionary politics on a grand scale. His majestic murals chronicle the history and life of the Mexican people. Rivera came of age during the Mexican Revolution of 1910, a time when artists and writers were often the conscience of their people. In the words of one biographer, "Revolution turned him into a revolutionary painter – compelled to paint for the masses." And mural painting was an art form oriented for the masses. Anyone in the street could see them and no admission could be charged. Rivera's murals adorn the walls of public buildings, so they have remained in the hands of the Mexican people. The murals detail all aspects and incidents of oppression in Mexico, from the Spanish who first conquered the land, to the landowners who ruled Mexico on a platform of corruption and great poverty. Magnificent works of art, the murals are also a powerful testimony to the struggles of the Mexican people.

In Durham there is a store called the Scrap Exchange. Founded by Pat Hoffman in 1993, The Scrap Exchange gets companies to donate materials they no longer need. These are then sold to the public at very low prices. Among items always available are material, paper in all sizes and colors, wood pieces, foam in all shapes, ribbons, and funky containers. Material for the Arts, in New York City, has a similar mission. They provide surplus office equipment and supplies, furnishings, art materials, and other donated items to nonprofit cultural organizations and art programs free of charge. The program is a joint project of the Department of Cultural Affairs and Department of Sanitation. If you don't have a place like this nearby, perhaps you can get together with other people and trade materials.

ℰ mandalas: symbol of the spirit

When composing mandalas, you are trying to coordinate your personal circle with the universal circle. In a very elaborate Buddhist mandala, for example, you have the deity in the center as a power source, the illumination source. The peripheral images would be manifestations or aspects of the deity's radiance.
In working out a mandala for yourself, you draw a circle and then you think of the different impulse systems and value systems in your life. Then you compose them and try to find out where your center is. Making a mandala is a discipline for pulling all those scattered aspects of your life together, for finding a center and ordering yourself to it. You try to coordinate your circle with the universal circle.

~ *Joseph Campbell,* The Power of Myth

Mandala is the Sanskrit word for circle. In the Eastern religions of Buddhism, Hinduism, and Jainism, the *mandala* is used as a tool for contemplation to encourage the spirit to move forward along its path of evolution. The creation of a mandala is a powerful ritual, accompanied by prayer and meditation. Psychologist Carl Jung discovered the mandala through dreams and artwork, not knowing it had existed in Eastern religions for thousands of years. Jung used them often with patients. He believed the mandala was vital in healing psychological fragmentation because it both restored a previously existing order and gave expression or form to something completely new. No one mandala would ever be exactly the same as another, because each is an integration of a series of images from its creator that are projected from the psyche.

Mandalas can be created to reflect on anything worthy of attention. Start with a white circle of paper the size of a dinner plate. Have crayons, paints, and colored pencils available. In the center, draw, paint, or collage a symbol of your spirit, spirit world, spirituality, or faith. Then, intuitively decide what you might want to surround this image with. What will best support your spiritual journey at this time? Find a way to represent that. Or, you might start with an image in the center that symbolizes something you want to change in the world. Again, what images will conjure up the support you need for this aspiration to manifest itself?

ℰ reaching out to others: sharing inspiration

You can do this as a twist on "show and tell" during a family gathering, an evening with friends or with coworkers. You might be amazed at how this simple activity opens up new avenues of conversation and deepens levels of understanding.

Ask everyone to bring in something that inspires them in their daily life or something from their spiritual or religious tradition to share with others. It might be something written, an object in their home, a ritual, a practice, a poem or prayer, a song – anything. Give each person three to four minutes to share his or her inspiration with the group.

℮ images with intention

When the artist is alive in any person, whatever his kind of work may be,
he becomes an inventive, searching, daring, self-expressing creature . . .
He disturbs, upsets, enlightens, and he opens the way for a better understanding.

~ Robert Henri

Get some nice cloth cut into a small (4" x 4") piece, cord or string, herbs like lavender or tobacco, a small piece of paper, and a writing implement. On the piece of paper, draw an image symbolizing a great hope or intention that you have for yourself or your community. Try not to use words. Fold or roll up the paper and place it in the center of the cloth. Sprinkle some herbs over it and say a blessing if you wish. Wrap the cloth up and bind it with the cord or string. Put it in a place where you'll see it every day and be reminded of the prayer inside.

This is something you can also do with a few friends. Get enough cloth, cord, and herbs for everyone. Give everyone a slip of paper and ask them to write a prayer for themselves. Let them choose a piece of cloth (you can also have folks bring their own cloth and exchange with each other.) When everyone is finished, ask them to stand in a circle with their bundles cupped in their hands in front of them. Ask if anyone has a prayer they'd like to offer for all of the bundles. You can also exchange them and have members of the group keep another person's bundle for a specified period of time.

℮ "photographs"

This is fun to do when you find yourself with others, in a moment or a place you want to remember. In pairs, have one person be the blindfolded "camera" and the seeing partner be the "photographer." The photographer leads the camera to a spot he wants the camera to see and photograph. When the camera is in front of the potential picture, the photographer takes off the blindfold so the camera can take a photo in his mind. Then the blindfold is replaced. Partners should do this three times before switching. Encourage the photographers to choose images that are unique or beautiful in some way. If you want a challenge, ask the photographer to lead the camera back to a central spot and then find the subjects of his photographs.

@ group paintings

This helps engage a group in making art with great freedom. For example, you can do it at the beginning of a staff meeting, during a holiday celebration at home or at work, or with any group of young people. For this you will need water-based paints, brushes, jars for water, and one large piece of paper for each person. Have everyone sit in a circle if possible, or two circles if the group is larger than eight people. Give everyone a piece of paper and put the paints in the center of the circle. Ask everyone to choose or create a color they like and start painting. If they need more direction, ask them to sit quietly and think back over something powerful that happened to them during the day or the week. Without trying to paint the memory itself, encourage people to paint how it made them *feel*.

Let people paint for a few minutes. Then tell everyone to pass their painting to the person on their left and resume painting. (Don't tell them ahead of time that they'll be painting on each other's paper!) Continue this pattern – everyone painting for a few minutes and then passing their paper to the left – until each paper makes it all the way around and winds up back with its original owner. The sheets can be cut up and made into cards. Have people add their own prayers or quotes to the cards, and then exchange them.

@ collage

Collect an assortment of magazines, paper, drawing supplies, and whatever else you find that can be used for collage. Poster board makes a great base for a collage. Collage is a great medium to start with if you or others feel anxious about doing art. When a group is coming together for the first time, it can be a great way for each person to portray themselves to others. This is particularly valuable if the group is from diverse backgrounds, regions of the country, and/ or ages. Here are some possible themes:

- Convey something about your roots.
- Represent God or spirituality to you.
- Reflect what you love most about your life.
- Reflect what you do and why you do it.

℮ creative gatherings

"Art parties" used to be held twice a year where I live. These were a chance for local artists to display their work. The parties began when a group of young artists were frustrated with the lack of gallery space interested in their work. Most of the art space in town were more interested in established artists. So, these folks took matters into their own hands, organizing a party in their own house. They used the walls of every hallway and room to display visual art of all mediums. They made great food, put out a jar for donations, and told guests to bring their own drinks. Some art was for sale; some wasn't. After a couple of years, performance art was added in the basement. Everyone was invited to share their talent, whether music, dance, poetry, video, or improv theater. By the end, the art parties were attracting hundreds of people.

- If you were going to throw an art party, where would you do it?
- Who might help you? What artists do you know?
- Whom would you invite?

a note about making art with others:

Give yourself plenty of time to set up and clean up, and don't be afraid to ask for help. If you're using someone else's space, go the extra mile to make sure no damage is done. A big plastic tarp works well for floors. Have extra newspaper and paper towels or rags on hand.

Do what you can to create an atmosphere of freedom. You might have people work in silence or with quiet music. Some people will dig right into making art; others will want to just sit and watch for a while. You can suggest something else or encourage people to follow their intuition. Be patient; sometimes people will find a role for themselves, like washing paint brushes or mixing paint colors or cutting strips of paper.

℮ images of community

I see myself as an urban artist, using the entire environment that I work in, which includes the people in that environment. If I am talking about transforming an environment – changing, enhancing, making it more beautiful – then I am also talking about changing the people who live in that environment as well. The elements of my design are not just line, form and color but all the

---

good materials to have

<u>Paper</u>, white and colored, that is good for paint, collage, and drawing, and construction paper. You can also make art on paper bags or newspaper.

<u>Paint</u>, watercolor and/or water-based.

<u>Pencils</u>, <u>crayons</u>, and/or <u>markers</u>. You'll often find these cheaper in drug or toy stores than art supply stores, which tend to sell more high-end supplies.

<u>Brushes</u>, old jars for water, and empty egg cartons for mixing paint colors.

Be creative when gathering additional supplies:

<u>Food</u>: cereal, pasta, beans

<u>Nature</u>: leaves, flowers, grass, branches

<u>Hardware</u>: old screws, nails, scrap metal, wood

<u>Material</u>: fabric swatches, old curtains, bedspreads, clothes, ribbons, yarn, string

<u>Office</u>: rubber bands, paper clips, scrap paper, old magazines

Always be on the lookout for things that will come in handy for art projects and remember that anything goes. Find a good container in which to store everything.

environmental and social factors that are inherent in the space and that cannot be separated from it. That's changing everything and not just the facade.

~ *Judy Barca*, Making Face/Making Soul

It is powerful to witness how people join together to create imagery and forge a renewed sense of power in the process. The act of determining and producing images of oneself and one's hopes fosters connections that bind people together in new levels of connection. In cities and towns across the United States and around the world, symbolic representation helps communities express pain, chip away at old walls and open up new venues for communication.

℮ images of grief

There is a long history of women creating stories of family and community in their quilts. Today, this art form remains a tangible and collective process. The AIDS quilt is one example of how images have told untold stories and served as powerful symbols. It was started in 1985 in San Francisco by Cleve Jones. To memorialize the one thousand San Franciscans who had died of AIDS up to that point, he and others taped pieces of paper with their names to the walls of the federal building. Stepping back from the tribute, Jones saw the resemblance to a quilt, and the idea of a memorial was born. Jones made the first panel to commemorate his best friend.

The AIDS quilt brings people together in a way that helps to dissolve some of the fear, anger, and despair. When it was laid out in its entirety in the fall of 1996, just eleven years after it began, the quilt stretched nearly a mile, from the foot of the capitol building to the Washington Monument. Seventy thousand people were memorialized on thirty-eight thousand panels. The quilt brings us face to face with the immense pain of so many deaths, disease, and the homophobia surrounding the virus. Mary Fisher, an HIV-positive mother of two who founded the Family AIDS Network and put a new public face on AIDS when she spoke at the 1992 Republican National Convention, explained the following about the quilt in her book, *I Will Not Go Quietly* (New York: Scribner, 1995):

> *Until the Quilt is finished, it is wise for those of us who remain to gather at the memorial from time to time, if only to remember – not so much for those who have fallen as for ourselves . . . No matter how often we have been in its presence, we come to the Quilt tentatively, reverently, as one comes into the presence of something greater than oneself. We move from panel to panel, not only remembering but wondering. We see a name and we ask, "Why?"*

images of peace

The Boise Peace Quilt Project started in 1981 when three people decided to make a friendship quilt for people in what was then the Soviet Union. The idea was to extend a concrete statement of their hope for world peace and their desire for friendship with "ordinary Russian people." The first quilt was presented at the Russian Embassy in Washington, D.C., and then found its way to its intended home in Alitus, Lithuania. Since then, the Boise Peace Quilt Project has continued to make peace quilts for people in other parts of the world and to give Peace Quilt awards for peacemakers who are "blazing new trails to survival for our global family." Past quilt recipients include Rosa Parks, Cesar Chavez, Mr. (Fred) Rogers, Julia Butterfly Hill, and Senator Frank Church. A documentary about the project, "A Stitch for Time," was nominated for an Academy Award in 1988.

- What are your greatest hopes for peace?
- What medium might you use to express your hopes?
- Who else would want to join in the creation?
- To what part of the world would you send these hopes?

images of a neighborhood

Street Level-Video was founded as part of a public art program in Chicago supported by the National Endowment for the Arts. Street Level Youth Media worked with local youth, gangs, adults, and community groups to organize a video installation block party. Fifty young people were taught how to use video cameras and then make videos about their neighbors' community. These were displayed on monitors set up along the street during the block party. On milk crates, in empty lots, and on the stoops of people's homes, seventy-five monitors offered an electronic look at the neighborhood's collective identity, linking one private experience to another in a public venue. According to one reviewer from *ArtForum* magazine, the narratives revealed, "A preoccupation with borders, generations, and isolation, but also hopes of reclamation and tolerance . . . what was visualized on the videotapes was realized on and reflected back to the block."

- How do the people in your neighborhood experience each other's lives?

medicine wheels

The Medicine Wheel dance has had a strong beginning. In the late 1970s, Spirit gave me a powerful vision. In this vision I saw a hilltop bare of trees. A soft breeze was blowing, gently moving the prairie grass. I saw a circle of rocks that came out like the spokes of a wheel. Inside this large circle was another circle of rocks, nearer to the center. As I was looking at this vision, I knew this was the Sacred Circle, the hoop of my people.
– Sun Bear, *Dancing with the Wheel*

The Native American medicine wheel is laid out on the ground with stones and other natural elements. It is a vital element in cultures where the earth is respected and protected. Each element can help human beings remember their sacred connection to nature. It begins with a circle and four spokes for the four directions: east, west, north, and south, symbolizing the universe and each person's place in it. Each of the four directions represents a different attribute. The wheel, then, becomes a cosmic diagram.

- How could you deepen that understanding and connection? Who would help you?
- If you wanted to organize a block party with a creative component how would you begin?

@ images of the other

Face to Face: Photographs by Don Camp and Laurence Salzmann was an exhibit that chronicled the relationships between Jews and Blacks in Philadelphia. The two men – one Black, one Jewish – photographed individuals from both backgrounds whose lives had intersected in some way. The images run the gamut from congenial and familial to aloof and even suspicious. The exhibit portrayed Black-Jewish relationships in all their complexity, exploring issues of identity, history, belief, and community. Photographer Don Camp wrote about the process as follows: "Myths and stereotypes, about ourselves and others, are still our primary source of information. We find ourselves unable, or unwilling, to investigate each other's presence and reality . . . I chose people to photograph who were simply unafraid to explore each other's presence."

- What group(s) are you most interested in learning about?
- How would you exchange this learning? In what format?
- How and where would you display the results of your exploration?

@ images of youth

From the Hip, a national photo documentary celebrating youth activism and service, was initiated by Tony Deifell and the Campus Outreach Opportunity League. It began when 280 young photographers and writers across the country took camera and pen in hand and sought answers to two questions: Does the public know who young people are? and What actions are they taking to strengthen their communities? The result? A thirteen-story collection of images and words by and about young people that serves as a visual diary of their work in communities. The young artists told stories of the Berkeley Free Clinic; the Tommy Hill housing development in Newport, Rhode Island; and Fusion Cafe, a hangout for young people in Jacksonville, Florida. They chronicled the lives of a needle exchange program volunteer in New York's Lower East Side; a teen theater group in St. Paul, Minnesota; and participants in the Sex Offender Treatment Program in Giddings, Texas. Brilliant photographs and straightforward story writing created a moving and highly original portrayal of young people in the United States.

- What story of community service and youth would you tell about your community?
- Is there one project or organization or person you would choose to focus on?
- How would you document their activities?

resources for images

American Museum of Visionary Art, 800 Key Highway, Baltimore, Md. 21230-3940. (410) 244–1900. www.avam.org

Boise Peace Quilt Project, P.O. Box 6469, Boise, Idaho 83707. (208) 378-0293. www.peacequilt.org

Cameron, Julie. *The Artist's Way*. Los Angeles: Tarcher/Putnam, 1992. Cameron presents a twelve-week program for reclaiming creativity based on two primary tools: the morning pages and the artist date.

Campbell, Joseph, with Bill Moyers. *The Power of Myth*. New York: Doubleday, 1988. www.jcf.org

Chicago, Judy. *Holocaust Project: From Darkness into Light*. New York: Penguin Books, 1993. A personal account of a journey through the history of the Holocaust and creating art in memory of it. www.judychicago.com

Cornell, Judith. *Mandala: Luminous Symbols for Healing*. Wheaton, Ill.: Quest Books, 1994. Guide to making sacred art for healing the body, mind, and spirit. Historical information, inspiring meditations, and exercises for making mandalas and beautiful images. www.kripalushop.org/kripalu/programs/bios/JudithCornell.html

Diaz, Adriana. *Freeing the Creative Spirit: Drawing on the Power of Art to Tap the Magic and Wisdom Within*. San Francisco: HarperCollins, 1983.

Fisher, Mary. *I Will Not Go Quietly*. New York: Scribner, 1995. www.maryfisher.com

Ghiselin, Brewster, ed. *The Creative Process*. Berkeley: University of California Press, 1985. Originally published in 1952, this book contains original commentary from thirty-eight writers, artists, and scientists on creativity. Contributors include Einstein, Mozart, van Gogh, and Nietzsche.

Goldstein, Ernest. *The Journey of Diego Rivera*. Minneapolis: Lerner, 1996. A biography with a special focus on Rivera's murals. www.diegorivera.com/murals

Guggenheim Bilbao. www.guggenheim-bilbao.es/ingles/home.htm

Jones, Bill T., with Peggy Gillespie. *Last Night on Earth*. New York: Pantheon Books, 1995. Jones's fascinating life history, told autobiographically with beautiful photographs.

Kent, Corita, and Jan Steward. *Learning by Heart: Teachings to Free the Creative Spirit.* New York: Bantam Books, 1992. Principles, techniques, and tools to help tap your creative energy.

Kimmelman, Michael. "Of Candy Bars and Public Art." *New York Times,* 26 September 1993. A review of the Culture in Action project, including the Street-Level block party.

Krishner, Judith Russi. "Street-Level Video." *ArtForum*, December 1993.

Materials for the Arts, 410 West 16th Street, New York, N.Y. 10011. (212) 255-5924. www.ci.nyc.ny.us/html/dcla/html/mfa.html

Muschamp, Herbert. "A Masterpiece for Now." *New York Times Magazine,* 7 September 1997. Article about the Guggenheim Museum in Bilbao, Spain and its architect, Frank Gehry.

Sark. *A Creative Companion: How to Free Your Creative Spirit.* Berkeley, Calif.: Celestial Arts, 1991. Inspiring words and stories to free your creative muse. www.campsark.com

Scrap Exchange, 548 Foster Street, Durham N.C. 27701. (919) 688-6960. www.scrapexchange.org

Street Level Youth Media, 1856 West Chicago Avenue, Chicago, Ill. 60622. (773) 862-5331. http://streetlevel.iit.edu/

making art . . . .

Jeanette Stokes

Jeanette Stokes is a Presbyterian minister and the director of the Resource Center for Women and Ministry in the South, an organization she founded in Durham, North Carolina in 1977. Through that organization and her life, she is committed to weaving together feminism, theology, social justice, creativity, and spirituality. She spends her days creating innovative programs in areas of feminist spirituality and creativity, painting, writing, meditating, and dancing.

As a child I made art for entertainment. I started again in 1992 when I was forty-one. I had these three big disappointments: I didn't get pregnant, I didn't get a job that I wanted, and I didn't get a funded sabbatical. Someone gave me a copy of the *The Artist's Way*. First, I started writing every day. That is a practice I have continued. Then, my friend Jewel invited me to come over and play with watercolors one day. I liked it so much that I went out a week later and bought myself some brushes, paints, and paper and started painting on my kitchen table.

In 1995, I quit my job. It had devolved. I felt like I was nothing but a workshop organizer and publication producer. It had been fun and creative for a lot of years, but I was doing the same thing over and over again, and I didn't like it anymore. I knew I had to quit, because it had gotten boring, repetitive, and tedious. I was completely burned out.

I rented a studio immediately, which seemed like an extravagant thing to do since I wasn't generating any income, didn't have any way to pay for it, and didn't really think of myself as an artist. But I wanted a more direct relationship with my own energy, my own inspiration, my own creativity. I spent a lot of time painting and writing. Then I took a bookmaking and a paper-making class and started making books.

The Artist's Way says that if you start writing every day and listen to what you're saying you want, you won't be able to stand hearing yourself say the same thing over and over again without doing something about it. For me, art is about wanting something and then getting what you want: wanting red, right here in this spot, right now. The more I practice wanting red, right here, right now and putting it there, the better I am at hearing and trusting what I want in life. I've come to believe that one of the ways the divine communicates with us is through our wanting. So I make lists of things that I want, not so much to get them but just to be able to watch the process of having things I say I want actually come to be. Making art helps that process.

> I've come to believe that one of the ways the divine communicates with us is through our wanting.

When I'm tired at work, the image that comes to mind is trying to push dead weight. If I do that in relationship to art, what I get is really bad. The process doesn't feel any good, I have no relationship to the product, I just hate the whole thing. We do wonderful art and wonderful work when the energy comes out of the middle of us or off the top. When it's dredged up from these really tried, resentful places in us, it's not good.

I'm interested in the present moment, and art supports that. The skills that we employ in work situations are like the skills that I see among my friends who are trying to finish a dissertation: you keep doing it, long after you love it. You wind up with a lot of burned-out people. Most of the people I know who are overachievers keep pushing way past the good energy. We value organizational efficiency very highly. I don't think there's anything efficient about making art. If I threw out as much work at my job as I throw out art in my studio . . . and yet I expect every one of my working hours to be productive. Work has become so focused on being productive. That may be one of the enemies of creativity.

For organizations to be more creative, they have to get in touch with what they really want, be willing to take risks and try new things, and be committed to the goal of getting their heart's desires met in the work. The process of wanting, noticing, responding to what I want, saying what's true at the moment, taking risks, trying things, being okay if they don't work out – those are all skills that are practiced in making art. And they're really good skills in human relationships as well.

To me it's all about God, it's all about spirit, it's all about mystery. I don't think any of us really know what we're doing or why we're doing it. We don't even know why our handwriting looks the way it does! They're the doodles God gave me. When I paint, all I do is doodle with a paintbrush.

I never understood why people would say, "I didn't write that; God wrote that and I wrote it down," until I started painting. I look at what I've painted and I remember painting it, but I don't know why I made the marks I made. Why we see the world the way we do and why we want what we want. It's all very holy and very sacred to me. This is why I get nearly hysterical if someone says, "No, no, don't paint trees like that; let me show you how to paint trees."

I lose track of the sacred much more easily in a work situation, in the face of trying to get things accomplished. When I'm making art, partly because I'm not trying to make a living at it, I remember there is no place I'm trying to get to; there's nowhere to go. It's like a love relationship, it's like life. All there is is living.

I'm interested in the present moment, and art supports that. The present moment is the perfect teacher; it is always with us. Making art is about being in the moment. I asked a professional artist about this and she said the only way for anyone to do work that is any good is to be present to the process. If you focus on the product, it is not possible to turn out something worthwhile. Making art is the way that I am the most often in contact with what I would call spirit or God.

Jeanette can be reached at stokesnet@aol.com

images.

Part Three

Embrace

Turning Outward, Building Connection

As individual people, and as a society, we search for authenticity and integrity. To fully realize the best we can be as a planet, we need the mirror of those we know, and those we do not know.

How do we take in the levels of horror and pain and strangeness in the world, and still engage? If we try to shield ourselves from what is happening down the street or halfway around the world, this isolation often just brings more pain. Once the eye is open, we must see. Once we hear, we must respond.

So, how do we find the strength to turn toward struggle, instead of away from it? By embracing the golden rule that lies at the heart of virtually every spiritual path. Do unto others what you would have done unto you. To listen, to hear, to see – all acts of transformation. However seemingly insignificant, acts of kindness and justice transform us from the inside out. When we respond to the need, within ourselves and in the world, it gives us strength.

This is a vital aspect of our spiritual lives, this reaching beyond the self, beyond what is familiar, to find that what we thought was separate from us is actually part of us. Fear and pain are universal. So is the power of our loving embrace.

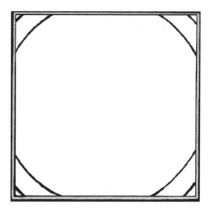

circles

We need smaller groups now. That's all I can talk of and it's not nearly enough . . .
Hope a new class of people who will know what's necessary . . . It's these small groups of people
who will lead in the eventual help. . . people who will be able to make the change to a higher place . . .
Their small risks will become law.

~ Lewis Mumford, *quoted in* The Last Days of Lewis Mumford *by Tonia Shoumatoff*

The circle is a feminine shape; a feminine sound. It is a protected and consecrated space,
a space where all things and all people are equal. The circle is at the very root of equality.
It is the symbol for equality. The circle is at the root of true humility where each is seen as
important to the whole and none is more important than any other. God is a circle whose
circumference is nowhere and whose center is everywhere . . . We stand at the center of the Circle, always.
All ceremony begins with honoring the Circle. All ceremony, all prayer, all celebration,
all rituals, all moments in time. We are related to things, visible and invisible.

~ Scout Cloud Lee, The Circle Is Sacred

what are circles?

Circles are small groups of individuals who gather regularly, with intention, to support each other, renew themselves spiritually, and explore areas of common interest. Spiritual circles are as old as time and part of many different traditions. Seekers have always benefited from a community that reinforces their journey and supports the quest for authenticity: the Jewish havurah, Christian mission groups, the Buddhist sangha, twelve-step programs, Bible study groups, women's spirituality groups, and many others. When convened and facilitated with intention and dignity, circles spark intense dialogue, ongoing challenge, and powerful relationships.

For anyone interested in social transformation, the idea of the circle takes on new meaning. We know that social change and political movements do not begin at mass rallies, in town meetings, or with the forming of organizations. They begin around someone's kitchen table, on the front porch, or at the local diner. True change becomes possible when a small group of people make commitments to each other, commitments that allow them to do something they would not do on their own. These groups matter because they provide a space in which people can heal from the past, learn to honor what is truly present, and envision a radically different future.

turning point

When I first began to develop a practice, I wondered what kind of communities supported individuals in their quest for wholeness. To find out, I visited holistic health and yoga centers, read a lot of books, and attended workshops. Everywhere I went I met people considering similar questions: What does a life aligned with the spirit feel like? How could I bring more peace into my day-to-day life? What practices would help me feel less full of myself and more full of God? I was surrounded by thoughtful, alive, and intelligent people having the conversations I'd been yearning to have. I was discovering what it felt like to live life in the present, and I was grateful. For a time, an inner calm arose and I was able to sink into a comfortable place that was both new and vaguely familiar.

Soon, however, I began to feel uncomfortable. This world of spiritual renewal was overwhelmingly white and very well resourced. People were facing the suffering in their own lives with courage but there was little conversation about any larger challenges facing society. The message I heard over and over again was, "The only thing you can change is yourself." I believed this, but at the same time I believed it was a cop-out. What relevance did all of this mindfulness have for the world around us? I began to wonder where all of this spiritual retreating was leading.

I felt torn. My vocational commitments were justice-based, but my ability to sustain those commitments, I now knew, would require the energy I was cultivating in the realm of the spirit. My daily practice was an individual one, but broad change required collective action. In 1995, I started an organization called stone circles. Our mission would be to find ways to integrate spirituality and faith into social change work. I wanted to share the gifts of the inner life with all of the brilliant but overworked activists whom I worried might kill themselves before they'd saved anybody else. And, I wanted to I find a group of people who cared deeply about both personal and social transformation.

I began to talk to folks about my desire for a circle. I asked them what they thought of a small group of activists, loosely defined, coming together for spiritual renewal. Did they need it? Would they come? Most people were intrigued, if not a little confused, so I scheduled a potluck dinner at my house and wrote a short statement of my intentions. I was not sure if it made sense but people called and said they would come. To be truthful, this response made me nervous. It's one thing to walk in the wilderness alone; it's quite another to bring a whole group along with you. But it was too late to turn back.

A few days later, these friends and colleagues were seated in my living room. We talked about our faith and spiritual backgrounds, some of the questions we were wrestling with, and what kind of community we wanted to support our seeking. Most folks were interested in meeting on a monthly basis, and the "First Circle" was born. We met for over two years and the experience touched each of us in different ways. Much of this chapter, and parts of other chapters, have come directly from my experience with this group and the two other circles that followed. I feel blessed to have had the members of these circles as companions for life's journey.

? questions for reflection . . . .

Who are the people with whom you can share joys and struggles? How did you find them?

Have you ever tried to bring these people together? With either planned or unstructured activities?

What communities or "circles" have supported you in your life? How did they come together?

What made these groups meaningful to you?

℮ your own footing: the need for community

We are all longing to go home to some place we have never been – a place, half-remembered, and half-envisioned, we can only catch glimpses of from time to time. Community. Somewhere, there are people to whom we can speak with passion without having the words catch in our throats. Somewhere a circle of hands will open to receive us, eyes will light up as we enter, voices will celebrate with us whenever we come into our own power. Community means strength that joins our strength to do the work that needs to be done. Arms to hold us when we falter. A circle of healing. A circle of friends. Someplace where we can be free.

~ Starhawk, Dreaming the Dark

Consider what purpose a small group like a circle might serve in your life. Are you craving a spiritual community, a forum for open dialogue, or a way to convene people around a particular issue that you care about? First, see if there are any groups in your area you might join. Ask around, check out bulletin boards and your local papers. Call people and go to a meeting or gathering. Find out what other people are already doing.

You might also consider creating a circle as part of a group that you are already in. This could be a group related to your workplace, your house of worship, or a hobby you have. It might be an identity group (women's circle, men's group, et cetera), a book or garden club, or even a sports team. You can also consider creating a circle at a site where you are volunteering. There is no end to the list of groups that can benefit from carving out time to pay attention to the intersection of the inner and outer life.

You'll know if an existing group is ready for the intentionality of a circle if some part of the group has:

- Expressed desire to deepen their connections to one another and to their work, take the next step toward authenticity and intimacy
- An interest in exploring spirituality and faith
- Been raising big questions
- Experienced a crisis and found no satisfactory process to address it
- Talked about possible routes for social action

As you think about initiating a circle, it will be easier if you are cultivating a commitment to your own spiritual path; have enthusiasm and respect for the people in your group; know of one person outside of the group who can support you; and have a willingness to learn more about group process.

℮ a circle forming

*What we call spirituality, it's matter of taste. What's spiritual for you,
might leave me cold. I can't read someone's mind and know what's going to work.
Do your best to find a small circle of people with whom you can create a
community, with whom you can travel a road together. And build in way so that you're
learning about yourself, about the world, about fortitude and character, matters of faith.
Share that with a minimum of two other people, and as many
as eight or nine other people. That will be your spiritual circle for a time.*

~ Rabbi Sid Schwarz

If you decide you want or need to initiate something new, and you have the
energy to get a circle off the ground, consider finding a partner to join you. It
is easier to share the load, and the risk, when there are two initiating a circle.
Begin by talking with each other about healthy, successful group experiences
you have had. Make a list of the key ingredients of these groups. It will help
guide you.

Decide on your optimal number and reach out accordingly; you don't
want to invite thirty people if you're looking for a core group of twelve, and
twelve is actually a great number for a circle. Have a conversation with each
potential participant. Explain your reasons for starting the circle and your idea
of what might evolve from it. You don't need to promise a particular outcome
but it is useful to share some of your own reasons, and get a sense of other
people's needs.

Some people will be drawn to the idea because they are connected to a
religious tradition but interested in discovering the spiritual elements of that
religion and/or connecting with people of different backgrounds. Others may
have little or no connection to organized religion and desire a way to bring
spirituality into their lives. Some might be most interested in ways to slow
down, while others will crave companionship and support for their journey.

*My whole transformation was catalyzed by being in a circle.
I definitely feel more sure, more grounded, and more supported in the work that I'm doing.
Before I was running on two wheels: one was acting, one was reacting. It was all about motion.
What the circle brought in was two other pieces – groundedness and the emotional piece that
helped me better understand myself. So now I'm cruising on all fours.*

~ Daughtry Carstarphen

ⓔ format

The circle was structured by the intentions of its members;
we explored what compelled us. I miss what those gatherings added to my life,
the intimate spiritual community and the time and intention to reflect,
meditate, learn, move, write, share, make art, and eat in that community.

~ Heather Zorn, member of the Second Circle

The format of the circle should flow directly from the desires of the group members. Combine activities from this book with those you create yourselves. You need a minimum of two hours for meaningful interaction. As the group becomes closer and more social, suggest that people arrive fifteen minutes early to socialize. Another option is to have potlucks that start thirty minutes before the meeting.

It's good to have consistency in the format and in the way in which the space is set up. Here is a simple design that works well:

1. Opening period of silence and meditation, and/or opening ritual
2. Check-in: short updates from everyone in the group on their lives and spirits
3. Discussion or activity, based on the topic chosen
4. Announcements and preparation for next meeting (location, topic, and facilitator chosen)
5. Closing ritual

ⓔ roles

In the beginning, people will look to the convener(s) of the circle as the leader. If you are interested in having the group rotate facilitation, express that at the first gathering so people know what to expect. You may want to commit to planning the first three gatherings and then have facilitation rotate after that. People can also pair up and facilitate together. The facilitator(s) should plan the agenda of the gathering and let people know what, if anything, they need to do to prepare.

ⓔ your first gathering

Start your circle with an introductory meeting or potluck supper. Find a comfortable, quiet space. This could be your house, or, if folks are very spread out, a room in a centrally located office building or community center that you can reserve. If you're using a space outside the home, think about how you can transform the space so that it creates the atmosphere you are seeking.

The first gathering is a time for everyone to meet each other, find out what this is all about, and articulate their beliefs and needs. Have everyone introduce themselves. Explain that you'd like the group to talk about two questions, as a way of exploring their own purpose in coming to the gathering, and what their own needs are:

- What made you decide to come?
- Currently, what is your relationship to faith and/or spirituality?

These are large questions, so people may find it easier to discuss this one-on-one. Break into pairs for ten minutes to answer these questions. Then, come back to the large group and share some of your thoughts with each other. Finally, pose a third question to discuss as a group.

- What would you like to get out of this circle?

At the end, suggest a date for the second gathering and ask people to think about whether or not this is something they want to participate in. Ask people to call you if they decide they don't want to participate. Don't be surprised if a couple of people are enthusiastic and then decide later not to join. There are an infinite number of reasons for deciding not to join a group, most of which will not involve you. The timing may be wrong for someone to delve deeper into this topic, or they might not have felt comfortable with the rest of the group. If you are curious and feel comfortable, ask them about it.

your second gathering

The Circle provided me an opportunity to be with people who had the same values and who even shared the same history. The jury is still out about impact. A lot is contingent on what the person does with the action, the knowledge. I've become a stronger person and more of a believer. Before it was easy to say I'm atheist or agnostic even though I wasn't. Because I had not the grounding, the language, or the support to say what I believed. But through all the work and interaction, I now have that strength, and that's made me self-aware, more confident, ready to challenge more things.

— Ed Chaney, member of the First Circle

Ask people to come to the second meeting prepared to go into more detail about their needs and expectations. They can discuss the following statements in pairs:

- This circle will be a success for me if . . .
- The support I need for my journey from this group is . . .
- One thing I might like to share from my own experience is . . .

groups with mission

Church of the Savior, which runs a vast array of social service programs in Washington, D.C., believes strongly in small mission groups. These groups offer one powerful model of what is possible. They have at least two purposes: (1) to serve the surrounding community, and (2) to support the inner and outer lives of those doing the work. In *Servant Leadership, Servant Structures*, the story of Church of the Savior, author Elizabeth O'Connor relays the importance of these groups that:

create safe space in which the members could tell their stories – what has happened to them in the past, what is happening in their hearts in their present life situations, and their dreams, fears and hopes for the future. These groups allow for deeper and deeper levels of trust, which in turn allows people to give more and more of themselves . . . Much more than the confession of our light or our darkness is involved. What is involved is the recovery of love, itself, the communion that is the deepest need of every life, the unlocking of that infinite capacity that each one has to be a friend and to have a friend.

circles of change

Spirit in Action is a national organization working to support the development of a powerful and visionary progressive movement. Their program, Circles of Change, enables people to make valuable connections between spirituality and progressive organizing. The Circles are designed so people will find a space to explore individual concerns, develop group awareness, and contribute to a collective effort for social justice. To do this, Spirit in Action is developing a model that has both structure and flexibility. Each Circle includes work on core elements of:

- community building;

- honoring and welcoming spirit and spiritual practices from all traditions;

- visioning of the world we want to live in and the movement we want to build;

- analysis of the state of the world;

- oppression / liberation work;

- hope, despair, and transformation;

- action.

(continued on next page)

Come back to the large group and share what you learned. You might be tempted to build consensus or even complete agreement. Resist this. You just want to ensure there is enough common ground and interest to move forward. At the end of the gathering, decide when and how often you want to meet, and where. Weekly may be too often, monthly not often enough. You may not find a day or a time that's perfect for everyone. You can start by calling out days of the week, "Who cannot make it on Monday evenings?" (Look for a show of hands.) "Tuesday evenings?" And so forth, until you find a time when most or all people are free. Another method is to pass out a blank calendar of a week (all seven days, each broken down by hour) to everyone and ask them to block off times that do not work for them.

℮ group norms

Early on, take time as a group to develop norms for how the circle will operate. You can let the group suggest its own list or offer the following as a starting place: nonjudgment, openness, space to take risks, attention, permission to challenge, and confidentiality. You can foster more accountability by agreeing that people will call someone if they are going to miss a meeting.

Over time, you want to create an atmosphere of trust that will foster open dialogue. Issues of spirituality and faith are rarely talked about and they are not easy topics to discuss. Some people feel comfortable sharing struggles and joys early on; others take more time.

And every group goes through many stages in its development. As your circle evolves, challenges and conflicts are bound to arise. If they are dealt with openly and honestly, they will help you deepen your relationships with one another. This is part of the learning, but it's easier if you know some of what you can expect. For more guidance, see the Appendix, "Facilitating Spiritual Work with Groups," which outlines other challenges that may arise, as well as possible responses.

This advice comes from Leigh Morgan, an organizational development consultant who was part of a circle for two years:

Talk about what type of community you want the group to be and revisit that periodically. Every time you revisit it, people can deepen their understanding of what that original vision meant and adjust as needed. It's also important to set some norms for membership and be clear about roles and expectations.

I think some people mistake trust for friendship. The absence of trust can be seen when members don't use "I" statements, distance themselves from how they feel about an issue, or don't take ownership of their own thoughts and feelings. When that happens, the group tends to avoid conflict, because no one will really name what is going on. One way to develop trust is to just name what is happening.

I think shared leadership is important. That notion looks and feels different, to different people, but providing opportunity for people to take different leadership roles is important. It's helpful to remember that a group will go through different stages, and there will be times when the energy isn't going to be high. This is to be expected, and it seems like there's a real parallel here with one's own spirituality – knowing there are going to be peaks and valleys and noticing and learning from this instead of fighting it. It's doing at a group level what you hope to do with yourself.

℗ themes for circle gatherings

You can use many of the themes laid out in the book – mindfulness, ritual, stories, and so on – as topics for your gatherings. Below are some additional ideas.

in the beginning

Early on, spend time sharing information about your spiritual or faith backgrounds. Use the following to help people to reflect on their faith or spiritual base and tell a story from their childhood:

- Name two ways in which the spiritual or faith tradition that you grew up with was enlightening or uplifting.
- Name two ways in which it was alienating or disturbing.

objects that tell a story

Read the preface from James Carse, *Breakfast at the Victory: The Mysticism of Ordinary Experience,* which tells a beautiful story about a pair of boots, significant in the lives of two men. Ask everyone to bring an object that tells a story about their life: a major decision, a transition, or a turning point. It can also be something associated with what Carse calls "modest events" – times and experiences whose importance may only be known much later. Go around and share your stories, placing the objects in the center of your meeting space.

photo night

This was offered by Mitty Owens, a member of the First Circle. Have everyone bring photos and/or mementos that reveal something meaningful about their past, family, childhood. Discuss the following questions in relation to your formative years:

- What excited you as a child?
- What "rooted" you and gave you a sense of place or belonging?
- What scared or intimidated you?
- What concerned you?

food

Have everyone bring a dish that is important to their cultural or faith tradition, or one that was important in their family when they were growing up. Before eating, ask each person to explain what they brought and its significance. Ask someone to prepare a blessing for the feast. You might also ask everyone to bring in copies of their recipe for the group.

prayer circles

Ask folks to bring a prayer to share with the group (enough copies for everyone) and mention that it can be one they've written themselves. Begin with a few minutes of silence; then ask folks to talk about prayer and its significance in their lives. Have people share the prayers they brought. These may be read aloud by one person, by the whole group, or silently. Leave a minute or two for silent reflection between each one.

Invite people to share their joys and concerns, so that others may add their prayers and energy. Many Unitarian Universalist Fellowships do this and it always seems to be a time when members feel most connected to one another. You may choose to go around in a circle and let each person share his or her joys and concerns. Again, leave time for everyone to pray about them before going on to the next person; or you may just have one period of silent prayer at the end. Close with a song, reading, or moment of silence. You might also choose to spend a few minutes composing individual prayers.

℮ communal responsibility: what do sacred texts say?

This is a great way for people to get to know other traditions. Divide into groups of three and give each group a passage to study. Suggest that they read the passage out loud first and then consider the primary lesson or message of the passage. How would you apply it today? How have you heard it interpreted? How is it ignored? Come back together and ask each group or person to offer a reflection in light of the passages.

Possible passages to use:

Genesis 47:13–26	land use and economics
Exodus 4:1–31	reluctant leadership
Leviticus 25:1–17	jubilee and redistribution of wealth
Matthew 5:38–48	love your neighbor and your enemies
Luke 10: 29–37	the good Samaritan
Bhagavad Gita 3:8–10	selfless service
Tao Te Ching 29, 30, 31	improving the world, governing, peace

℮ the circle ending

Nothing lasts forever, certainly not your circle. Sometimes it's hard to know if you're hitting a slump or hitting the end. You might go through a low period, full of uncertainty before gaining steam again. If things seem to be slowing down, set aside time to talk about it as a group. Ask people to be honest about their commitment and interest level. The circumstances of our lives change constantly. People may mean well but be unable to continue. You might decide to gather less frequently, for example, quarterly instead of monthly. If it seems that the circle has served its purpose, plan a last gathering as a final celebration. Give everyone a chance to reflect on what the group has given them, what they've learned, what's changed in their life as a result, and what they'll miss.

sangha

There are three jewels in Buddhism: the *Buddha*, which stands for the teacher; the *dharma*, which is the teaching or the way; and the *sangha*, which is the community of practice. Buddhist vows include the promise to take refuge in all three. The Sangha provides a place for collective wisdom to unfold, as it draws together individuals who are on a similar path. Many Buddhists believe that you need the Sangha to support a true practice. In his book An Invitation to Practice Zen (Tuttle, 1989, p.116), Albert Low, remarks *"Few people are able to commit themselves totally to anything; there is always some part of themselves that is left out and that nags, criticizes, or looks desperately around for alternatives. When one practices with a group, there is less likelihood of this problem becoming serious enough to interrupt the practice. To some extent the conflict abates and energy that is normally used in struggling with alternatives can be applied to practice."*

resources for circles . . . .

Baldwin, Christina. *Calling the Circle: The First and Future Culture*. New York: Bantam Books, 1998. Extensive information and stories on calling the circle in various contexts of work and community. http://underwire.msn.com/underwire/social/inprofile/97Profile.asp

Canfield, Jack, Mark Victor Hansen, Maida Rogerson, Martin Rutte, and Tim Clauss. *Chicken Soup for the Soul at Work: 101 Stories of Courage, Compassion and Creativity in the Workplace*. Deerfield Beach, Fla.: Health Communications, 1996. "Chicken Soup" groups have sprung up as a forum for spirit-filled storytelling at work. Contact: 64 Camerada Loop, Santa Fe, N.M. 87505. (505) 466-1512. www.jackcanfield.com

Carnes, Robin Deen, and Sally Craig. *Sacred Circles: A Guide to Creating Your Own Women's Spirituality Group*. San Francisco: HarperCollins, 1998. A look at how women's groups are thriving around the country; full of practical ideas and suggestions for starting your own circle. www.sacredcirclesthebook.com

National Havurah Committee, 7135 Germantown Ave, Philadelphia, Pa. 19119-1842, (215) 248-1335. www.havurah.org

O'Connor, Elizabeth. *Servant Leadership, Servant Structures*. Washington, D.C.: The Servant Leadership School, 1991. www.seekerschurch.org/mission/index.htm

Public Affairs Television. *Talking About Genesis: A Resource Guide*. New York: Doubleday, 1996. A companion book to the public television series, *Genesis: A Living Conversation,* this resource guide includes commentary, reflections, and activities from over thirty different contributors. www.pbs.org/wnet/genesis

Rosen, Brant. "Community as Fellowship: The Reconstructionist Havurah." *The Reconstructionist* 60 (spring 1995), 57–65.

Spirit in Action, 274 North Street, Belchertown, Mass. 01007. (413) 256-4612. www.spiritinaction.net

Study Circles Resource Center, 697 Pomfret Street, Box 203, Pomfret, Conn. 06258. (203) 928-2616. www.studycircles.org

Whitmyer, Claude. *In the Company of Others: Making Community in the Modern World*. New York: Tarcher/Perigee, 1993. An anthology of writings on community: seeking it, making it, finding it, and living it. Includes essays by M. Scott Peck, Ram Dass, Starhawk, Thich Nhat Hanh, and many others.

spiritual discipline . . . .

Leigh Morgan

Leigh Morgan is an organization development consultant with GlaxoSmithKline. She has also worked with the North Carolina Commission on National and Community Service and the Carolina Justice Policy Center, where she staffed anti-death penalty and violence prevention initiatives. Leigh believes in bringing her full self to her work so that she can enable the people and organizations she consults with to reach their full potential.

Across religious traditions there is a common desire to lead an ethical, moral life, to treat yourself and others well, and to find meaning in life. Yet, too often that commonality gets lost, because we focus on our own religious tradition. And, too many religious traditions tend to divide people more than they bring people together. This seems to be antithetical to celebrating the different experiences that people have on the planet. Spiritual groups like circles can serve to build, rather than divide, and can address the problem of narrow-minded religious expression. An intentional spiritual community with people from different backgrounds is so important in this regard – to remember and really experience the joy of different spiritual expressions.

> **In the circle, we created a community with a sense of shared meaning around spiritual- ity and the role of spirituality.**

I joined a circle during a time when I was struggling with the breakup of a relationship and was in a lot of pain. When the circle came along, it was a wonderful opportunity to begin to learn more about myself and what this idea of "spirituality" meant to me – especially in relation to others, the community, and my work. All arrows were pointing me to some kind of intentional spiritual community.

It sounds like an oxymoron, but I've developed a sense of spiritual discipline. Since being in the circle, I have seen a difference in the depth of spiritual experiences that I have on a daily basis. Also, I'm going to church now, and this is a very positive movement for me. I'm actually reclaiming a religious tradition as what I want to make it, whereas before I had some anger and cynicism toward Western religious traditions, especially Christianity. It feels like I've "come out" as a spiritual person. And I find that I am kinder and more compassionate to others and myself on a more regular basis. I stop to look at flowers a lot more. The little things are be- coming more significant in my life. I think life is about little things anyway; paying attention to them is important to me now.

I think all people crave to find meaning and purpose and connection in their daily lives. But so often people don't talk about it, or they're not able to express it, or when they do, they get slammed. In the circle, we created a community with a sense of shared meaning around spirituality and the role of spirituality. Groups are healthy when there's a sense of interdependence – where I, as an individual, can be better because of my relationship with others in the group.

A lot of groups don't get to that point. There may be a high trust level, but members don't take that extra step to say, "How can we, as a group, help each individual be all that he or she can be?" To me, that is ultimate potential for an intentional group or community. The individual epiphanies come when there's a sense of "more than me." At this point, you can imagine that the group is going to take off and do great things. It takes a long time, a lot of trust, and an intentional commitment to define a group in this way. It rarely happens by accident. We sat on the floor a lot, hung out in each other's kitchens, and had a lot of meals together. Little things like that helped to create a good atmosphere.

It sounds like an oxymoron, but I've developed a sense of spiritual discipline.

I try to trust that it is important and relevant to talk about my own experience. So, if there is a difficult situation or conflict, I speak to how I'm experiencing the situation in the moment. That can be such a powerful tool for moving through conflict. Usually other people are feeling the same thing, or my comments help others express something opposite. I think it's a skill that I have that anyone can have. Part of it comes with training and experience, also.

It's been like learning how to ride a bike – you have to practice enough in order to balance. This is a great metaphor for being spiritually centered. You have to spend time at it, fall over, get up again, et cetera. Having others remind me to keep going in my spiritual journey has made such a positive difference in my life.

joining a havurah . . . .

Margot and Ellis Horwitz

My parents, Margot and Ellis Horwitz, commute between suburban Philadelphia and New York City. Ellis is general counsel for Itochu International, a Japanese trading company; Margot is a freelance writer, author, and longtime community volunteer. In 1990, they joined a havurah. *Taken from the Hebrew word for fellowship, a havurah is a small participatory, self-run group of Jews who gather on a regular basis to study, pray, celebrate holidays, support each other, and socialize. My parents'* havurah *is a group of five couples from their synagogue that meet regularly to study the Hebrew Bible and engage with issues evolving in Reform Judaism.*

MH: I grew up in a fairly observant, Conservative Jewish atmosphere where holidays were spent with extended family and friends. We went to Hebrew school and went through confirmation. Most of our Judaism was home-based. I did not go to synagogue every weekend because I spent so much time there in religious school. I lived in an area that was mostly Jewish, though some of my close friends were Catholic, and we each enjoyed each other's holidays.

EH: Our system was a lot more casual. We practiced a variety of Judaism that was sort of made to order. We did not keep kosher (Jewish dietary laws), but if we had bacon, it was eaten on paper plates. Holidays were observed; my mother made a big deal about Passover. Nobody in my family went to synagogue much, but I started going to Hebrew school at a young age. I worked hard on the *bar mitzvah* training, because it was important to my family. After my *bar mitzvah*, there was a modest amount of pressure to continue on to confirmation,[1] but it was clear I wasn't into doing that. As I moved into my teenage years, our observance tapered off even more.

I knew Margot and her family took Judaism a whole lot more seriously than I did. I knew the level of commitment and observance was going to be much higher than what I was used to, and that I was going to make significant compromises to accommodate the things that were important to her. I knew what I was getting into, except, of course, you never know what you're getting into until you're in it.

MH: We tried different synagogues to see where we felt most comfortable. In the beginning, we tried mostly Conservative synagogues. Then we went to a *bar mitzvah* at Main Line Reform Temple, and Dad said, "I feel good here," and we never left. Even if left to my own devices, I'm not sure I would have pushed for a Conservative synagogue. The Reform movement was very into social action, and that gripped me. It was less traditional than my background, but Dad was into it, and I was, too.

> I thought a smaller group would be complementary to what I was getting out of the synagogue ... I have more of a sense of the five books of Moses and how important they were and continue to be ... The *havurah* has deepened my Judaism.

EH: Mom was approached by a friend about being in a *havurah*, and I was very cool to the idea. The people were all very heavy-duty Jews, and I didn't even know what a spice box[2] was until I saw one at the *havurah*. I looked at it as an unpleasant duty to perform to please Mom. As time went by, I got to know the people better, I got to like them, and I found many of the evening's readings and discussions stimulating and enjoyable. There is discipline involved. To the extent that you want to maintain your self-respect, you feel the need to prepare. So I make an honest effort to do the readings ahead of time.

I don't find synagogue particularly interesting. I only go on the high holidays, maybe two Friday nights a year. It's something you do because of tradition or obligation, or some combination. It doesn't contain nearly as much stimulation as the *havurah*, which is fairly self-directed. Everybody has a say so about what we're going to do next time. We operate by veto. I feel like most of the time we're doing stuff the vast majority has agreed it would be good to do.

MH: Main Line Reform Temple is a big place, and even though I have been involved (on the board, and so forth), I thought a smaller group would be complementary to what I was getting

[1] a ceremony at age sixteen when Jews "confirm" their allegiance to Judaism
[2] used during the Havdalah service which marks the end of Shabbat

out of the synagogue. I don't think it takes the place of the synagogue, because I feel there is a place in any Jewish person's life to be part of a larger religious group. I enjoy having the Torah read as a community; the whole liturgical aspect is important. Sitting in services, it opens my eyes to Judaism in a different way. I have more of a sense of the five books of Moses and how important they were and continue to be. There are a lot of great truths in the Torah. The *havurah* has deepened my Judaism.

EH: It has resulted in my spending a lot more time thinking about, reading about, and discussing topics of a Jewish nexus than I ever had before. It may be connected with the modest and sporadic interest I have in the early history of Middle Eastern peoples. I can't see myself having been a founding member or exerting any effort to assemble it. Other people said, "We're interested in building something." That they have expended the energy to form this and really keep it going and have such a strong commitment is pretty fascinating. And, it's fascinating that someone like me, who felt so little appeal in the beginning, has come a ways toward feeling like it's got value.

> Other people said, "We're interested in building something." That they have expended the energy to form this and really keep it going and have such a strong commitment is pretty fascinating. And, it's fascinating that someone like me has come a ways toward feeling like it's got value.

circles.

celebration

Celebration is a forgetting of ego, of problems,
of difficulties, in order to remember the common base
that makes another's sufferings mine
and in order to imagine a relief of that suffering.
There can be no compassion without celebration
and there will be no authentic celebration
that does not result in increased compassionate energies.

~ Matthew Fox

what is celebration?

People, groups, and communities need celebration. It is hard for people to endure, to be strong for one another, without it. Celebrations fill us with hope and remind us of the broader arc of life. When we celebrate, we celebrate each other. Birthdays, weddings, anniversaries, even funerals are a celebration of someone's life. The world livens up when we find ways to celebrate graduations, the completion of major projects, or a new job. At the same time, celebration reminds us of the breadth and depth of the community around us. Some days, struggle can seem near-constant and the high points feel too far spread out. Celebration is a forgetting of ego, of problems, of difficulties. Rather than wait for those "mountaintop" experiences to present themselves to us, we can actually help create them with three simple ingredients: respect for ourselves, love for others, and a desire to create some common expression of joy.

Our spirits may have a lot in common, but our journeys on earth vary widely. As we worship together, we see on an intimate level how another person experiences spirit or praises God, then the potential for joint action becomes limitless. Even commemorating hard or tragic circumstances is a way to share something of ourselves and gain strength in the process. The task of transforming the world is rooted in faith, and it will take more than just one faith to achieve the changes many of us are seeking.

turning point

In 1995, I convened my first interfaith celebration. The need for this kind of gathering was intuitive, and mid-December seemed to be an appropriate backdrop. Growing up Jewish, I often felt relegated to the sidelines during this time of year; no doubt this is true for others who do not celebrate Christmas. More importantly, I was having trouble reconnecting with what I love about that time of year, all of the festivity, the lights, the good cheer. I was tired of getting swept into the frenzy of gift buying, cookie making, and housecleaning. As I thought about people preparing for their own particular holiday – Christmas, Hanukkah, Ramadan, Kwanzaa, and the winter solstice – I wondered what it would be like if people from different traditions attempted to celebrate together, in the context of both our commonality and our differences.

As I thought more about creating an interfaith celebration, I became aware what a leap of faith it was. I'm not sure I'd ever even *been* to an interfaith service before. I began by asking others if they would consider ways they might participate. Some were understandably perplexed by the idea or at least unsure what it was I was proposing. A few agreed to take the leap with me. I found space at a community center, sent out an invitation with minimal explanation, and then set on the task of developing the event.

For weeks, I researched prayers from a myriad of religious and spiritual traditions. It was the best way I knew of deepening my own understanding of what might be possible. Armed with a folder three inches thick, I realized the event needed a theme to have any kind of coherence. I kept returning to the haunting beauty of the winter solstice. Since ancient times, the returning of the light on the longest night of the year has been marked with great celebration, and this theme is echoed in many of the other winter holidays. I began to craft a program around this notion, blending prayers and poems from many sacred traditions and rituals designed by teams of intrepid individuals who had agreed to share from their own tradition.

Setting up the space the afternoon of the celebration, I began to notice my nervousness. What would happen? I thought. I honestly had no idea. I took refuge in the circle of chairs I was setting up and marveled at the simplicity of the candles and stones in the center. People began to arrive, some of whom I knew and some I didn't. We added more chairs. I gave a short welcome, explained that the prayers printed in the program would be read by whomever felt moved to speak at that moment, and we began. When we got to the first prayer, there was an awkward silence. And then someone spoke up, reading the printed prayer in a confident tone. Two friends presented the principles of Kwanzaa, while another one drummed. One participant spontaneously led us in a dance; another offered an impromptu song. We lit the Hanukkah menorah. As we drank cider and munched homemade desserts afterwards, I marveled at what can transpire when people come together in a prayerful and playful way.

This celebration has grown and changed over time. One year we had a large group of young people from a local church youth group; their voices added a vibrant energy. We do more singing now, and we have incorporated movement as well. Some elements have stayed constant. The service always includes a candlelight prayer ceremony. As the participants light the candle of the person next to them, they speak their joys and concerns for the world into the circle. And we always close with the singing of "Amazing Grace."

? questions for reflection . . . .

What kinds of celebrations exist in your life?

What do you love best about celebrating?

Have you ever been to a celebration that you would consider nonreligious, and had a spiritual experience?

When, if ever, have you worshipped in a different faith tradition or been a part of an interfaith celebration?

What moved you about it?

℗ your own footing: preparing for interfaith celebration

Recall whether you have any memories of sharing a holiday, worship service, or celebration with someone whose spiritual or faith background was different from your own. Do you remember what it was like to be with this person's family or in their community of worship? You might recollect how you felt, what was new and strange and what felt familiar.

Are you interested in sharing worship with someone of a different faith now? See if you can attend a worship service or celebration with someone of a different faith background, and invite them to accompany you to your place of worship if you have one. Enhance your visit with preparation. Write down what you are curious about, what you have been intrigued or perplexed by. Read some books on the faith or spiritual tradition and make a list of the questions you have. See if you can find the answers before you go. Imagine what the visit might be like. Recall other times you have felt uncomfortable or on the margin of a community. Consider what you were raised to believe about people of other faiths and what, if anything, you still believe to be true.

℗ an opportunity to rejoice

What events or transitions do you already celebrate? What others could you imagine marking with a gathering? My brother planned a large party when he finished the final draft of a novel he had been working on for four years. Instead of waiting for it to be published, he took the opportunity to thank the people who have helped edit it and gave everyone else a chance to see what he had been working on. It was a way of respecting the time he had put in and the support he'd gotten from other people. He says:

What about the day that, say, Modigliani painted Jeanne Hebuterne? Did he sell it for three million dollars? No, he had a glass of red wine. He sat there and he felt good.

> *There have been people who have given hours upon hours to my manuscript and become indelible parts in it: their words literally come from*

the mouths of the characters. Then there have been people who have nurtured me during the writing, partially by asking me how it was going during this very solitary practice, and partly by making me laugh, letting me play with their kids, teaching me things I did not know that became the model for how exciting learning can be.

Some of them will like certain parts better than others. Some people will take their copy of the manuscript home (as a parting gift) and put it in the corner for eight years. Some will read it the next weekend, possibly because they don't have small children.

When, how, where, and who publishes my writing comes second to my having written. To me, celebrating means taking the occasion to say what's been important in my life, and to share the whole arc of that experience with others, not as a self-important ego basking in the limelight, but not as a mute little soldier, either – in real, clear spiritual terms as an equal, who was for this time an engaged artist and a channel.

℮ seasonal celebration: autumn equinox

Many groups plan celebrations to mark the seasons. One circle decided we wanted to celebrate the transition from fall to winter, often a depressing time for many people. We began by brainstorming a list of ideas: do something with pumpkins, string colored yarn in the trees, dance, weave together, build energy we can store for the winter, chant, drum, use leaves, see winter as a time of positive retreat, make a dream catcher, welcome the darkness, praise, harvest, focus on the heat of the earth and its warmth, bring fall foods to share. In the end, our celebration went like this.

As we entered the space, everyone was asked, "What do you leave behind?" This was a chance to let go of something that would no longer serve us as we moved into a new season. Silently we visited four altars that we'd set up – one for each of the four elements: fire, air, water, and earth. Each altar was a table covered in cloth holding objects symbolic of that element. The room was lit by candles. Then, we honored the four directions by turning to each and naming its qualities.

We gathered in a circle, and each of us spoke about what we were thankful for at this time of year. After a few minutes in individual silent prayer, one member led us in a guided meditation on darkness and light. The meditation emphasized our connection to the earth, the coming fall, and how winter could be a time of

come sunday . . . come saturday

Interfaith celebrations can be held as part of related events. stone circles has held many interfaith gatherings at conferences, for example. Once, we collaborated with the Bridges Project at the Center for Documentary Studies to convene an interfaith celebration in conjunction with a photography exhibit. "Come Sunday" was a photographic pilgrimage to the Black churches of Brooklyn. Held on a Saturday after the exhibit opened, we called the celebration, "Come Sunday . . . Come Saturday." We gathered on the grass outside of the center. The celebration consisted of readings, prayers, songs, and movement from Baha'i, Buddhism, Christianity, Hinduism, Islam, and Judaism, as well as original poetry. After the celebration, people had a chance to view the photographs.

positive retreat. Afterwards we talked about our experience with the meditation in groups of three.

Next, we created a dream catcher together. One member had already cut a piece of grapevine and created the outer circle. With brightly colored yarn, each of us wove part of the dream catcher and then we tied a piece of ribbon we'd brought with us onto the edges. We decided the dream catcher would be present with us at all of our subsequent gatherings. We closed with drumming and singing, and finished by feasting on food to accompany the time of year: squash, apples, pumpkins, cider, heavy bread, and soup.

℮ interfaith celebrations

Interfaith celebration is a particularly unique way to bring groups together. It does not take the place of single-faith worship or individual spiritual practice; it enhances it. Gathering people who believe in a different idea of God or who read different sacred texts or pray differently can open doors of understanding if respect is there. Seeing how another human being experiences spirit, faith, or God can deepen our relationship with and pride in our own tradition or path. This can be particularly revolutionary given how often cross-religious communication ends up as a divisive or even violent enterprise.

Interfaith celebration requires a willingness to move from participant to observer and back again to participant. If, during interfaith worship, a Christian begins to praise Jesus, a Hindu or a Jew can become an observer, taking that opportunity to learn more about someone else's faith tradition. If I recite a prayer in Hebrew, non-Jews in the room may not participate, but they can listen and perhaps understand more about Judaism. And, in collective silence during an interfaith celebration, each of us can find our own expression of God, our own words of prayer, our own acts of praise. It provides space for diversity within an atmosphere of unity.

If you're part of a group that wants to organize an interfaith celebration, you might begin by allowing everyone to become familiar with each other's faith. You can do that by asking everyone to bring something from their faith or cultural background to share. It might be an object that tells a story, a prayer or song, a ritual in which everyone can participate, or something else entirely. Set up the room so everyone can sit in a circle. Facilitate the sharing Quaker-style: silence sets the tone and then individuals can take their turn sharing whenever they feel moved.

Another useful step is to help people clarify and understand what they mean by certain terms. The first piece is done individually. Tell the group you are going to write a word on the board or a large piece of paper, and you want them to write, think, or draw stream of consciousness on what the word means to them. They will have a couple of minutes for each word. Write only one word at a time:

Faith   *Spirituality*   *Religion*   *God*   *Justice*

After you've gone through all five words, ask people to come back and discuss what they wrote, word by word. Remind people that there is no right and wrong here; they are here to learn from each other's definitions and to notice similarities and differences.

organizing an interfaith celebration ~ six steps

1. set goals

Think about your primary reasons for convening this type of gathering. Do you want to create common ground between various faiths? Is it important to involve a wide spectrum of people? Do you want to focus on educating folks about various religious and spiritual traditions? Do you want to make sure the celebration is participatory?

2. planning group

Find people from a range of faith and spiritual backgrounds. Having a clergy member present can be great, as long as they are clear about the intent of the service. Clergy or others who have had experience with interfaith dialogue or worship will be particularly helpful. It's also great to involve folks who have a celebratory presence and those who are never afraid to offer a spontaneous song, dance, or ritual. And, you will need folks to help set up, greet people, hand out programs, assist with refreshments, and clean up.

3. content

Do some brainstorming on content as a group. Ask folks what is most special to them about worship and if they've ever been to an interfaith celebration. You may even want to lead a short guided meditation, asking everyone to sit quietly and think back to a meaningful worship experience they've had. Ask people what they most want to see included in the service. Do they have a favorite prayer or know of a dance that a large group of people can do?

The more interactive the service, the better. People in the planning group can collect readings, poetry, prayers, and songs. Encourage people to write something themselves, and to look in likely and unlikely places for inspirational passages. If you're planning a lot of music, you might consider inviting everyone to bring a percussion instrument. In addition to those in the planning group, you may know people who are committed to their religion or spiritual practice and who may want to share something from their tradition – poetry, a passage from a sacred text, a song, or movement.

4. logistics

The location will set the tone for the event. Consider a religiously neutral site like a school, dance studio, art gallery, university commons room, recreation center, library, or community center. Any space can be transformed with flowers, material, sacred objects, and candles. Consider seating possibilities and make sure there is a rain site nearby if you're planning an outdoor location.

Serving food afterwards gives people a chance to meet others with whom they've just shared the experience. Ask people on the planning group to make or bring desserts and light snacks.

5. invitations and programs

Invitations to your celebration can be as simple as a postcard. Make sure to include all the vital information: time, date, location, directions if the place is difficult to find, a note if refreshments will be provided, and a phone number to call for more information. Explain if you want folks to bring anything, like a candle or an instrument. And if you are going to charge or ask for a suggested donation, make sure to note that on the invitation.

A program is a great addition to the event itself and serves as a reminder for people long after the celebration is over. Include the text of the readings and songs so people will have these as part of their own collection. The program does not have to be anything fancy, unless you have a design/graphic arts person in the planning group who wants to work on it.

6. the day of

Take time before the celebration to collect your thoughts, maybe with a walk or a meditation. Give yourself plenty of time to set up and get ready. If you are serving food, make sure you have what you need. Ask everyone who is participating to get there at least a half-hour early, more if they need to set up anything. Provide a table or space in the center of the room where people can put any ceremonial objects they are going to use. If your location is hard to find, post signs in the appropriate places. Run through the program with everyone and make sure folks have what they need.

℮ celebrating a cause: the children's sabbath

Many communities and organizations now use celebration as a way to heighten awareness around a specific issue. For example, since 1991 the Children's Defense Fund (CDF) has sponsored the National Observance of Children's Sabbaths to promote education and health for children. They are a unique opportunity for interfaith and interdenominational worship. On the same weekend in October, tens of thousands of congregations across the country – mosques, churches, and synagogues – recommit themselves to the needs of children. These religious institutions design a special worship service, organize activities with service agencies, or convene educational programs. The goal is to inspire people of faith to take long-term actions to protect the health and well-being of children through outreach, direct service, or advocacy. CDF provides organizing assistance and resource materials for those interested in participating, including an outline for a sample interfaith service.

℮ vigils: the solemn side of celebration

Vigils of prayer and silence are powerful ways to pay tribute. They help communities resist hopelessness and deal with grief. In communities all over the country, there are examples of people coming together in spirit – to face and fight levels of violence or to cope with tragedy. For example:

- Many neighborhoods have organized prayer vigils as part of their efforts to fight gangs and drug activity. Interfaith groups now also hold vigils at murder sites or before a prisoner is to be killed with the death penalty. Religious and lay people come together to bring a sense of peace and hope to their community.

- Take Back the Night marches give survivors of sexual violence, and their allies, a chance to walk in the dark, with support around them. Marches often include stops along the way for poetry, testimony, chanting, or ritual.

- When hate crimes were on the rise in Germany in the early 1990s, thousands of citizens took to the streets for a silent candlelight vigil. People up and down the East Coast gathered for two minutes of silence a day during the summer of 1995 to offer prayers for peace in Bosnia.

The Annual Interfaith Worship and Healing Service of the Sabbath of Domestic Peace is cochaired by a minister from the Philadelphia Baptist Association and the executive director of the Board of Rabbis of Greater Philadelphia. Sponsored by a different faith tradition every year, the Sabbath of Domestic Peace is an interdisciplinary, interfaith coalition that encourages and supports the involvement of religious congregations in the effort to prevent and reduce domestic violence. The Sabbath of Domestic Peace was started in 1995 by SaraKay Smullens, a family therapist, and Mimi Rose, the head of the Sexual Assault and Domestic Violence Unit in the District Attorney's office.

resources for celebrations . . . .

Alternatives. *To Celebrate: Reshaping Holidays and Rites of Passage*. Ellenwood, Ga.: Alternatives, 1987. Alternatives is a nonprofit organization providing resources for responsible living and celebrating. Contact: Alternatives for Simple Living, P.O. Box 2857, Sioux City, Iowa 51106. (800) 821-6153. www.simpleliving.org

Beversluis, Joel. *A Source Book for the Earth's Community of Religions*. Grand Rapids, Mich.: CoNexus Press, 1995. Comprehensive guide includes reference materials, reflections, prayers, essays, and analysis. www.silcom.com/~origin/csb2.html

Budapest, Zsuzsanna E. *The Grandmother of Time*. San Francisco: Harper & Row, 1979. A book of celebrations, spells, and sacred objects for every month of the year. Draws on goddess spirituality. www.zbudapest.com

Children's Defense Fund. *Childrens Sabbath Resource Manual*. Washington, D.C.: Children's Defense Fund. This guide to organizing a Children's Sabbath is published yearly and available for Catholic, Jewish, and Protestant congregations. Contact: Religious Affairs Division, CDF, 25 E Street, N.W., Washington, D.C. 20001. (202) 662-3693. www.childrensdefense.org/moral-children-sabbath.htm

Eck, Diana. *Encountering God: A Spiritual Journey from Bozeman to Banaras*. Boston: Beacon Press, 1993. One woman's beautiful account of journey from her Christian childhood in Montana to the East. Eck is the originator of the Pluralism Project.

Magida, Arthur J., ed. *How to Be a Perfect Stranger: A Guide to Etiquette in other People's Religious Ceremonies, Vol. 1 and 2*. Woodstock, Vt.: Jewish Lights Publishing, 1996. All basic questions are answered here: custom, attire, behavior. The first volume covers the ceremonies of all the major religious traditions; the second volume, edited by Magida and Stuart M. Matlins, covers those religions and denominations with smaller memberships. www.jewishlights.com/books/397.html

National Conference for Community and Justice, originally founded as the National Conference for Christians and Jews, promotes understanding and respect among all races, religions, and cultures. They sponsor interfaith dialogues and publish a yearly listing of major holidays from different faith traditions. Contact: 71 Fifth Avenue, Suite 1000; New York, N Y 10003. (212) 206-0006. www.nccj.org.

Pluralism Project, Harvard University, 201 Vanserg Hall, 25 Francis Avenue, Cambridge, Mass. 02138. (617) 496-2481. www.fas.harvard.edu/~pluralsm/

Sabbath of Domestic Peace. www.angelfire.com/sd/sabbathdomesticpeace

Teish, Luisah. *Jump Up: Good Times throughout the Seasons with Celebrations from Around the World*. Berkeley, Calif.: Conari, 2000. Folks tales, wisdom, and stories of celebrations and festivals from all over the world, with a special focus on Africa and the Carribean. www.jambalayaspirit.org

————. *Carnival of the Spirit: Seasonal Celebrations and Rites of Passage.* New York: HarperCollins, 1994.

Tobias, Michael, Jane Morrison, and Bettina Gray, eds. *A Parliament of Souls: Conversations with 28 Spiritual Leaders from Around the World.* San Francisco: KQED Books, 1995. A companion to the twenty-six-part television series of the same name, the interviews in this book offer insight into a range of personal faith journeys and the dilemmas and truths that unite them. www.dnai.com/~gray/Pos.html

celebrating faith and neighborhood . . . .

Arun and Sunanda Gandhi

Sunanda and Arun Gandhi run the M. K. Gandhi Institute for Nonviolence in Memphis, Tennessee. Born in South Africa and the grandson of Mohandas K. "Mahatma" Gandhi, Arun was working as a journalist in India when he met Sunanda, the nurse who cared for him after surgery. The institute, which they cofounded in 1991, provides training and education on the theory and practice of nonviolence.

AG: I came from a really strange spiritual background. Grandfather believed very early in his life that the only way we can bring peace to the people is by bringing unity in religions, bringing all the religions closer together. Which did not mean that he wanted them all to become one, but that there should be respect and an understanding for each other's religions. There's a wonderful saying from his writings, "A friendly study of all the religions is the sacred duty of every individual." And he emphasized the word "friendly." He made that friendly study of all the major religions of the world and incorporated from each one of them what he thought was useful in his daily prayer service.

SG: Not only prayer service, but in his life.

AG: His beliefs, he made it a part of his mission. I grew up with prayer services every morning and evening, including hymns from every major religion of the world: Christianity, Islam, Judaism, Buddhism, Hinduism, all of them. We had the prayers in a room or under a tree where hundreds of people gathered to participate. That's what we have followed, respect for all the different religions.

> Grandfather believed very early in his life that the only way we can bring peace to the people is by bringing all the religions closer together.

SG: I actually grew up with a very traditional Indian spiritual upbringing. It was ritualistic and bound by certain traditions. But somewhere deep down in me, there was a reckoning consciousness for service. Although in the traditional India taking a profession like nursing was looked down upon – girls from good standing did not go into a service profession like that – I chose to go into it, and it was one step against the tradition of a very well-blessed family. From there on, I started realizing the leaning of my heart, of serving people and being with them. I met Arun and we married. Then I saw people in his family, and all the people who came into our lives, their dedication to service, total dedication. It made me realize *that* was my path, my spirituality, my way of understanding religion.

AG: We need to understand what we mean by spirituality. We have a very limited notion of this, and we mix it up with religion. My own perspective of religion and spirituality is that religion is more ritualistic. Spirituality to me is something that goes above religion, where all the different belief systems meet, and they respect and understand each other. When we reach that level of spirituality, where we can appreciate and accept each other, then we are on the right way of serving.

But as long as we get bogged down in religious rituals and insist that our way of life is the only way and no other can be accommodated, then we are not really practicing religion. All the scriptures talk about love, compassion, understanding. That's the foundation of every scripture in the world. And yet we don't incorporate that in our lives. We have misinterpreted many of the religions. The most important thing is to translate that religion or scripture into our lives, into our daily actions. Not just go and mouth it two or three times a day in church or temple or mosque or wherever and then forget about it.

SG: We do all these things, the rituals and the practices, like robots. We follow them because we're so used to it. We don't try to shake ourselves out of it. If we look around, we'll find much more to life, if we seek that love and that understanding. But we have already made up our minds about people. Just because someone looks different than us or has different ways of walking, we have preconceived notions without even trying to start a dialogue and find out, "If you are different, why you are different?" Once we start to do that, it becomes so apparent that what seems to be different is really not different.

> **Spirituality to me is something that goes above religion, where all the different belief systems meet, and they respect and understand each other.**

If we are told that the flight is cancelled or delayed, you get into the line, people rush from behind and get in front of you. That's the time when you start wondering, "What is happening, now?" And your beliefs, for that split second, start getting a little doubtful in your mind. Then you try to think, as much as you are stressed, the other people are stressed, and they have their own ways. And sometimes you try to smile your way out of it, or laugh. Or sometimes you let the stress get hold of you. But these are normal human reactions.

AG: I think it's an ongoing process. It's not something you can learn within a week, or even ten years. It's a process that has to go on throughout your life. And every day is a new learning day. Every night is a new learning night. A lot depends on how open you keep your mind and how willing you are to learn from other people. If you close your mind and don't have any willingness to accept other influences, you stagnate. There was this very powerful lesson that Grandfather taught me. He said, "As you grow up, your mind should be like a room with many open windows. Let the breeze flow in from all of them, but refuse to be blown away by any one of them." We need to absorb things from all different sources, keep whatever we find useful, and grow from it.

You must look at yourself like a farmer. A farmer goes out and plants the seeds in his fields, and then he waits and prays for those seeds to germinate so that he gets a good crop. What we are doing today is planting those seeds, and we hope those seeds will germinate and we'll get a good crop.

SG: You can help the natural environment and the natural surroundings, like a farmer, to allow that seed to germinate, and not just leave it to its own fate. That little seedling needs a helping hand. Be a support system.

AG: The important thing to remember is that we can't change the whole world, but we can change ourselves and we can influence people around us, so we should concentrate on that. When we try to change the world, or take up big issues, that's when we get burned out. Set yourself goals that can be achieved and achieve those goals, and then move to another goal. Take it one step at a time. The tendency I find in most young people is that they want to change the whole world. I've noticed that most young people are always looking at political conflicts all over the world, but not many people seem to focus on economic conflicts or social conflicts that are going on, even in their own neighborhoods.

SG: I'll cite an example. In earlier days, we found that there were many neighborhood watches. The crime situation in Memphis is really very, very grave. Unfortunately, it ranks sixth in the nation in crime, and everybody is worried about it. We were going to troubled neighborhoods and talking with people, just having dialogue with them. We said, "You have neighborhood watches, and you have neighborhood meetings where you talk about all the problems that you have. We have attended those neighborhood meetings, and people are getting frustrated and tired of them. Slowly the meetings are becoming smaller and smaller."

We suggested, why not let us have a street party? Now, once or twice in a month we have a potluck party. Everybody comes out, brings something, has fun, and plays games. Children are there, and so are the next-door neighbors. We get a chance to know who they are, what they are doing, what their family situation is. In the beginning people were a little doubtful about it, but recently we have found that they're really having wonderful results. People have started knowing each other; people have started taking an interest in one another instead of just gossiping about each other.

> Why not let us have a street party? Now, once or twice in a month we have a potluck party. People have started knowing each other; people have started taking interest in one another instead of just gossiping about each other.

AG: When we get too bogged down in problems and negativity, we become very oppressed and depressed, and we don't know what answers to find. We need to have a more positive attitude toward things

In applying nonviolence to our personal lives, we have to learn two things. The first is to use our anger constructively, rather than destructively. We have to find ways of channeling that energy properly. And the second is to build relationships with people that are based on respect and understanding, not on selfishness. That's not a relationship; it only adds to the conflict and violence. We have to learn how to have relationships with each other because we are human beings; we are part of one whole. People in the West tend to believe that we are independent individuals, that we can do whatever we like, and that's our business. But we are not independent; we are interdependent, and we have to look at ourselves as part of a whole big picture. We are all part of this whole creation, interlinked with each other.

SG: Many of the people who are on this quest for nonviolence help me understand that it is the truth all of us are after. Truth has many facets. And yet there is only one truth that we are all seeking.

festival for the earth . . . .

Richard Goldberg

Richard Goldberg holds a doctorate in biomedical engineering and teaches at the University of North Carolina at Chapel Hill. He develops assistive devices for people with disabilities in the local community, and he previously did research on echolocation used by bats. Richard is also on the board of directors for the Haw River Assembly, a grassroots environmental organization, and he's been a Big Brother to Demario since 1992. He lives with his wife, Edie, and son, Benjamin surrounded by forests in Chapel Hill, North Carolina.

I've always been an environmentalist. But it's through the Haw River Festival where I started to view nature in a more spiritual way. The festival is an environmental education program for fourth graders that seeks to go beyond traditional formats by establishing connections with and an appreciation for nature – just by having them notice things with all their senses. And at the same time it builds community among the volunteers.

The fourth graders get to use their senses. It was really apparent last week, because the river was so loud and if you put on your "deer ears" and faced the river you heard all river, and if you turned around, you heard all birds. And the kids found, without prompting, a snake that was pretty well camouflaged. Kids got excited over every turtle, cicada, and other living thing they saw and heard. I'd hoped they would take that away with them, and I think they did.

> I believe all living things are connected, and all living things are connected to nonliving things.

In some ways it isn't political, because you're only working with one kid or ten kids at a time, but I feel it *is* political, because you're trying to change the way people view the earth. I help plan the festival, and I'm also on the board. It challenges me to do things I've never done before, so I learn a lot about myself, like how to get up in front of one hundred and twenty kids and sing. It's a real positive, supportive atmosphere where every person, no matter what the age, is important. I brought Demario, and for someone like him, who had been kicked out of school for insubordination numerous times, it's really important to get all the positive reinforcement.

The atmosphere lets people experiment and try new things that they've never done before. On a practical level, it's why the program runs as well as it does. There are a number of volunteers who had come to the festival as fourth graders. If you ask them what they remember, they'll say they remember some games and playing with clay. But it affected them on a deeper level, which is why they return to the festival as volunteers.

I believe all living things are connected, and all living things are connected to nonliving things. There's some force that makes that connection. Maybe "related" is the wrong word, but they are a reflection of each other. They're sort of in parallel and what works on a spiritual level will also work on a scientific level. From a spiritual level, I believe all things are related, and the science agrees with that.

celebration.

place

I believe in beauty.
I believe in stones and water, air and soil,
people and their future and their fate.

~ Ansel Adams

Free spaces are settings between private lives and large-scale institutions
where ordinary citizens can act with dignity, independence and vision . . .
environments in which people are able to learn a new self-respect,
a deeper and more assertive group identity, public skills,
and values of cooperation and civic virtue.

~ Sara M. Evans and Harry C. Boyte, Free Spaces

what is place?

The connection between human beings and the places we find ourselves in is reciprocal; one reflects the other. The places where we live and work and play and gather shape our levels of happiness, productivity, distress, comfort, and tranquility. Everything about these places – from the quality of the air and light to the colors and textures to the level of noise and the degree of inspiration – influences our capacity for thought, rest, and relationship.

In addition to our homes, work spaces, and other gathering spaces, we all pass through the metaphorical public square – however we define it, whether we give it a passing glance or a long look. I believe it is this public space that most greatly impacts our notions of community, of connectedness, of what is possible. When cities and towns fall into physical decay and disrepair, so do our spirits. In many areas, public places are rapidly disappearing or being developed for exclusive use. Space is what allows us to come together for a common purpose. We cannot hope to build strong, loving communities without places where people can gather, talk, exchange, scheme, learn, plan, and celebrate.

turning point

When I was a kid, the ocean was the safest, most life-giving place I knew. I vividly recall the sting of being left out on the playground or teased for my kinky hair. What saved me on those days was my affinity for place. I would close my eyes tight and picture the beach. I would conjure up the spray of the blue-gray waves and the feeling of tiny pebbles and shells between my toes. Somehow I knew that visualizing this place of peace – the chief place I felt a sense of wholeness or completion – would ease the inevitable pain of separation from my friends. Where healthy visualization ends and escapism begins, I do not know. But I do know that both my sense of place and my ability to honor that connection was a great gift, uncovered early and still a valued resource in my life. Long after I forget a person's name, I will recall the nuances of the place where we met or had an inspiring conversation. I can be in a place one time and recall scores of details about it years later. I can find my way around cities I have not been in for over a decade.

I have a great affection for the place I live now – Durham, North Carolina. This is almost ironic considering that I spend about one-third of the year on the road. But with all this traveling, regardless of where I've been and with whom, there has not been a time when I wasn't relieved to see the green trees and Carolina red clay from the window of my airplane seat. I love Durham for all that it is – culturally rich, reasonably progressive, friendly, and very, very real – and for all that it isn't – too fast, too expensive, too full of itself. I love that I can barely go anywhere without seeing somebody I know (though I do crave some anonymity now and then).

And I love how the past, the present, and the future are so closely connected. You can see this in so many places, even on a road like Alston Avenue. Alston starts out as a busy four-lane road in the neighborhood surrounding North Carolina Central University, Durham's historically Black university. It quickly becomes a two-lane back road, winding its way past storefront churches, groves of pine trees, boarded-up gas stations and thriving communities. After a few more miles, signs of the New South appear. There is land available for sale, as well as buildings with names like Tricenter South and West Park Corporate Center. These complexes sit squarely across the street from old homes and uncultivated fields, interspersed with signs for barbecue and flower shops.

When I am home in Durham, I tend to stay within a two-mile radius of my home. I hunker down in the retreat atmosphere of my apartment and often walk to work. And I have a few of what Ray Oldenburg would call "third places," those beyond work and home, where I meet up with friends. My local grocery store seems to double for a hangout and there are a couple of great places to sit and drink a cup of coffee. Mostly, it seems, Durham is just a good place to be.

 questions for reflection . . . .

What places are central to your life?

When you encounter stress, where do you envision yourself being? How about when you are lonely?

How would you describe your relationship to these places? To place in general?

What makes you feel connected to where you live?

your own footing: places that matter

Everybody has places that matter, even if we've only been there once or twice in our lives. These are the places where we feel most alive, most like ourselves. They are places of inspiration. Make a list of these places for yourself – the places that matter. Notice if they are close or far from where you live, inside or outside, accessible or hard to get to. Find a map of the town or city where you live and post it on the wall. Mark the places you identified on the map; then add those places that are far away.

Most people have at least one place that was an important part of their childhood, whether it was a bedroom shared with a sibling, the creek nearby, the playroom at a house of worship, or a friend's backyard. Through words or images, reflect on these spaces that were important in your childhood. Consider the spaces – inside and out – that had the most influence on you. Who else was a part of these places? Were any of them a secret? Why?

Do you have places you tend to overromanticize, like a place you've been on vacation or one connected to a special occasion? Is there a place you have tried to use as escape, only to find that whatever you were attempting to leave behind came right along with you?

℮ everyday places: home and work

We spend significant time in the places where we live and work, but how much ownership do we feel over these spaces? If we can begin to create places that mirror our values and express our desires, we'll be more likely to create community places that do the same.

Draw a diagram or map of the *living space* in which you spend the most time. It might be your bedroom, a living room, or even an entire apartment or house. Do this from memory, when you are not in the space. Think about what's most important about this space to you. What do you like the most about it? What do you like the least?

Take the diagram and stand in the middle of the space. What did you remember to include in your diagram? What did you forget? Look around. What is the space set up for? What are the activities this room/space invites? Now, think about how you and/or your partner, family, or housemates use time at home. Write down the three activities that are most important to you and the three activities that consume the most of your time at home, if they're different. How does the room arrangement match up with how you spend your time? There may be some real differences between what you *think* you should have versus what you really *want*. Are there gaps between how you use this space and what it feels most conducive to? For example, maybe you have a guest room that rarely gets used and you've been craving a place to work or create at home. Do you need to change anything to greater align this space with its primary purposes?

Repeat this exercise for your *work space*. Is it a desk, a cubicle, an office, a classroom, a house, something entirely different? Start with your own space, realizing you may have minimal control over what the larger place looks and feels like. Brainstorm ways to develop a relationship with shared space such that it can feel like your own.

℮ creating sacred space

We create sacred space to bring our spirit into harmony with life
in our daily environment. When our mind is clear and we are fully present to life
and the world around us, we are in sacred space. And creating sacred space, by ritually
changing and rearranging our outer environment, is a means both of focusing our mind –
becoming present to the sacred, which is always within us –
and of anchoring and aligning the flow of Spirit in our physical environment.

~ *Margo Anand,* The Art of Everyday Ecstasy

There are many ways to transform "ordinary" space at home or at work into space that feels sacred. Think about what changes the feel or look of a space to you. You can use tapestry or cloth to change the appearance of a floor, table, or other surface. A shift in lighting is easily accomplished by adding candles, small table lamps, or different-colored lightbulbs. Maybe you can change the angle of your desk. Large pillows make sitting on the floor more appealing for guests, coworkers, clients, and so forth. Elements from the natural world add life, from plants and flowers to stones, sand, water,or wood.

One way to begin creating sacred space is by building an altar. A meditation altar might consist of a candle and a statue of significance. Altars can be created in honor of a specific intention or an event. Billie Burney, a friend and colleague, offers the following story about her ancestor altar:

When I decided to create my altar, the first thing I did was look at my house and figure out a space that was safe, a space where someone couldn't accidentally knock something over or trample on it, but a space that was central to the room. An ancestor altar is something that anyone can establish. A lot of people have them, and they don't realize it. They may have a section of their house with a lot of photographs of relatives, maybe a candle. They don't realize they've already begun an altar, a way to honor those people.

With my altars, I'm more aware of my living space and the energy that I invite into my house. With my mom passing, my ancestor altar will eventually provide a place where she and I can talk. It makes you more aware that even if people aren't around in a physical sense, they're there in a spiritual sense, which gives me hope. The ancestor altar is designed to embody the "asé" of family members and friends who had transitioned. Asé is a word of African origin that means essence or power.

If you have a parent who's deceased, or a grandparent or friend, create an altar for them. Get a white cloth, a white candle, some incense, and a glass of water. Spend at least fifteen minutes a day having a conversation with that person. Share some food with them. Keep the water fresh. Give them fresh flowers. It's a powerful thing to know your ancestors can still help you if you open yourself up to it.

wicca, the four elements, and the four directions

Witchcraft is a religion based on nature and the movements of the sun and the moon. Pagan or Wiccan groups honor the earth's natural calendar and celebrate the bond between humans and the earth. Starhawk, a peace activist and leader in feminist spirituality, offers the following from her book *The Spiral Dance: A Rebirth of the Ancient Religion of the Great Goddess.*

[Witchcraft] *is not based on dogma or a set of beliefs, nor on scriptures or a sacred book revealed by a great man. Witchcraft takes its teachings from nature, and reads inspiration in the movements of the sun, moon, and stars, the flights of birds, the slow growth of trees, and the cycles of the seasons.*

The Goddess has infinite aspects and thousands of names – She is reality, the manifest deity, omnipresent in all of life, in each of us. The Goddess is not separate from the World – She is the world, and all things in it: moon, sun, earth, star, stone, seed, flowing river, wind, wave, leaf and branch, bud and blossom, fang and claw, woman and man.

(continued on next page)

℮ the third place

The "third place" is a term coined by Ray Oldenburg, author of *The Great Good Place,* to describe what he calls "core settings of informal public life." According to Oldenburg, we have our home, and our workplace(s) and then, in a thriving society, we have a third place. These are the places where people can gather, inclusively, to talk, relax, debate, and hang out – places like coffee shops, beauty salons, corner bars, community centers, diners, and the proverbial general store.

The best third places are the ones where people feel at home, where conversation flows freely, and where accessibility is unlimited. In the third place, people have an opportunity to digest the news of the day and form their own opinions in the company of others. It provides the setting where a sense of shared experience can develop and sustain itself. So, the third place plays a key role in society and the preservation of true democracy. It is the small institution that creates a bridge between one's individual private life and the larger society. Without it, we have a tendency to become isolated from where we live, too self-contained, and rather homogeneous in our associations. Cafes and taverns have been the breeding ground of revolution; it has been said that neither the American nor French revolutions would have occurred without these essential gathering places.

Where are the third places in your community? Where do people gather and who gathers? Consider the popular hangouts – restaurants, coffee shops, bars, community centers. What happens there? If we are interested in strengthening a sense of community, we must begin with these third places where community is built and sustained. Here are some examples of third places that seem to have been deliberately designed to build community:

The White Dog Cafe is the brainchild of Judy Wicks, a one-time VISTA volunteer who came of age during the sixties. What began as a muffin shop in West Philadelphia is now one of the most vibrant and committed restaurant enterprises around, sponsoring an ever-evolving series of community events and volunteer opportunities. "Table Talk" invites speakers of all backgrounds and areas of expertise to share their knowledge and engage in discussions over an early morning breakfast. There are trips to sister restaurants in Vietnam, Cuba, Iraq, and other countries with whom the United States has tenuous relations, as well as in other neighborhoods throughout Philadelphia.

- What restaurants, cafes, or diners near your home or work bring people together?
- Do they host any events like music, poetry, speakers, and so on?
- What are your favorite places to go? Why? What could you imagine happening in the space?

St. Joseph's AME Church. Founded in the late 1800s, St. Joseph's was the heart of Hayti, Durham's Black community, for generations. During the Civil Rights Movement, St. Joseph's was often the congregating spot for organizers, marchers, and citizens. When much of the neighborhood was destroyed through various "urban renewal" projects, the church was saved through a community-led effort to place it on the National Register of Historic Places. Hayti Heritage Center, built next to the church, is a gathering space for art-related events, poetry readings, art exhibitions, an after-school youth program, and various concerts. St. Joseph's just underwent $2.5 million worth of renovations, which created a 350-seat performance space to host traveling and local entertainment, meetings, and lectures.

- What religious institutions in your neighborhood act as gathering places?
- What do they offer? Who meets there?
- Are you affiliated with a place of worship? Who uses the space when services aren't being held?

Village of Arts and Humanities was initiated by artist Lily Yeh in 1986. What began as a mural project and sculpture garden in North Philadelphia is now a series of parks, community gardens, a community center, performances, events (dance, theater, and ritual), and exhibitions. There are arts education and after-school programs, GED and vocational training programs, and resident-led construction projects to renovate nearby buildings and homes. Working with residents, Yeh and the Village have developed a crafts industry that markets images associated with the Village and sells baked goods and vegetables. They are acquiring more vacant lots for community gardens and parks. Yeh's ongoing collaboration with neighborhood artists and residents is an example of the best that community-based art has to offer.

- What changes have occurred in your neighborhood over the past year?
- Who was responsible for them?

wicca, (continued)

Like many earth-based spiritual traditions, Wicca draws a connection between the four directions – East, South, West, and North – with the four elements: air, fire, water, and earth. This relationship is invoked at most rituals and ceremonies. Each of the elements augment human power with their energy. Air belongs to the east, and it rules over the mind, creativity, knowledge, and communication. This direction offers inspiration and insight. Fire is the element of the south. It is faithful and energetic and rules the spirit, healing, and the sun. Water is the element of the west. Its power is intuitive, receptive, and compassionate. Water rules emotions, love, and courage. Earth is in the north, and it is the seat of wisdom. Earth rules the body, nature, silence, birth, and death.

- Are there public parks? Who takes care of them?
- Is there a space for public art close to your home? Whose art is there? How did it get there?

The <u>Highlander Research and Education Center</u> in New Market, Tennessee, was started in 1932 by Myles Horton and Frank Adams with a mission to train leaders in the South and preserve local culture. It has been training grassroots activists in a variety of arenas ever since. In the heart of Appalachia, one of this country's poorest regions, workshops and discussions at Highlander gave people a sense of their own power and their connection to one another.

In the 1930s and 1940s, Highlander worked to develop the skills, strategies, and networks of labor organizers and displaced factory, mill, and mine workers. In the 1950s and 1960s, Black and white activists congregated at Highlander to build bridges that would create a movement. It was, in fact, one of the only places in the South where Blacks and whites could meet openly and safely. Martin Luther King Jr. as well as Rosa Parks spent time at Highlander. Carrying this spirit and commitment forward, Highlander continues to provide training and to act as a true gathering spot for activists. Since the 1980s, Highlander has organized around the issues of environmental degradation, global economic restructuring, and youth leadership.

- Where do people go to talk about serious issues confronting your community? What places are safe for this?
- Similarly, are there places where people of different ethnic backgrounds and classes can gather on equal footing?

<u>Warehouse 21</u> is a multifaceted, youth-driven initiative in a four-thousand square foot warehouse on the edge of downtown Santa Fe, New Mexico. The warehouse includes a recording studio, small meeting rooms, and a large open space for concerts and workshops. Created in response to a lack of arts institutions with a commitment to young people, they offer a number of opportunities, run mostly for and by young people. Activities include free and low-fee arts workshops; "Broad Issues," an independent and alternative newspaper; weekly dance parties and youth concerts; video forums; and *Ground Zero*, a weekly radio show.

- Where do young people in your community hang out?
- What empty or abandoned buildings do you pass by on a regular basis?
- For what were they once used? What else can you see happening in that space?
- Who in your community needs a place to gather?

℮ reaching out to others: exploring place

One interesting way for a group to get to know each other is by seeing a place through each other's eyes. This is particularly powerful if you are engaged in some kind of action or community service that is locally based. First, ask each person to answer the following questions in writing.

- What is your favorite public place in your city or town? Describe it. How did you find it?
- Why do you love it? What goes on there?
- What place most inspires you?

Then, divide into groups of three and share your answers. Come back together as a group. Notice where the answers overlap and where they are different. You might also post a large map of your city or town and begin marking these places as people describe them. What can people learn about each other and about your community? If people are interested, suggest meeting for an afternoon to visit these spaces together.

Another variation on this: Ask each person in your group to choose a public place in your community that interests them or a place they'd like to change, and research its history using the following questions:

- How old is this place? How did it come into being and why?
- Who was instrumental in its creation or development?
- For what was the space initially intended?
- Who uses the space now, and for what? How is it maintained?

Come together to share what you've learned. If time allows, visit these places and do your "reports" onsite.

℮ earth: the place beyond the place

*Loving relationships are rooted in trust, truthful communication, and mutual respect. Our rela-
tionship with the Earth can also be described in these terms.*

~ *James A. Swan,* Sacred Places

The earth is our foundation, the place we all share. It is the very ground we walk on. It is vital to remind our feet, our hands, our eyes, and our heart that the earth holds everything upon it. We forget the earth was here long before we were. Before we built roads and skyscrapers, malls and houses, there were fields and forests and the desert. Natural places can be our greatest teachers about change, cycles, and sustainability. The passing of the seasons, the life

pilgrimages:
the journey to
a holy place

Pilgrimages have been around for thousands of years. In making our way to holy or sacred space, we are transformed, both by the journey and the destination. Followers of Buddhism visit the Buddha's birthplace, the place of enlightenment, and where he died. Catholics travel faithfully to the Shrine of Our Lady of Guadalupe in Mexico City where it is said the Virgin Mary appeared in 1531. Hindus take a sacred plunge into India's Ganges River. Every year on Easter, Christians follow the Stations of Cross, reenacting the last days of Jesus. And Jews find renewal in a trip to pray at the Wailing Wall in Jerusalem.

Perhaps the largest of all pilgrimages is that of the Hajj, the trip to Mecca that all Muslims who are able must complete at least once in their lifetime. Mecca, a city in Saudi Arabia, attracts millions of people every year from all over the world. First, Muslims must enter *ihram,* a state of purity and cleanliness. Then they go to the Ka'bah, the first temple, which is circled counterclockwise seven times. People then travel through the desert of the

(continued on next page)

and death of a flower, the pattern of a tree's trunk – the greatest lessons life has to offer can be found in offerings from nature. As we observe, respect, and live in harmony with earth's natural rhythm, we learn to surrender to that which we cannot control.

As mainstream society moves further away from the natural world, we lose touch with its structure, regularity, and rhythm. In the spring, living things revive and are renewed. Birds lay eggs, plants send out new shoots, and animals emerge from hibernation. With this rebirth, we feel hope, freedom, and a sense of possibility. In summer, nature is at its peak, creating and sustaining life. In the fall, we have reminders of summer and we prepare for the winter ahead, a time of turning inward. Many trees let go of their leaves and the land lies fallow for a time. What is your favorite season? Why? Of which changes are you most aware, internally and externally?

℮ learning from the earth

Ask the beasts, and they will teach you; the birds of the air,
and they will tell you, or the plants of the earth, and they will teach you;
and the fish of the sea will declare to you.
Who among all these does not know that the hand of God has done this?
In God's hand is the life of every living thing
and the breath of all humankind.

~ Job 12:7–10

As a kid, our house had a lot of woods behind it and a creek,
and I used to love playing out there. I had all that growing up.
The other day it occurred to me that being in nature is such a spiritual place,
because I'm away from all the distractions and all the human creations in the
regular world. Just being around all natural objects that were created by God
or some other force, makes me feel closer to spirit. It's where I go to think.
It's where I go to get away from things. It's my personal retreat.

~ Richard Goldberg

To begin to understand what wisdom lies in the simple forms of nature, we must spend time with them. Pick one, get close to it, and begin.

soil

Pick up a handful of dirt. When it's in your hand, what does dirt remind you of? What is the dirt like closest to the place where you live? How far away is it from your front door? For what is it used? How would you bring it inside with you? What would you do with it? Do you know how dirt contributes to other life forms and the overall ecosystem?

river

Go to the river nearest your home and sit beside it. Where does this river start and where does it end? Have you ever been to either place? What lies on its banks? For what is it a boundary? How high is the river and how fast does it flow? What alters its course? What is the sound of water moving? Of what does it remind you? *Throw a leaf into the river.* What happens? *Try a stick. Then a small stone. A bigger rock.* What impact does each of these have on the water?

tree

Find a tree you like and touch it in different places. What kind of tree is this? How old do you think it is? What do the roots look like? How would you describe the relationship between the branches and the trunk? How are they similar? How are they different? Do the branches remind you of something? How easily do they move? *Look at the bark. Get even closer.* What images do you see? What does this tree shade?

ocean

When you find yourself by the ocean, make the most of it. How quickly do the waves seem to come into the shore? How high are they? How wide? What patterns do you see in the waves? Do they remind you of anything? What does the ocean sound like? Is there a rhythm? How does it change? What colors do you see? What do you smell? *Pick up a handful of sand.* How many variations does the sand have? Can you separate the grains? Of what does the texture remind you? From where do you think it came? *Dig deeper into the sand.* What changes?

sun

Choose a cool day when the sun is out. Sit outside where the trees do not block the sun. Look straight ahead. What evidence of the sun do you see? Where do you see shadows? Where do you see light? *Wait five minutes.* Has anything changed? What is different? *Close your eyes.*

pilgrimages:
the journey to
a holy place
(continued)

Mina Valley to the hill where the Prophet Muhammed gave his last sermon. They perform *sa'i*, or "hastening," traveling seven times between two hills near the Ka'bah to replicate Hagar's frantic search for water for her son, Ishmael. Muslims also throw stones at pillars symbolizing Satan and the rejection of evil. Pilgrims feast together and trim a lock of hair to symbolize the end of the Hajj.

Where on your body do you feel the sun's warmth? *Turn your face toward the sun, leaving your eyes closed.* What changes?

As you begin to investigate your place in the world, find some ways to enlist family, coworkers, and friends. Next time you invite a group of friends over for dinner, ask everyone to bring one thing that they have from the natural world that is meaningful to them. Have each person tell a story about it: where it came from, how and when they got it, and what it means to them now. Create a living collage with all of the objects. Leave it in a place where everyone can see it for a while.

You might ask a group of coworkers to join you in spending your lunch hour away from the office. This might be in the woods, in a nearby park, by a river, or in the mountains. Spend part of the time in silence. Find things you've never seen before. Together, make a mental list of what is new.

℮ start a community garden

I love people to a certain extent.
But sometimes I want to get off in the garden to talk with God.
I have the blooms and when the blooms are gone,
I love the green.
God dressed the world in green.

~ Minnie Evans, self-taught artist

What better way to cultivate a shared sense of place than by planting and harvesting with others who live near you? Particularly in cities where green space is at a premium, community gardening is thriving everywhere. Will Atwater is the garden director at SEEDS, a community gardening organization in Durham. He offers the following suggestions for groups wanting to start their own garden.

1. As a group, start by visualizing the kind of garden you want to have. Where can you see the garden? Will it have vegetables? Flowers? Both? Will you break your space into individual plots or garden as a group, which requires more cooperation? (For groups starting out, Will recommends that each person or family tend their own spot.)

2. Find a location that is accessible to everyone. Make sure it gets at least half a day of sunlight. Find out where the closest water source is.

3. Do a soil test for quality. In many states, the local agriculture extension office will provide soil testing kits free of charge. You collect samples of the soil and send it to them, along with information about what you want to grow.

They will analyze the soil and make helpful recommendations for planting. If you find a good location that doesn't necessarily have great soil, Will recommends building a raised bed and bringing in your own soil.

4. Find a planting guide at the bookstore or library. This will tell you when to plant what, how long it will take for a plant to grow to maturity, how much water it needs, and other vital information.

To see whether there is already a community gardening group in your area, contact the American Community Gardening Association. See "Resources for Place," on page 221.

@ stewardship of place: your piece of earth

We can tell a lot about our society, our town, or our culture by how it treats the earth. Strengths and weaknesses are mirrored in this relationship. When communities are aligned with values of cooperation and unity, stewardship for the planet emerges as a central tenet. As we cultivate a sense of reverence for each other and for ourselves, we nurture the same for the earth. Similarly, when we show disregard for the natural world, it pervades many aspects of our being. As we assert our power for personal gain or economic growth, domination prevails – over others and over the earth.

The impact of this is evident everywhere. The area where I live is experiencing unparalleled growth in almost every direction. North Carolina's population is projected to be over 8.5 million people by the year 2020, an increase of 31 percent in just thirty years. What implications does this have for our future? Every major road has been widened at least once since I moved here in 1992. Mega stores pop up where there used to be fields. Homes are built at a staggering rate. Only now, amidst this frenzy, have policy makers begun to talk about managing growth. But an inordinate amount of land has been cultivated at lightning speed; entire ecosystems that cannot be replaced have been wiped out.

Permaculture is a global, grassroots movement toward sustainability, cooperation, and equality. It is based on an ethic of (1) caring for the earth in such a way that all life systems continue and multiply, and (2) human access to resources necessary for existence, without accumulation of wealth or land beyond need. According to the Bay Area Permaculture Group, "Permaculture designs and nurtures agriculturally productive ecosystems which have the stability, diversity and resilience of natural ecosystems." Developed in the

jubilee

All of the world's religions stress the interdependence between humanity and creation. Leviticus 25:3–5 tells us, "Six years you shall sow your field, and six years you shall prune your vineyard, and gather in its fruits; but in the seventh year there shall be a Sabbath of solemn rest for the land." On every seventh day, the Sabbath, humans must rest. Any attempts to control forces of production, namely labor and the land, are interrupted. Leviticus 25 outlines the concept of a Sabbath for the earth. During the sabbatical year, or the seventh year, the land must be allowed to lie fallow. After forty-nine years, there is a jubilee year. In this fiftieth year, God commands that all land is returned and redistributed, preventing any mass accumulation of land. Through this biblical text, we can see the ideal relationship between how we treat each other and how we treat the earth. As one relationship deteriorates, so does the other. Just as people need rest, so does the earth.

1970s in Australia by Bill Mollison and David Holmgren, Permaculture adopts techniques and principles from old and new traditions. These include renewable energy sources, soil and water conservation, sustainable agriculture, and appropriate technology.

Environmental groups speak of "carrying capacity" – the largest number of any given species that a habitat can support indefinitely *without environmental damage*. For example, when forests are clear-cut, the surrounding region's capacity to purify the air; moderate temperatures; stabilize soil; protect watersheds; preserve biodiversity; and preserve cultural, spiritual, and recreational space is greatly reduced. Start by figuring out who in your community might have answers to the questions below. Try your county or state department of environmental protection and natural resource agencies. Here are some questions to ask:

- What is the capacity of your local watershed to absorb waste and pollution while providing safe drinking water at the same time? (A watershed is any area of land that drains into a lake or river and provides water for drinking, farming, and industry.)
- Are agricultural and natural ecosystems adequately protected?
- How are natural, recreational, and historical areas in your community preserved?
- How will the local biological diversity be protected?
- How available is public transit in your area?
- Where are the wild, untouched areas in your community? What do you know about them?

resources for place....................

American Community Gardening Association, 100 N. 20th Street, 5th floor, Philadelphia, Penn. 19103. (215) 988-8785. www.communitygarden.org

Bernstein, Ellen, and Dan Fink. *Let the Earth Teach You Torah*. Philadelphia: Shomrei Adamah, 1992. A practical guide for learning and teaching Judaism's approach to the environment, ecological crises, and the wisdom of the earth. Shomrei Adamah runs educational programs and retreats. Contact: 5500 Wissahickon Ave., #804C, Philadelphia, Penn. 19144. (215) 844-8150. http://members.aol.com/shomadam

Berry, Thomas. *The Dream of the Earth*. San Francisco: Sierra Club Books, 1988. A collection of essays on the environment and how humans might reconcile with the earth.

Evans, Sara M., and Harry C. Boyte. *Free Spaces: The Source of Democratic Changes in America*. New York: Harper & Row, 1986.

Findhorn Community. *The Findhorn Garden: Pioneering a New Vision of Man and Nature in Cooperation*. New York: HarperCollins, 1975. The amazing account of the ecological community in Findhorn, Scotland, begun on just a plot of land in a trailer park. www.findhorn.org

Hayti Heritage Center, at Saint Joseph's Historical Foundation, 804 Old Fayetteville Street, Durham, N.C. 27702. www.hayti.org

Highlander Research and Education Center, 1959 Highlander Way, New Market, Tenn. 37820. (423) 933-3443. www.hrec.org

LaChapelle, Dolores. *Sacred Land, Sacred Sex: Celebrating Deep Ecology and Celebrating Life*. Silverton, Colo.: Finn Hill Arts, 1988. Resource for returning to the magic within the earth and within ourselves. Includes a broad range of commentary, history, poetry, and practical suggestions.

Linn, Denise. *Altars: Bringing Sacred Shrines Into Your Everyday Life*. New York: Random House, 1999. A guide to creating altars in your home to represent various intentions and aspirations.

Mollison, Bill. *Permaculture: A Practical Guide for a Sustainable Future*. Washington, D.C.: Island Press, 1990. www.permaculture.org.au

National Religious Partnership for the Environment is a coalition of religious organizations and denominations united by a biblical and religious responsibility to protect the environment. Each denomination develops the strategy and materials it needs to reach its constituency. Contact: 1047 Amsterdam Ave., New York, N.Y. 10025. (212) 316-7441. www.nrpe.org

Oldenburg, Ray. *The Great Good Place*. New York: Paragon House, 1989.

Sierra Club. *Saving for the Future: A Guide to Local Carrying Capacity*. Washington, D.C.: Sierra Club. Contact: Sierra Club Local Carrying Capacity Campaign, 408 C Street, NE, Washington, D.C. 20002. (202) 547-1141. www.sierraclub.org

Starhawk, *The Spiral Dance: A Rebirth of the Ancient Religion of the Great Goddess*. New York: Harper & Row, 1989. Earth-based rituals from the practice of Wicca. www.starhawk.org

Streep, Peg. *Altars Made Easy*. New York: HarperCollins, 1997.

Village of the Arts and Humanities, 2544 Germantown Ave., Philadelphia, Penn. 19133. (215) 255-3949. www.villagearts.org

Warehouse 21, 1614 Paseo de Peralta, Santa Fe, N.M. 87501. (505) 989-4423. www.warehouse21.org

White Dog Cafe, 3420 Sansom Street, Philadelphia, Penn. 19104. (215) 386-9224. www.whitedog.com

Williams, Terry Tempest. *Refuge: An Unnatural History of Family and Place*. New York: Pantheon, 1992. In this moving personal account, Williams parallels the environmental turmoil resulting from the rising of Great Salt Lake in Utah with the turmoil of her mother's losing battle with cancer. www.mtholyoke.edu/proj/cel/williams.html

our black church . . . .

Charles McKinney

Charles McKinney is a program and research associate in the Office of Intercultural Affairs at Duke University. He is finishing a Ph.D. in history at Duke University. Raised Pentecostal in southern California, Charles now attends Mount Level Baptist Church in Durham, North Carolina. He originally wrote this piece for the Afroam List Serve, April 7, 1995. Charles lives with his wife, Natalie, and their son, Ayo, in Durham, North Carolina.

I went to church last Sunday. Hardly a noteworthy action. It's a straight-up little "country" church: off the paved road, in a sanctuary that's too small, replete with mothers and loud children, and predominated by men and women who remember the Great Depression. Yet, as I took in the service, a number of things occurred to me about church, religion, and Black people.

I've always enjoyed going to this particular church. It's always had the right combination of singing, preaching, and good ol' worship (grandma would say "wu-ship"), but on this day, something about the whole thing moved me. As the men's chorus stood to sing "Can't Nobody Do Me Like Jesus," heads nodded and shouts of "Amen!" arose to greet the senior men as they struggled out of their chairs. They were affirmed and it showed in their singing. The slow, methodical singing and the heartfelt foot-tapping was contagious. The chorus and the audience fed off one another; the men singing their hearts out, and the audience responding with shouts of "Amen!" and "Preach!" After a number of extended choruses, the men sat down to shouts of joy and appreciation.

> It is a community of old and young, male and female, brought together by cultural, social and religious bonds. It is a place we come to when we want to charge our batteries for the week.

So, I'm sitting there, in this little church, trying to figure out why I enjoy it so much. As a budding historian, perhaps I get a kick out of the old people. When you think about it, the practice of worship for Black people hasn't changed very much in a couple of centuries. Perhaps the rhythms and sounds that I hear evoke images of old slave men and women – heads bowed and eyes closed as they perform the West African ring shout. Maybe they make me think of the religious processionals of the motherland, as the elders poured libations under a starry sky. Maybe the old people remind me of my own family – a grandmother and grandfather (on both sides of the family) who claim that they got through only by the grace of God. Maybe that's why I love this place so much.

Then it hits me. I love this place because it is a community. It is a community of old and young, male and female, brought together by cultural, social, and religious bonds. It is a place we come to when we want to charge our batteries for the week. The young come together with their elders – both to inject new blood into the church and to glean some of the elders' wisdom and insight into life. The old people come to be affirmed and recognized as individuals who have made it through. They have stories they want to tell us, little tidbits of life they want to give us, and this is the place where it happens. Can you think of any better place to affirm the elders and teach the young?

It's a place that we've carved out where it's all right to tell someone that you're thinking about them or praying for them throughout the week. And, for the spiritually minded among us, it's a place we can come in order to get another set of helpful hints (and admonitions at times) on how to get through to the end of the day. Yeah, that's what I like about this place.

being retreat . . . .

Ted Purcell

Ted Purcell is the Baptist campus minister at Duke University in Durham, North Carolina. Previously, he spent fifteen years in that role full-time at North Carolina State University in Raleigh. In 1989 he accepted the half-time position at Duke, which allows him to follow his calling as a retreat leader and a spiritual director. He spends much of his time addressing ecology as a spiritual issue.

I love being outdoors, in close connection with the natural world. I was a natural introvert, but there was such a sense of welcoming and hospitality that I felt acceptance. I associated it with peace and comfort, as well as adventure. I have this recurring vision that someday I might be connected with a retreat center. It's a confluence of several streams in my life – a convergence of hungers.

I think that retreat vision is very much about home, being at home with myself, or at home with God. It's about finding community. It's about living a contemplative life in the beauty of creation. I've found that many people resonate with that dream. At first I thought that the retreat vision was about a place that I would build or go to. Then I realized that I needed first to *be* a retreat, to focus more on the inner life of prayer.

That's the ferment that led me to Duke and a half-time position. I gave up half my salary and bought back half my life. It corresponds with a pull toward a more contemplative life. I really feel the need to have copious amounts of unobligated time. I had thought of ministry as being available to other people for the sake of God, and

> One of the reasons we need wilderness is that we need to preserve places, not only for the other species but for the cultivation of the human spirit. Our culture tends to regard the earth more as a commodity to be consumed than as a community to which we belong.

I realized that what's more basic was being available to God for the sake of other people. Along with that, I felt this growing sense of call about being near to the earth and, in light of the environmental crisis, to make some response to that. This calling to "ecological spirituality" was especially encouraged by the friendship and writing of Thomas Berry. I also appreciated the experience of working with the Land Steward- ship Council of North Carolina, whose mission was to educate people about the Jewish and Christian theological ethics with regard to the care of creation. There are many people whose spirituality is earth-connected – people who are not connected with institutional religion but find deep meaning and a sense of the sacred in the natural world. One of the reasons we need wilderness is that we need to preserve places, not only for the other species but for the cultiva- tion of the human spirit. Our culture tends to regard the earth more as a commodity to be consumed than as a community to which we belong.

I like the way Sam Keen said it in *Fire in the Belly* (New York: Bantam Doubleday, 1992): "The new human vocation is to heal the earth." I would add myself that it's the *original* human vocation. Keen says that we can't heal what we don't love, and we can't love what we don't know, and we can't know what we don't touch. It is a call literally to reconnect with the earth, to see ourselves not just *on* but *of* the earth, to have a sense of intimate presence with the earth.

We need to go back to the *other* Bible – the sacred book of nature. There was a time in Christian tradition when we spoke of the two sacred books: what has come to be written scripture and the sacred book of nature. Our scriptures are full of references to nature, so there's a tremendous symphony and unity between the written scripture and the natural world; each points to the other. Go out into the woods with a view of this being a place of sacred revelation. And, just as you would oppose any movement to burn the Bible, you need to oppose the desecration of earth that is taking place. We're poor stewards, influenced by ignorance, arrogance, and greed. We're exploiting the earth in a way that has damaged the life systems of the earth.

If you look at the primal elements – earth, fire, water, and air – and what those mean symbolically in different religious traditions, they're very powerful. No wonder Thomas Berry speaks of the earth as the primary revelation. We wouldn't have scriptures that are now in printed form without the primary revelation of the creation. It raises the great questions; it teaches the great lessons: "Who are we? What is the purpose of humankind? How can we live in relationship, in interdependent community, with the other forms of life?"

There's no more powerful spiritual metaphor in my existence than the image of home and homecoming . . . If there's one area where I can make some contribution to other people and the earth, it seems to me it is this area. Being closer to the earth nurtures my own spirituality, my relationship to God. In retreats and seminars, I invite people to tell their earth stories about

> There's no more powerful spiritual metaphor in my existence than the image of home and homecoming . . . being closer to the earth nurtures my own spirituality, my relationship to God.

special places or special experiences they've had. These stories often reflect the human longing to feel at home in relation to the earth, to heal the sense of alienation, to love the creation.

I can't think of a more radical act of faith than to rest. A lot of it comes from my understanding of Sabbath, which includes in the original commandment a call for earth to rest. There's a powerful connection between our restlessness and the ecological crisis. If you want to do something radically significant as an activist, just rest. Sabbath rest has many implications for the environmental crisis. Deep rest is a countercultural act. It involves connecting with the hospitable presence of the natural world as a place of solitude, a place of silence. Our contribution to the healing of the earth comes right back to us in a mutually enhancing way as we work and pray for the healing of the planet. Sabbath rest is about "resting in God," entrusting ourselves to something larger, and drawing nurture from that relationship with the holy.

Ted can be reached at ted.purcell@duke.edu

a lifelong commitment . . . .

Evelyn Mattern

Evelyn Mattern, SFCC, is a member of the Sisters for Christian Community. Over the last two decades, Evelyn has worked with the Roman Catholic Diocese of Raleigh and North Carolina Council of Churches as a lobbyist and advocate for the rights of farmworkers and other disenfranchised populations. Evelyn also taught English for ten years at St. Augustine's College in Raleigh and in the North Carolina Community College system.

My family wasn't church-going people, but they were very ethical. My mother would talk freely about what she believed, and the presence of God was part of her life. My grandmother wanted us to go to Catholic school, so from the age of six, life was integrated with religious meaning. I took it very seriously. I entered the convent, partly from not such good motives. I had this idea that I wouldn't be okay if I didn't give my life to God, so I did.

When I was in graduate school in the mid-sixties, Vatican II, a [Catholic] Church Council was telling us to look at the world. Students were burning draft cards, and I met Daniel and Philip Berrigan: brothers and Catholic priests who had been involved in the anti-war movement and other peace issues. My own brother was facing Vietnam. The Civil Rights Movement, Vatican II, and Vietnam came together, and I saw what God's work was in the world.

So I became an activist. And I paid a price for it. I wore a full-length habit with a black veil, but I also felt the need to be in anti-war demonstrations. The civil disobedience squad wouldn't arrest me, but they'd call up the Mother General. I remember the Sisters saying "You went to a demonstration with your habit on?!" and I asked, "Well, did you want me to take it off?"

In religion there are these two elements. First, the stabilizing element – all dictators want a religious people, because they're going to be obedient. But then there's this other dimension – the prophetic or disruptive dimension. People like the Berrigans gave me confidence to examine that dimension and apply it to our world today.

In 1972, I started going into the women's prison. I had volunteered to work with the Defense Committee for the political trial of the Berrigans and other peacemakers. I saw how similar their view of the world was to mine. They ended up in prison, and I thought, "Well, I'll probably end up in prison, so I better start getting comfortable with it." I started going to the women's prison one night a week, teaching creative writing. That was another world. I developed a notion of what the North Carolina criminal justice system was like.

Then, I heard our new bishop was open to peace and justice work, so I developed a response to migrant farm workers. I rode around to all the Catholic parishes in the eastern part of the state to survey the population. Everyone said, "The issues are in the next county, look in the next county." I sensed a tremendous amount of denial. It was a denial of presence. Women can be looked through, prisoners can be looked through, Black people can be looked through, migrant farmworkers can be looked through, even though they're all over the place. I was determined to get some kind of religious ministry to migrant farmworkers. When I left five years later, I had in place a full-time migrant minister who would spend 40 percent of his time in direct service and 60 percent on social change. That was my goal for all peace and justice efforts, to get people thinking in terms of policy change, not just Band-Aid. It was the Dorothy Day idea: you have your soup kitchen, but you also try to make your changes in the "dirty rotten system." She said that, so it gives me permission to call it that.

> I remember the Sisters saying "You went to a demonstration with your habit on?!" and I asked, "Well, did you want me to take it off?"

I began to see how the system doesn't really work for most people. I spent nine years lobbying at the state legislature and that radicalized me. I realized the legislators don't represent the people of North Carolina; they don't look like the people of North Carolina. Most are there to increase their wealth and power and connections. The political process did not touch enough people to suit me. I wasn't sure change could come through the political process unless there were some deeper cultural changes.

One of the best things I've gotten to do is hear people's stories. There are incredible people who have taken incredible risks, often in very quiet ways. They've managed to be very quiet leaders. I love hearing those people's stories with the intention of inspiring other people to look and say if this person can do it, I can do it. I'm always interested in people's communions of saints – people dead and alive – whom I look to with the question, "What would so and so do in this circumstance?" Even my religious community. We're very scattered in a way, but if I were totally alone, trying to live the way I'm living, I wouldn't be strong enough. There are times when you really need to know there are other people on the path with you. We share enough of a vision that I feel accompanied by my community.

And, I feel I have to pray regularly, I have to have solitude regularly, I have to do spiritual reading regularly, and I get very nervous if any of those isn't happening. A regular morning for me is to get up early, to read first and do a little yoga, and meditate through centering prayer for a half hour. At night I try to do some reading. Every now and then I take a day. It's a spiritual need, or maybe it's just temperamental: an introvert trying to operate in an extrovert world. And in the summers, I take three months off, and I go into monastic mode. Up early, more time for prayer, more time for physical work, more time for study. Not every day is the same, but I like to do prayer and writing in the morning, reading in the afternoon, work and a walk in the evening.

That's why I call myself a hermit. It's not that I don't see people, but this society we live in is crazy, and it would eat every minute of your time and every iota of your attention. You can't let it. My claim on time for God, time for spirit, is to say I'm a hermit.

> And, I feel I have to pray regularly, I have to have solitude regularly, I have to do spiritual reading regularly, and I get very nervous if any of those isn't happening.

place.

appendix:

Facilitating Spiritual Work with Groups

5 Ways to Go Deeper with Groups

Retreat Centers

stone circles

Facilitating Spiritual Work with Groups......
Principles

It a tremendous privilege to do spiritual work with groups; it has the potential to transform the way people see themselves and their work. You are creating a new learning community, and that community becomes your responsibility during the time you spend together. It gets easier with time and practice, and you will learn as you go. Here are some things to keep in mind:

begin with key questions

What is your primary objective for this work? What do you think other people might be interested in? Consider the overall mission of the group or organization you will be working with. Where does spirituality fit into that? Be honest about were the connection might seem problematic. If you are proposing this work be done with the group, think about who makes the decisions and how you might present your ideas to them. Think about who else in the group can help you.

prepare an outline

Now that you know your goals, you can create an outline. Consider the context and how much time you will have. Start with what moves you and think how you can share that with others. In the beginning it's always better to overplan; as you gain more experience, you will have a better sense of how long things take. Go over the outline at least twice and preferably three times. Visualize each component in your head, imagining how a group will actually *do* what you have planned. Build open time for discussion into your outline.

balance individual and group activities

Spiritual exploration and deepening takes place in many ways. Some people will have a revelation during individual reflection while others will gain new understanding through dialogue with one other person or a larger group. The more varied the formats you use, the more likely you will appeal to a variety of learning styles. Try to combine individual reflection activities – meditation, silence, writing, art – with an activity for small groups of three to five individuals each and/or the entire group. You can start with the following framework and vary it as you gain more experience. This outline is designed to fit into an hour and a half:

- Opening ritual to bring the group together (five minutes)
- Introductions or check-ins if the group knows each other (fifteen minutes)
- Individual reflection activity (twenty minutes)
- Small group activity or dialogue (twenty minutes)
- Large group reflections on the experience (twenty minutes)
- Closing circle or ritual (ten minutes)

set up an intentional space

Think about what kind of space the activity calls for. Will you be gathering in a circle? Make sure there is enough space to accommodate everyone. Is the space quiet and safe enough to encourage reflection and dialogue? Is it private? Do you want to do anything to alter the space? All spaces can be transformed with cloth draped in the center of the room, on the floor, or on a low table; plants, flowers, and other imports from the natural world; sacred objects that you bring and that you ask others to bring; candles or low lighting; and music.

think well about the whole group

You want to create an atmosphere that will allow for deep listening, effective communication, and a healthy group process. And, you want to make sure that the group maximizes everyone's participation. Cultivating good facilitation skills – being able to read a group's energy and create space where people can access deeper and different parts of themselves – takes time, and it will serve you throughout your life.

As you move through an activity, pay attention to how the experience is resonating with people. The challenge is to pay attention to two things at once: how the overall content of the session is going and how different individuals in the group are reacting to the session. You will learn to pay attention to nonverbal cues of the whole group, while still listening to what is being said. Make notes. Notice who is speaking and who is not. Don't hesitate to check in with people one on one during a break if you sense discomfort or boredom; both can be a sign that deeper issues are surfacing and someone may welcome an opportunity to talk. If not, respect individual privacy while letting the person know you are available if and when they do want to talk.

set a tone of inclusivity and safety

You can create a safe environment by drawing out opinions and helping everyone participate. Calling attention to diverse perspectives is particularly important with faith-based work. Be on the lookout for the "tyranny of the devout." Those who are most sure of and comfortable with their beliefs are often most likely to express them. Pay attention to those who don't seem as comfortable expressing their beliefs and help them find their voice in the group; they may need some extra support. If some folks seem to be generalizing and unwilling to speak personally, ask people to use "I" statements so that they speak for themselves.

Listen carefully to what people are saying; others will follow your lead. You want to be ready for the "a-ha" moments, those times when connections get made for the first time or someone comes face-to-face with a new truth or idea. If the discussion gets heated, the circumstances may be ripe for a teachable moment. When well-managed, intense situations have enormous potential to impact individuals and further group interaction. Your first instinct may be to "fix" something. The more you try to steer the conversation or bring it to a close, the more you risk limiting the group's learning process. Allow for chaos and do not attempt to control everything. People will be looking to you for cues; the more relaxed you are with conflict, the more you give the participants permission to relax into whatever is happening. (See "Stages of Community Building" at the end of this section.)

decide which questions are important

Asked in an environment of community and trust, questions give people a chance to begin telling their story. If there is already a base of openness in your group, you can begin with questions that involve a little bit more risk. If, on the other hand, this will be a brand-new experience, you'll want to start with some lower-risk questions. Always try to ask strategic, open-ended questions to get people talking. These are the questions that go beyond "yes" or "no" answers. For example, ask, "What do you remember about faith growing up?" Remember that even if the questions feel familiar, it will be a new experience to share their responses with a group of people.

don't panic when no one speaks

Try to get comfortable with silence. Don't be afraid to call on someone who hasn't spoken up and be aware of who monopolizes conversation. ("Thanks for your comment; I'd like to make sure we hear from other voices in the room.") In some cases, if people aren't talking, it might be because the topic is too risky and/or people are reluctant to share in a large group. In that case, there are four possible actions to take:

- Reframe the question or activity
- Break the group down into small groups of three or four
- Use an individual reflection exercise that allows people to think about it first on their own
- Share an example from your own life.

give people the option to opt out

Keep in mind that not everybody will share the same level of comfort or enthusiasm for an activity. Sharing information about oneself and one's faith brings up lots of issues for people, many of which tend to be unresolved. And people may not desire this arena (or any arena, for that matter) for exploration. As a result, people should be given the option not to participate without having to explain why. It's critical that you give the group some choices. Build this into the process of setting up an activity.

If it's a writing exercise, for example, encourage art as an alternative. If you're doing movement, encourage people to be still when they need to be still. We are used to following directions. Giving people permission to tune into and follow their intuition is a gift that opens up other doors. You are inviting people to become aware of and trust their own needs.

reflect on what you did

Take a deep breath. Relax. When you feel ready, think about how you feel. How did the group respond? Which parts of the activity did people seem to enjoy? What might be an appropriate next step?

Decide whether you want to know how people received what you gave them. This will help you plan what might come next for this group, provide useful information for work with other groups in the future, and give you an indication of where you need to grow. If possible, create time for both written and oral evaluation. Written feedback is useful because often people will write things they'd never say out loud. Oral feedback is helpful because people may reach new conclusions during conversation. You might also consider two complementary types of evaluation: postactivity evaluation and long-term evaluation.

postactivity evaluation

Evaluation immediately following an activity or gathering helps people reflect on what they got out of the activity. Use questions that keep people focused on their own experience of what happened. Here are some examples:

- What did you learn about yourself today? About others?
- What things did you like about this exercise/activity? What would you want to see repeated? What would you change?
- What questions do you still have?

long-term evaluation

Long-term evaluations are useful because the strongest effect may be felt long after the activity or group gathering is over. There are so many factors that can lead to one's spiritual development, and not all of them are easy to gauge. Following are some questions to help people to reflect on what is different about their life over the long term.

- What have you gotten out of the experience that you expected?
- What have you gotten that you didn't expect?
- What else did you expect to get out of your participation that you haven't gotten yet?
- Over the past year (six months, et cetera), what stands out?
- How do you think this experience has changed your daily life, if at all?

℮ stages of community building: M. Scott Peck

Psychologist and author M. Scott Peck provides a powerful model for community building; it is an incredibly useful framework for thinking about group process. A more detailed account can be found in his book *The Different Drum: Community Making and Peace.* He outlines four stages:

stage 1

Pseudocommunity. This is the stage where everyone is nice to one another. There is a lot of agreement, and conflict is avoided. Most individuals are looking for safe ways to interact within the group and deciding which pieces of themselves to reveal. During this stage, the group is very dependent on the leadership for guidance. You will often find people making lots of general statements (as opposed to "I" statements, which indicate ownership), and

As one of my mentors, George Lakey, says, "You'll never go wrong if you love your material, love your participants, and love yourself." Don't worry, however, if this love isn't always reciprocated. You challenge people when you ask them to think about hard topics or to explore themselves. As a result, you can become a target for whatever this stirs up for them.

Working with groups is a skill that can be learned, improved, and shared. You get better with practice, by reading about other people's experiences, and by watching people. Many organizations and individuals run workshops on how to be a good facilitator or trainer. The best that I know of is George Lakey's "Training for Change" workshops. Based in Philadelphia, Lakey and his team of trainers run workshops all across the country and around the world. See "Resources" for contact information.

there is little desire to challenge or be challenged. Once some of the generalizations are challenged, individual differences emerge, and you have . . .

stage 2

Chaos. Don't be nervous. Chaos is a vital part of any group process; a must, in fact, if people in the group are going to deepen their connection with each other. This is the time when individual differences begin to come out, and chaos, according to Peck, "always centers around well-intentioned but misguided attempts to heal or convert." People don't want to be healed or converted, so they resist. The first time a group goes into chaos, the communication is sometimes loud and disrespectful. People are playing out old patterns of communication and defending their positions and their place. The leader's job is to (1) pay very close attention to the chaos, and (2) gently guide people out of it at the right time. This is like watching people arguing loudly in a building that they don't know is on fire. Once they're ready for direction, you can show them where the door is. The only good way out of chaos is through . . .

stage 3

Emptiness. This will seem even harder than chaos for a while. Emptiness is almost like a death required for rebirth. It is a powerful time when people begin to get rid of that which is keeping them from communicating effectively and building real community. This is a time when people will need to release their expectations, preconceptions of the group, prejudices, assumptions, judgments, ideology, solutions, the need to heal/convert/fix someone, and the need to control the group. So it means individuals are going to share some of their hardest stuff. And then you finally reach . . .

stage 4

True Community. This will feel very different from the pseudocommunity you were in earlier. You can tell real community because people listen to each other better and longer, and participants are more comfortable revealing pieces of themselves. Chaos is a stage that groups may reach over and over again, but it will be different each time. As the group stays together, the people in it will find ways to make the chaos more productive. Incorporating silence or reflection, for example, will make the chaos more graceful.

5 Ways to Go Deeper with Groups . . . .

There are many ways to facilitate deeper reflection with groups. Below are five ideas: freewriting, guided meditation, stations of reflection, paired dialogue, and mandalas.

℗ 1. freewriting

In freewriting, each person writes stream of consciousness on a specific topic. Punctuation, grammar, and sentence structure do not matter. Freewriting helps people express themselves and releases individuals from traditional notions of what it means to keep a journal. It also allows people to return to their own wisdom, which helps a group remember how different each person's perspective is. This can be particularly valuable when one or two voices have been dominant.

   Encourage folks not to edit, but to keep writing even if it seems there is nothing else left to write. Natalie Goldberg says, "go for the jugular," meaning, go for the core of what you're thinking. She also recommends that you keep your pen moving for the entire time. In freewriting, the invitation is to release any concept of how ideas should fit together and feel the freedom to switch thoughts at will. Later you may be amazed at the connections that occur.

Setting. Any quiet space will do. Bring enough paper and writing utensils for everyone. If there aren't enough tables or other writing surfaces, bring clipboards or hardback books for people to write on.

Timing. Set aside a minimum of thirty minutes to do freewriting with a group. This is enough time to do two or three freewrites and still have time for people to share at the end. Each time you present a question or theme, give people five minutes to write. Have a watch or timer on hand. It helps to give a warning like, "thirty seconds left, start to finish your thought or sentence." After each theme, open up space for people to share what they've written. There should be no pressure, only encouragement. Or, you might ask people to pair up after writing and share that way.

Beginning. Here are three warm-up activities to get people writing.
1. *Lists.* Have people brainstorm a list of words that makes them feel powerful in their life and in their work. Or a list of words you love, secrets you have kept, your favorite days, and so on.
2. *Highlights.* Have everyone write about three highlights of their day so far; or their week, their month, their year.

freewriting for long-term planning

Using freewriting in long-term planning gives everyone a chance to envision the future. Ask people to imagine themselves, and the group, at a time in the future, perhaps five or ten years from now. Then, have everyone write for ten minutes on the following questions:

What is different in your life? What has changed in society?

What is different about this group or organization?

What do you hope has been accomplished?

Give them a couple of minutes to look over what they wrote and decide what they want everyone to hear.

3. *Photographs.* Cut out photos of many subjects: families, current events, travel, conflict, adventure, home life, nature, and so forth. Spread the photos in the middle of the room so all images are visible and ask everyone to pick one that catches their eye. Give people five minutes to write about the photograph. You might ask them to tell a story: What happened right before the photograph was taken and/or right after? Or, ask them how the image makes them feel, what it reminds them of.

After a warm-up, you'll find that many people are ready to keep writing, and you can introduce the main theme of the freewriting session. Here are some ideas to get you started:

TOPIC	QUESTIONS
Work	Why do you do what you do? What is the hardest thing about doing what you do? What is one thing you'd like to accomplish this decade?
Rest	What does calm feel like to you? How do you know when you're relaxed? To whom would you like to give the gift of rest?
Challenge	Describe a rough time you've had in the past year or two. What helped you through this? Who was important?
Place	What place on earth gives you the most peace? The most power? What place are you most concerned about?

Ending. Allow time for people to share what they wrote at the end. You might also ask people to circle the handful of words or phrases that jump out as being particularly powerful or a surprise.

Some people hate to write and will avoid it at all costs. Literacy levels vary widely and learning disabilities are more common than people without them know. It can cause great embarrassment or pain if someone is made to feel that writing is the only choice. Provide suggestions for other ways to reflect on the questions at hand (perhaps through art – have some supplies on hand – or thought or movement).

And don't worry if not everyone takes to this activity. Some people will be hungry for this opportunity and others will stare around the room blankly. During one journaling workshop, everyone seemed very intent, except for one individual who was clearly *not* writing. He approached me later and apologized. A few weeks later he called to tell me that he'd been journaling ever since the workshop and to invite me to do a workshop on journaling for a new youth service program he was starting.

℗ 2. leading a guided meditation

Guided meditation helps a group of people relax and it can also yield important information. You can start with written guided meditations such as the full-body relaxation in the "Mindfulness" chapter, or one from another book. As you do more and more guided meditations and get a feel for how they work, you can start writing your own.

Practice a few times by yourself and on one other person before doing this with a larger group so you can get a feel for the words, the pauses, and the flow of the meditation. You can record your meditation and then listen to it, noting what works for you and what doesn't. Or, ask your volunteer to give you feedback afterwards on the timing, the pace, the sound and volume of your voice, and what worked for them and what didn't.

Setting. Ask everyone to assume a comfortable position. Dim the lights or turn them off if it's during the day. It's better to have a little light than complete darkness. That way, people won't fall asleep. Don't be surprised if there is some moving around during the first few minutes as people get comfortable, change positions, and loosen clothing.

Timing. You need twenty to thirty minutes – a few minutes to get settled, ten to fifteen minutes for the meditation itself (many are longer), and a few minutes at the end for people to return to the present moment and stretch their bodies. You want to take your time but not go so slowly that you give people's minds a chance to drift. As you gain experience, you'll learn the right pace and how much time to leave between phrases.

Ending. Guided meditations should end with a way to come back to the present. You want to make sure that people don't get up too quickly, or they will get dizzy. Suggest that they move their fingers and toes, roll slowly over to one side, and then very slowly come to a seated position. A few minutes of silence at the end of a guided meditation is important for this transition.

As with dreams, it's easy to forget a lot of what happened in a meditation unless it is verbalized or written down soon after. If you use a guided meditation that is focused on something beyond relaxation, give people a few minutes to debrief through writing or by talking with one other person. You can ask folks to find a partner and then talk for a couple of minutes each about what they remember from the meditation.

example: meditating on challenge

Have people pair up and invite them to spend a few minutes talking about a challenge they are facing. Ask partners not to give advice but to listen well to each other. After five minutes, ask people to get comfortable for a guided meditation, either lying on the floor or sitting in a chair.

Start with the full-body relaxation in the "Mindfulness" chapter. After you've finished with the face and head, add the following:

> *Feel the sense of peaceful relaxation in your body . . . realize how much energy is available to you . . . and how much wisdom lies within your own heart . . . the challenge you have identified is not as big as it might appear . . . you have everything you need to face and resolve this issue . . . know that there are people in your life who want to help you . . . consider now who they might be . . . how might you ask them for help . . . the intuition within you already knows a creative response . . . consider a response you might not have considered before . . . if you had unlimited resources at your fingertips, what would you do? . . . what other possibilities come to mind? . . . what can you learn from these? . . .*

> Now let yourself open to focus on the one element that would help you with this challenge . . . it might be a person who could help, a conversation you could have, a specific resource that would change the circumstances of the challenge . . . know that this is available to you . . . even though it might not seem that way right now . . . allow yourself to put out a request for what you need . . . don't be afraid to ask for something that seems too large or impossible . . .

> *Breathe this request into your whole body . . . let the breath wash up and down like a wave, flowing over possibility . . . with your breath, notice how*

relaxed your body has become . . . know this is a state to which
you can always return . . . a sense of possibility and potential will
stay with you . . . return your awareness to the floor beneath you
and the room around you . . . leave your eyes closed . . . when
you're ready, begin to wiggle your fingers and your toes . . . stay
focused on your breath . . . slowly roll over to one side . . . very
slowly, when you're ready, sit up . . . notice how different your
body feels . . . when you are ready, open your eyes . . . move very
slowly as you stretch your legs and arms . . .

After a few minutes of quiet, have everyone reconnect with his or her partner and revisit the challenge that was discussed earlier. Ask people to talk about how they are feeling about it now.

- What, if anything, has shifted? What information did you get through the meditation?
- What else might you do in this situation?
- What else is available to you?

example: meditating on difference

I first participated in a guided meditation during a training for young people who were working on issues of economic justice. Since issues of class and race would have a great impact on our work, we spent a lot of time looking at issues like diversity and oppression. To begin examining how we'd been affected by stereotypes, we were led through a guided meditation and asked, from a place of deep relaxation, to recall our first memories of difference with regard to race and ethnicity. What were the words we remembered hearing? The images? What were we told by people close to us, such as family, friends, and teachers? What situations and events did we remember?

When we finished the meditation, we met in "affinity" groups; white people and people of color met separately to discuss the commonalities and differences of our experience. We talked about how society's messages about race had affected us, even before we were old enough to begin making adequate judgments about what we were hearing. And we were able to be honest about the stereotypes and messages that still impacted us as adults. When the whole group came back together, we shared the "data" we'd come up with, and it began to create a bridge of understanding that only got stronger with time.

@ 3. stations of reflection

This is a way for people to engage in individual reflection in the presence of others. The stations of reflection are created around thought-provoking questions. These questions can pertain to anything that is relevant for the group. You'll find two examples below, each for a different purpose.

Setting. Cluster chairs in five different areas; each of these areas becomes a station for one of five reflection questions. Altogether there should be a few more chairs than people so that people don't have to wait for someone to get up before moving to that part of the room. (For example, if you're working with a group of twenty-five, put six chairs at each station.) Set each question up in a way that makes it sacred. You might use pieces of material, candles, plants, flowers, or other items that are available to you.

Timing. You'll need an hour and a half for this exercise: time to introduce the activity, thirty minutes of individual reflection at the stations, thirty minutes in two different small groups, and time to close.

Beginning. Have the group gather outside of the space. Ask people to center themselves, perhaps by taking some slow breaths, or merely closing their eyes for a few minutes. Invite them to bring their journals with them. Read the paragraph below:

> *Please do this exercise in complete silence. When you enter the room, take a seat in a chair, reflect on the question in front of you, and then write what comes to mind. The order in which you answer the questions does not matter. If you don't want to write, you can use the time for reflection. Once you feel like you've finished with a question, move to a different question in another part of the room. You will have thirty minutes to finish all of the questions. I will make an announcement* (or ring a bell, et cetera) *when we are halfway through the time period. If a question touches you in a particularly powerful way, you might choose to spend a few extra minutes with it. The invitation here is to visit each station; try not to ignore any of the questions, especially those that might seem tough to answer.*

Be sure to announce the halfway point; you may want to make a second announcement when there are five minutes left.

Ending. After people have had a chance to answer all the questions, have them return to the question that was the hardest for them to answer. When they get to that question, ask them to talk and share experiences with others who showed up at the same question. If someone is at a question alone, invite them to join a different group.

Next, ask people to return to the question that was the most inspiring or powerful for them. Similarly, have them dialogue with the other people who show up at the same question. Complete this exercise with reflections in one large group. Ask people what it was like to do the exercises and what they learned.

example: reflections on a work experience

(For a group of people who have been working together and will continue to work together.)

- Remember a time over the past ____ (fill in time period) when you felt particularly good about your work. What did you like about it?
- What would you like to see this group achieve in the future? What do you believe this group capable of?
- Recall a time when you took leadership in this group. What did you learn?
- Recall a time when you felt very frustrated with this group. What prompted your frustration? How did you respond to it?
- For whom in the room are you especially grateful? What is it about them that you appreciate?

example: reflections on spirituality and society

(To use with any group, regardless of how well people know each other.)

- What is one significant event or turning point in your life that has helped shape your belief system?
- When, if ever, have you felt the presence of God or spirit in your life? Do you have a different name for it?
- What role, if any, do faith and/or spiritual practice play in the work you do? How have they been assets? How have they been barriers?
- What is particularly relevant to you about the role of faith in our society and culture? Where, if anywhere, does your own experience of faith or spirituality fit in this picture?
- Where do you see faith or spirit thriving in your community? Who is a part of this?

℗ 4. deepening through paired dialogue

Paired dialogues can be useful in a number of scenarios. They give people a chance to speak more in depth with someone whom they don't know very well, which often changes the dynamic of a group. Because we often talk more intimately with people who are somehow similar to us (with regard to ethnicity, age, gender, class background, sexuality, faith tradition, area of work) paired dialogue can help build community and nurture relationships across lines of difference. Paired dialogue is also valuable for riskier subject matters, when a fuller group conversation might be uncomfortable.

You can use this activity almost any time; for example, when a group is coming together for the first time to work or volunteer for something; when the group has faced a crisis or disappointment; or if a group has been working together for a while and desires to deepen in some way.

Timing. Paired dialogue can take as little as six minutes (three minutes per person, good for checking in during a larger group discussion) or as long as thirty to forty-five minutes (for more in-depth work together).

Setting. Get people into pairs, either randomly, by asking people to partner with someone they don't know well or haven't talked to in a while, or preassigning partners based on your best judgment. Make sure the pairs have some space between themselves and other pairs.

Beginning. Read the following directions once the pairs have assembled:

> *This is an exercise in listening with reverence but without reaction. First, decide who in your pair will go first. You are going to hear questions to answer. When one person is speaking, the partner should be actively listening, not talking. You can respond nonverbally in a way that conveys support to your partner. Our natural tendency is to agree or offer advice or a similar story, but this is different from a conversation.*

Then, ask a question for the first partner to answer, explaining they'll have three minutes. After three minutes, ask people to finish your thought and then switch so that the second partner has an opportunity to speak. Repeat the question for them. After three more minutes, you can ask the next question and proceed from there. Here are some examples to get you started:

OBJECTIVE	QUESTIONS
To build relationships by exploring each other's spiritual faith tradition	What faith or spiritual practice, if any, did you grow up with? What were your best memories of this tradition growing up? What about that tradition is still important to you now? Where are you now in your journey with faith or spirituality?
To explore the presence of spirit in one's life	What does calm feel like to you? What do you do that heals you? How can you tell when you feel grounded? How can you tell when you're not?
To face a hard issue in a group or organization	What do you believe is working well with the group? What is most frustrating to you? What do you need from others? What do you love about this group/ organization?
To prepare for an upcoming event	What are you excited about? What are you worried or scared about? What will help you be most prepared? What do you want to be able to say at the end of this?

℮ 5. mandalas

By using a *mandala* – a circular shape – you can help individuals focus on something that may be hard to reach through dialogue or words. Instead, they have an opportunity to focus on it through imagery. Here are three examples of good topics for a *mandala*:

- <u>Challenge</u> an individual is facing in themselves, a group, or his or her community
- <u>Intention</u> an individual has for himself or herself, a group to which they're connected, or his or her neighborhood
- <u>Fear</u> an individual has within or for the world in general

Setting. Start out with an art project that is fun and lighthearted, like group paintings. (See the "Images" chapter for more information on these.) Talk about what it means to create a mandala and mention that it can bring up emotion. You might even ask the group explicitly if they will make space for that.

Timing. This will take a minimum of an hour and a half.

Beginning. Ask people to sit quietly, relax into their breath, and identify the challenge, intention, or fear upon which they want to focus. Give people permission to sit with something that may be hard for them. Ask them to visualize a symbol for this. You may want to do this through the guided meditation. Using the information from the meditation, the group can begin making its mandalas. A symbol of their challenge, intention, or fear should go in the center of the mandala; make sure to save room around it. Request that everyone do this in silence.

After twenty minutes, ask people to show their mandala and talk about what they put in the center. This may be hard for some people. There may be laughter, tears, nervousness – whatever mechanisms people use to deal with tension. Go slow and honor the feelings that come up along the way. Next, ask people to spend time thinking about what might surround this challenge, intention, or fear. What do they want to see embracing it?

If you have time, you might have the group get into pairs and answer the following questions. Have them written on paper for everyone.

1. I'm glad/not glad to be talking with you about this right now because . . .
2. The challenge/intention/fear I'm working with right now is . . .
    (The following questions should each be answered three times. This is important. Given the sensitive nature of the subject, it is easy to give a general answer and move on. This is safer, of course, but does not get to the heart of the matter.)
3. This is most likely to come up when . . .
4. Not dealing with this might deprive me in the following ways . . .
5. The cultivation of acceptance would affect my challenge/intention/fear in the following ways . . .

Ending. Bring out the art supplies again. Ask folks to start thinking of what they want to surround their challenge, intention, or fear with, based on their answers to the questions above. They can then surround the center of the mandala with other symbols. Do this in silence. Leave time at the end for people to share their finished mandalas and to talk about what it was like to create them.

resources for group work

Bobo, Kim, Jackie Kendall, and Steve Max. *Organize! A Manual for Activists in the 1990's.* Santa Anna, Calif.: Seven Locks Press, 1991. Manual for grassroots organizers, with chapters on developing events, fund-raising, volunteers, meetings, public speaking, using the media, building coalitions, and more. Written by organizers from the Midwest Academy, a group that has trained more than twenty thousand activists since 1973. www.midwestacademy.com

Marcic, Dorothy. *Managing with the Wisdom of Love: Uncovering Virtue in People and Organizations.* San Francisco: Jossey-Bass, 1998. Based on Marcic's theory of "new management virtues" that an organization's health is fundamentally tied to the pivotal teaching of all religions: love your neighbor. www.marcic.com

Peck, M. Scott. *The Different Drum: Community Making and Peace.* New York: Touchstone, 1987. A look at community as an experience of self-awareness and profound connection. www.fce-community.org

Senge, Peter, et al. *The Fifth Discipline Fieldbook.* New York: Doubleday, 1994. Resource for developing leadership and creating true organizational transformation; filled to the brim with exercises, examples, and advice, this is an indispensable resource for those committed to building a learning organization. www.fieldbook.com

Shields, Katrina. *In The Tiger's Mouth: An Empowerment Guide for Social Action.* Philadelphia: New Society Publishers, 1994. Analysis and accessible approach for those working for change and in need of support and healing. www.newsociety.com

Spears, Larry C., ed. *Insights on Leadership: Service, Stewardship, Spirit and Servant-Leadership.* New York: John Wiley & Sons, 1998. Collection of essays and articles from a variety of individuals on the concept of servant-leadership and its possible applications.

Straub, Gail. *The Rhythm of Compassion: Caring for Self Connecting with Society.* Boston: Tuttle Publishing, 2000. A graceful look at the need for healing the human psyche and the world.

Training Center Workshops, 4719 Springfield Avenue, Philadelphia, Penn. 19143. (215) 729-7458. www.trainingforchange.org

Wallis, Jim. *The Soul of Politics.* New York: New Press and Orbis Books, 1994. A call for a new social vision that blends social justice with personal responsibility, but rises above both the liberal and conservative movements.

retreat centers . . . .

Avila Retreat Center, 711 Mason Road, Durham, N.C. 27712. (919) 477-1285.
www.win.net/~raldioc/avila/
Catholic retreat center that runs a great range of daylong and weekend
workshops. Also provides space for directed and private retreats.

Center for Life Enrichment/Nonprofit Holistic Resource Centers, 1509 S. Hawthorne
Rd., Winston-Salem N.C. 27103. (910) 768-0558; in Greensboro, (910) 299-
7999. www.thecle.com
Offers courses in yoga, astrology, ayurveda, reflexology, reiki, homeopathy,
meditation.

Elat Chayyim: A Center for Healing and Renewal, 99 Mill Hook Road, Accord, N.Y.
12404. (914) 626-0157. (800) 398-2630. www.elatchayyim.org
Inspired by the Jewish renewal movement. Runs weekend and weeklong
workshops in a variety of areas – dance, drama, writing, spirituality, Jewish
texts, and holidays.

Findhorn Foundation, Cluny Hill College, Forres IV36 ORD, Scotland; (44) 309
673655. www.findhorn.org
A residential learning center, ecovillage, and intentional spiritual community
in northern Scotland. Began in 1962 with three mystics who grew fertile
gardens, in part through spiritual meditation.

Gampo Abbey, Pleasant Bay, Cape Breton, Nova Scotia, BOE 2PO, Canada.
(902) 224-2752. Fax (902) 224-1521. www.gampoabbey.com
Monastery of the Kagyu lineage of Tibetan Buddhism. Pema Chödrön is the
resident teacher.

Greenfire, HCR 35, Box 436. Tenants Harbor, Maine 04860. (207) 372-6442.
Fax (207) 372-0561. www.greenfireretreat.org
Small community of women that enables the creative work of the deepest
self through retreats, structured and spontaneous events, and individual
consultations.

Green Gulch Farm, 1601 Shoreline Highway, Sausalito, Calif. 94965.
(415) 383-3134. www.sfzc.com/ggfindex.htm
Classes in Zen Buddhism, meditation retreats, workshops, and family events.
The famed Green Gulch Garden has a volunteer program and numerous
workshops.

Insight Meditation Society, 1230 Pleasant Street, Barre, Mass. 01005. (508) 355-4378. www.dharma.org
Wonderful place for the intensive practice of insight meditation; retreats from a weekend to three months.

Kirkridge Retreat and Study Center, 2495 Fox Gap Road, Bangor, Penn. 18013. (601) 588-1793. www.kirkridge.org
With their motto "Picket and Pray," Kirkridge is committed to the integration of personal growth and social change. They run retreats, workshops, seminars, and conferences.

Kripalu Center for Yoga and Health, Box 793, Lenox, Mass. 01240. (413) 448-3400. www.kripalu.org
Runs weekend and weeklong workshops. It is also possible to be in residence doing *seva*, or selfless service.

Omega, 150 Lake Drive, Rhinebeck, N.Y. 12572. (800) 944-1001. www.eomega.org
The nation's largest holistic learning and retreat center; a pioneer of new ideas.

Plum Village, Meyrac, Loubès-Bernam 47120, France (33) 53 94 75 40, and *Green Mountain Dharma Center*, Hartland-Four-Corners, Vt. 05049. (802) 436-1103. www.plumvillage.org
Retreat communities founded by Vietnamese Buddhist monk and activist Thich Nhat Hanh. Encourages mindful sitting, walking, eating, and resting.

Southern Dharma Retreat Center, 1661 West Road, Hot Springs, N.C. 28743. (704) 622-7112. www.main.nc.us/SDRC
Located in the western North Carolina mountains. Sponsors teachers from a variety of traditions for meditation retreats.

Vallecitos Mountain Refuge, P.O. Box 1507, Taos, N.M. 87571. (505) 751-0351. Fax (505) 751-1775. www.vallecitos.org
Wilderness mountain ranch in Carson National Forest, Vallecitos is a refuge for contemplative practice and spiritual renewal for environmental and social activists.

stone circles

stone circles are universally holy.
They symbolize sacred doorways,
the center of the universe,
the dwelling place of the life force.

stone circles helps individuals and organizations integrate faith, spiritual practice, and reflection into the work of social transformation and social change. We serve nonprofit, social change organizations, activists, and caring individuals through:

- workshops and retreats on contemplative and spiritual practice,
- organizational development assistance and training,
- practical and inspiring publications,
- community gatherings; and
- interfaith celebrations.

We use a range of tools including discussion, reflection, writing, movement, ritual, art, silence, brainstorming, readings, and music. These well-constructed pauses are designed to reconnect people and organizations to their core values and passions, to each other, and to their work. We are interested in your experiences using this book. Please send feedback, comments, and questions to:

stone circles
301 West Main Street, Suite 280
Durham NC 27701
SpiritActivist@aol.com
www.stonecircles.org
www.spiritualactivist.org

index